Junior Certificate Business Studies

Eurobusiness
Workbook

Third Edition

John Taylor B. Comm, HDE, HDEM

FOLENS

Contents

Editor: Kristin Jensen

Design and layout: Niamh Carey, Liz White Designs

ISBN: 978-1-84741-838-8

© 2011 John Taylor

Folens Publishers,
Hibernian Industrial Estate,
Greenhills Road,
Tallaght, Dublin 24.

Household Income

1. Complete the table below to show how different groups of people receive income.

	Regular income	Irregular income
Employed person		
Student		
Unemployed person		
Retired person		

2. Group the following forms of income under the correct heading.

Wages	Pension	Lottery win	Pocket money
Casual work	Child Benefit	Win at bingo	Jobseeker's Benefit

Regular income

_____

_____

_____

_____

_____

Irregular income

_____

_____

_____

_____

_____

3. Look at the different jobs listed below and suggest ways people might receive benefit-in-kind. Can you think of other jobs and the benefit-in-kind associated with them?

Job

- Aer Lingus pilot
- Sales representative
- Fitter with Guinness
- Cashier with AIB
- Luas tram driver
- Employee of the Clarion Hotel
- _____
- _____
- _____

Benefit-in-kind

_____

_____

_____

_____

_____

_____

_____

_____

_____

4. Look at the income record below for the Byrne family and answer the questions that follow.

BYRNE FAMILY	July	Aug	Sept	Oct	TOTAL
INCOME	€	€	€	€	€
Paul Byrne – salary	950	950	1,200	950	4,050
Margaret Byrne – salary	800	800	800	800	3,200
Child Benefit	30	30	30	30	120
Lottery win		1,000			1,000
TOTAL INCOME	1,780	2,780	2,030	1,780	8,370

(a) List the Byrnes' regular sources of income.

_____

_____

_____

(b) List the Byrnes' irregular sources of income.

_____

(c) How much is their total income for the 4 months?

_____

(d) Give one possible reason why Paul's income rose in September.

_____

5. Prepare the income record for each household for the 4 months January to April using the information below. All figures are per month.

	CURTIS FAMILY	WRIGHT FAMILY	DOOLIN FAMILY
Salary	Paul – €1,450 Mary – €640	James – €1,870 Susan – €1,400	Elaine – €1,500 John – €1,300
Bonus			Elaine – €400 (Apr)
Child Benefit	€130	€65	
Sale of car		€1,000 (March)	
Lottery win			€2,000 (Feb)
Sale of shares			€1,500 (Mar)

CURTIS FAMILY	Jan	Feb	Mar	Apr	TOTAL
Paul Curtis – salary					
Mary Curtis – salary					
Child Benefit					
Total					

WRIGHT FAMILY	Jan	Feb	Mar	Apr	TOTAL
James Wright – salary					
Susan Wright – salary					
Child Benefit					
Sale of car					
Total					

DOOLIN FAMILY	Jan	Feb	Mar	Apr	TOTAL
Elaine Doolin – salary					
John Doolin – salary					
Lottery win					
Sale of shares					
Total					

6. From the following information, prepare the income record for the O'Callaghan family for the 6 months January to June.

- P. J. O'Callaghan – salary €1,400 per month plus overtime in February (€350) and May (€350)
- Mary O'Callaghan works part time and will earn €450 in February, April and June
- Child Benefit is €130 per month
- Sale of old computer €300 in March

O'CALLAGHAN FAMILY	Jan	Feb	Mar	Apr	May	June	TOTAL
P. J. O'Callaghan – salary							
Mary O'Callaghan – salary							
Child Benefit							
Sale of computer							
Total							

7. From the following information, prepare the income record for the Meyler family for the 6 months July to December.

- Luke Meyler – salary €1,750 per month plus overtime in August (€340), October (€420) and December (€280)
- Sinead Meyler – salary €1,250 per month, but she intends giving up working outside the home on 31 October
- Child Benefit will be €150 per month from 1 November
- Sale of second family car in December for €4,500

MEYLER FAMILY	July	Aug	Sept	Oct	Nov	Dec	TOTAL
Sinead Meyler – salary							
Luke Meyler – salary							
Child Benefit							
Sale of car							
Total							

8. Below is the income record for the Brennan family. Redraft it after taking the following changes into account.

- Alan will receive a pay rise of 10% from 1 March

- Margaret will receive a bonus of €250 in April

- Interest on savings will be €60 in February

BRENNAN FAMILY	Jan	Feb	Mar	Apr	TOTAL
PLANNED INCOME	€	€	€	€	€
Alan Brennan – salary	1,350	1,350	1,350	1,350	5,400
Margaret Brennan – salary	1,400	1,400	1,400	1,400	5,600
Child Benefit	90	90	90	90	360
Interest from savings		40			40
TOTAL INCOME	2,840	2,880	2,840	2,840	11,400

BRENNAN FAMILY	Jan	Feb	Mar	Apr	TOTAL
PLANNED INCOME	€	€	€	€	€
Alan Brennan – salary					
Margaret Brennan – salary					
Child Benefit					
Interest from savings					
TOTAL INCOME					

9. Below is the income record for the Kenny family. Redraft it after taking the following changes into account.

- Peter will receive a pay rise of 20% from 1 April

- Norma will start job sharing in May and her salary will be cut in half

- Norma will receive a bonus of €500 in June (this can be included in her salary)

- A tax refund of €800 is expected in April

- Dividends from shares of €340 is expected in July

KENNY FAMILY	Mar	Apr	May	June	July	Aug	TOTAL
PLANNED INCOME	€	€	€	€	€	€	€
Norma Kenny – salary	1,650	1,650	1,650	1,650	1,650	1,650	9,900
Peter Kenny – salary	2,000	2,000	2,000	2,000	2,000	2,000	12,000
Child Benefit	220	220	220	220	220	220	1,320
TOTAL INCOME	**3,870**	**3,870**	**3,870**	**3,870**	**3,870**	**3,870**	**23,220**

KENNY FAMILY	Mar	Apr	May	June	July	Aug	TOTAL
PLANNED INCOME	€	€	€	€	€	€	€
Norma Kenny – salary							
Peter Kenny – salary							
Child Benefit							
Tax refund							
Dividends from shares							
TOTAL INCOME							

10. Word search

The grid below contains many of the new terms you have learned in Chapter 1 – Household Income. See how many you can find. The answers may read forwards, backwards or diagonally.

Income
Regular
Irregular
Benefit-in-kind
Perk
Grant
Overtime
Pension
Wages

A	B	C	D	E	R	P	G	F	E
I	N	C	O	M	E	E	D	H	M
B	T	N	A	R	G	N	N	M	I
I	E	J	K	L	U	S	I	N	T
O	P	N	Q	R	L	I	K	S	R
T	U	V	E	W	A	O	N	X	E
Y	Z	A	B	F	R	N	I	D	V
K	R	E	P	E	I	F	G	H	O
I	J	K	L	M	N	T	P	Q	R
I	R	R	E	G	U	L	A	R	S
T	U	V	W	X	Y	Z	A	B	C
D	W	A	G	E	S	J	E	F	G

Section A Questions

11. Matching terms and explanations

Column 1 is a list of terms to do with household income. Match them with the correct explanation from the list of explanations in column 2. When you have chosen your answers, place the correct letter beside the number below.

1. Pension		A.	Income received for work done
2. Overtime		B.	Regular payment to the parents of children still in education
3. Wages		C.	Regular payment to people who are out of work
4. Regular income		D.	Extra hours worked in a week
5. Jobseeker's Benefit		E.	Money paid by the government to students
6. Grant		F.	Non-cash forms of income
7. Benefit-in-kind		G.	Regular payment to people who have retired
8. Child Benefit		H.	Income received on a weekly or monthly basis

1. ☐   2. ☐   3. ☐   4. ☐

5. ☐   6. ☐   7. ☐   8. ☐

12. Match the following perks (benefit-in-kind) with the most appropriate occupation from the list below.

1. Free flights	A. Sales rep
2. Travel allowance	B. Restaurant waiter
3. Low-interest loans	C. Bank official
4. Free meals	D. Air steward

1. ☐   2. ☐   3. ☐   4. ☐

2 Household Expenditure

1. Rearrange the following list of expenditure items into the three expenditure groups.

car insurance	electricity	entertainment	groceries
house mortgage	house insurance	telephone	gas
car loan repayments	school expenses	new clothes	house redecoration
holiday	motor car expenses	internet broadband	rent
facial	phone credit	furniture	car service
TV licence	going online in an internet cafe		

Fixed	Irregular	Discretionary

2. Prepare the expenditure record for the Kelly family for the 4 months January to April.

Fixed:

Mortgage	€750 per month
Car loan	€170 per month
Broadband	€25 per month

Irregular:

Electricity	€60 (Jan)
	€70 (March)
Groceries	€80 per month
Telephone	€45 (Feb)
	€68 (April)

Discretionary:

| Entertainment | €76 per month |
| New furniture | €450 (April) |

KELLY FAMILY	Jan	Feb	Mar	Apr	TOTAL
PLANNED EXPENDITURE	€	€	€	€	€
Fixed					
Subtotal					
Irregular					
Subtotal					
Discretionary					
Subtotal					
TOTAL EXPENDITURE					

3. Prepare the expenditure record for the Temple family for the 4 months May to August.

Fixed:

Rent	€370 per month
Car tax	€150 (June)
House insurance	€35 per month

Irregular:

Gas	€56 (May)
	€65 (July)
Telephone	€50 (June)
	€64 (August)
Groceries	€70 per month
Petrol	€50 per month

Discretionary:

Entertainment	€85 per month
Weekend away	€700 (July)

TEMPLE FAMILY	May	June	July	Aug	TOTAL
PLANNED EXPENDITURE	€	€	€	€	€
Fixed					
Subtotal					
Irregular					
Subtotal					
Discretionary					
Subtotal					
TOTAL EXPENDITURE					

4. Prepare the expenditure record for the Keegan family for the 6 months January to June.

Fixed:

Mortgage	€600 per month
Car loan	€210 per month
House insurance	€45 per month

Irregular:

Electricity	€48 (Feb)
	€67 (Apr)
	€54 (June)
Groceries	€100 per month
Telephone	€84 (Jan)
	€92 (Mar)
	€86 (May)

Discretionary:

Entertainment	€65 per month
New furniture	€600 (Feb)

KEEGAN FAMILY	Jan	Feb	Mar	Apr	May	June	TOTAL
PLANNED EXPENDITURE	€	€	€	€	€	€	€
Fixed							
Subtotal							
Irregular							
Subtotal							
Discretionary							
Subtotal							
TOTAL EXPENDITURE							

5. Prepare the expenditure record for the O'Toole family for the 6 months July to December.

Fixed:

Mortgage	€350 per month
House insurance	€35 per month

Irregular:

Gas	€94 (Aug)
	€140 (Oct)
	€180 (Dec)
Telephone	€60 (July)
	€74 (Sept)
	€82 (Nov)
School expenses	€400 (Sept)
Groceries	€100 per month
Car expenses	€80 per month

Discretionary:

Entertainment	€55 per month
Holiday	€1,000 (Aug)

O'TOOLE FAMILY	July	Aug	Sept	Oct	Nov	Dec	TOTAL
PLANNED EXPENDITURE	€	€	€	€	€	€	€
Fixed							
Subtotal							
Irregular							
Subtotal							
Discretionary							
Subtotal							
TOTAL EXPENDITURE							

6. Prepare the expenditure record for the Meehan family for the 4 months January to April.

Mortgage   €470 per month

Car loan   €150 per month

Electricity   €52 (Jan)

                    €61 (Mar)

Telephone   €84 (Feb)

                    €92 (Apr)

Clothes   €140 (Mar)

Car service   €105 (Mar)

Groceries   €102 per month

Entertainment   €70 per month

New furniture   €1,000 (Feb)

MEEHAN FAMILY	Jan	Feb	Mar	Apr	TOTAL
PLANNED EXPENDITURE	€	€	€	€	€
Fixed					
Subtotal					
Irregular					
Subtotal					
Discretionary					
Subtotal					
TOTAL EXPENDITURE					

7. Prepare the expenditure record for the O'Reilly family for the 4 months September to December.

Telephone	€64 (Oct)
	€70 (Dec)
Groceries	€86 per month plus an extra €100 in December
Mortgage	€510 per month
Entertainment	€60 per month
Holiday	€800 in October
Car insurance	€47 per month
TV licence	€105 (Nov)
School expenses	€270 (Sept)
Gas	€72 (Sept)
	€85 (Nov)
Car expenses	€53 per month
Beauty treatment	€100 (Dec)

O'REILLY FAMILY	Sept	Oct	Nov	Dec	TOTAL
PLANNED EXPENDITURE	€	€	€	€	€
Fixed					
Subtotal					
Irregular					
Subtotal					
Discretionary					
Subtotal					
TOTAL EXPENDITURE					

8. Prepare the expenditure record for the Grealish family for the 6 months July to December.

Rent	€540 per month	
Gas	€34 (July)	
	€56 (Sept)	
	€102 (Nov)	
Entertainment	€84 per month	
Telephone	€65 (Aug)	
	€74 (Oct)	
	€85 (Dec)	
New furniture	€467 (Sept)	
House insurance	€329 (Oct)	
Car expenses	€120 per month	
Christmas expenses	€200 (Dec)	
Cable TV	€90 per month	
School tour deposit	€200 (Sept)	
Groceries	€143 per month	

GREALISH FAMILY	July	Aug	Sept	Oct	Nov	Dec	TOTAL
PLANNED EXPENDITURE	€	€	€	€	€	€	€
Fixed							
Subtotal							
Irregular							
Subtotal							
Discretionary							
Subtotal							
TOTAL EXPENDITURE							

9. Redraft the expenditure record below for the Ellison family, making sure to place each item under the correct heading. Calculate the subtotals for each section as well as the totals for the 4-month period. A blank document is provided below.

ELLISON FAMILY	July	Aug	Sept	Oct	TOTAL
PLANNED EXPENDITURE	€	€	€	€	€
Fixed					
House mortgage	450	450	450	450	
Electricity		45		70	
School costs			150		
Subtotal					
Irregular					
Entertainment	70	70	70	70	
Car loan	220	220	220	220	
Telephone	55		90		
Holiday		1,100			
Subtotal					
Discretionary					
Groceries	306	306	306	306	
Car tax		180			
House redecoration	150				
Subtotal					
TOTAL EXPENDITURE					

ELLISON FAMILY	July	Aug	Sept	Oct	TOTAL
PLANNED EXPENDITURE	€	€	€	€	€
Fixed					
Subtotal					
Irregular					
Subtotal					
Discretionary					
Subtotal					
TOTAL EXPENDITURE					

10. Redraft the expenditure record below for the Whelan family, making sure to place each item under the correct heading. Calculate the subtotals for each section as well as the totals for the 6-month period. A blank document is provided below.

WHELAN FAMILY	Jan	Feb	Mar	Apr	May	June	TOTAL
PLANNED EXPENDITURE	€	€	€	€	€	€	€
Fixed							
Car insurance	25	25	25	25	25	25	
Groceries	120	120	120	120	120	120	
Weekend away			590				
Subtotal							
Irregular							
Telephone		56		78		49	
Apartment rent	160	160	160	160	160	160	
School expenses		120			90		
House decoration						1500	
Subtotal							
Discretionary							
Electricity	110		98		88		
TV licence				152			
Gas		198		156		70	
Subtotal							
TOTAL EXPENDITURE							

WHELAN FAMILY	Jan	Feb	Mar	Apr	May	June	TOTAL
PLANNED EXPENDITURE	€	€	€	€	€	€	€
Fixed							
Subtotal							
Irregular							
Subtotal							
Discretionary							
Subtotal							
TOTAL EXPENDITURE							

11. The grid below contains many of the new terms you have learned in Chapter 2 – Household Expenditure. See how many you can find.

Q	W	E	R	T	Y	U	I	I	O
O	F	I	X	E	D	P	A	S	P
D	F	G	H	J	K	L	D	E	P
Z	X	C	E	V	B	N	I	R	O
M	Q	W	S	E	R	T	S	U	R
Y	U	I	L	O	P	A	C	T	T
R	A	L	U	G	E	R	R	I	U
S	D	F	P	G	G	H	E	D	N
Z	X	C	M	N	V	B	T	N	I
M	N	Q	I	W	E	T	I	E	T
T	Y	Y	U	T	I	O	O	P	Y
P	U	A	S	S	F	G	N	X	H
B	H	J	K	O	L	Z	A	E	X
C	V	B	N	C	M	Q	R	W	E
A	T	R	Y	U	I	O	Y	D	F

Expenditure
Discretionary
Fixed
Irregular
Impulse buying
Opportunity cost

Section A Questions

12. Match the explanations in column 1 with the correct terms in column 2.

1. Paid electricity bill   **A.** Fixed expenditure

2. Paid TV licence   **B.** Discretionary expenditure

3. Paid for new Xbox game   **C.** Irregular expenditure

1. ☐   2. ☐   3. ☐

13. Tick the correct box to show which class of expenditure each item is.

	Fixed	Irregular	Discretionary
(a) Mortgage	☐	☐	☐
(b) Groceries	☐	☐	☐
(c) Entertainment	☐	☐	☐
(d) House insurance	☐	☐	☐
(e) Electricity costs	☐	☐	☐
(f) TV licence	☐	☐	☐
(g) Petrol	☐	☐	☐

14. To a young person, which of the following are needs and which are wants?
Tick the appropriate box in each case.

	Needs	Wants
(a) TV for bedroom	☐	☐
(b) Food	☐	☐
(c) Computer games	☐	☐

15. Maureen has €5.50 to spend. She would like to rent a DVD and go to the youth club disco, but they cost €5.50 each. Maureen decides on the DVD. The opportunity cost of the DVD is:

(a) The €5.50 she paid for the DVD ☐

(b) The disco she did not go to ☐

(c) The enjoyment she gets from the DVD ☐

16. Column 1 is a list of terms concerning budgeting. Column 2 is a list of explanations for these terms. Place the appropriate letter beside the correct number below to match the two lists.

1. Fixed expenditure	**A.** Doing without the next best alternative
2. Irregular income	**B.** Non-cash income
3. Benefit-in-kind	**C.** Spur-of-the-moment decision to purchase an item
4. Opportunity cost	**D.** Expenditure where the amount is not related to use
5. Impulse buying	**E.** A lotto win is an example of this

1. ☐   **2.** ☐   **3.** ☐   **4.** ☐   **5.** ☐

Household Budgeting

1. Complete each of the following household budgets by filling in the missing figures. For each month, say whether there is a surplus or deficit.

(A) KEALY FAMILY	Jan	Feb	Mar	Apr	TOTAL
TOTAL INCOME	12,000	12,600	12,000	13,400	
Fixed expenditure – subtotal	4,500	4,500	4,500	4,500	
Irregular expenditure – subtotal	3,700	4,500	3,800	3,700	
Discretionary expenditure – subtotal	2,300	2,400	2,500	4,600	
TOTAL EXPENDITURE	10,500				
NET CASH	1,500				
OPENING CASH	100	1,600			
CLOSING CASH	1,600				

(B) WRIGHT FAMILY	Mar	Apr	May	June	TOTAL
TOTAL INCOME	15,000	16,700	14,900	14,900	
Fixed expenditure – subtotal	4,700	4,700	4,700	5,100	
Irregular expenditure – subtotal	5,500	6,100	5,800	4,200	
Discretionary expenditure – subtotal	3,700	2,200	2,200	4,900	
TOTAL EXPENDITURE	13,900				
NET CASH					
OPENING CASH	500				
CLOSING CASH					

(C) CONVEY FAMILY	May	June	July	Aug	TOTAL
TOTAL INCOME	12,950	12,950	12,950	12,950	
Fixed expenditure – subtotal	3,770	4,100	4,100	3,600	
Irregular expenditure – subtotal	4,500	5,300	5,700	4,700	
Discretionary expenditure – subtotal	3,100	4,150	3,990	3,400	
TOTAL EXPENDITURE					
NET CASH					
OPENING CASH	700				
CLOSING CASH					

2. Complete the household budget for the Keogh family for January to April by filling in the missing total and subtotal figures as well as the Total column for January to April.

KEOGH FAMILY	Jan	Feb	Mar	Apr	TOTAL
PLANNED INCOME	€	€	€	€	€
Mark Keogh – salary	1,200	1,200	1,200	1,200	
Jill Keogh – salary	1,300	1,300	1,300	1,300	
Child Benefit	40	40	40	40	
TOTAL INCOME	2,540				
PLANNED EXPENDITURE					
Fixed					
Mortgage	400	400	400	400	
Car loan	100	100			
Annual car tax			120		
House insurance	10	10	10	10	
Annual car insurance		380		280	
Subtotal	510				
Irregular					
Household costs	520	520	520	520	
Electricity	120		140		
Telephone		80		120	
Car running costs	150	150	150	150	
Subtotal	790				
Discretionary					
Presents			100		
Entertainment	100	100	100	100	
Holiday			1,000		
Subtotal	100				
TOTAL EXPENDITURE	1,400				
NET CASH	1,140				
OPENING CASH	120	1,260			
CLOSING CASH	1,260				

3. Complete the household budget for the Tobin family for May to August by filling in the missing total and subtotal figures as well as the Total column for May to August.

TOBIN FAMILY	May	June	July	Aug	TOTAL
PLANNED INCOME	€	€	€	€	€
Elaine Tobin – salary	2,100	2,100	2,100	2,100	
John Tobin – salary	1,850	1,850	1,850	1,850	
Child Benefit	120	120	120	120	
TOTAL INCOME					
PLANNED EXPENDITURE					
Fixed					
Mortgage	850	850	850	850	
Personal loan	240	240	240		
Annual car tax		156			
House insurance	25	25	25	25	
Annual car insurance		400			
Subtotal					
Irregular					
Groceries	480	480	480	480	
Gas		150		176	
Telephone	95		110		
Car running costs	120	120	120	120	
Subtotal					
Discretionary					
Wedding present		250			
Entertainment	180	180	180	180	
New furniture				2,000	
Subtotal					
TOTAL EXPENDITURE					
NET CASH					
OPENING CASH	240				
CLOSING CASH					

4. Complete the household budget for the Adeymi family for September to December by filling in the missing total and subtotal figures as well as the Total column for September to December.

ADEYMI FAMILY	Sept	Oct	Nov	Dec	TOTAL
PLANNED INCOME	€	€	€	€	€
Victor Adeymi – salary	2,100	2,100	2,100	2,100	
Cecile Adeymi – salary	1,850	1,850	1,850	1,850	
Dividends from shares			400		
TOTAL INCOME					
PLANNED EXPENDITURE					
Fixed					
Rent	654	654	654	654	
Health insurance	78	78	78	78	
Broadband	39	39	39	39	
Car insurance			360		
Subtotal					
Irregular					
Household expenses	540	540	540	540	
Electricity	160		154		
Mobile phone		120		132	
Car running costs	150	150	150	150	
Subtotal					
Discretionary					
Christmas presents				700	
Entertainment	150	150	150	250	
Deposit for holiday		1,500			
Subtotal					
TOTAL EXPENDITURE					
NET CASH					
OPENING CASH	300				
CLOSING CASH					

5. Prepare a simple budget for John Wilson for the 3 months January to March using the information below. Opening cash on 1 January is €100.

Planned income:

* John Wilson earns €1,100 per month

Planned expenditure:

* Apartment rent is €400 per month
* Insurance is €54 per month
* Groceries are usually €125 per month
* Telephone bills are expected to be €165 in January and €175 in March
* Entertainment is expected to be €70 per month

JOHN WILSON	Jan	Feb	Mar	TOTAL
	€	€	€	€
PLANNED INCOME				
Salary	€1,100	€1,100	1,100	3 300
TOTAL INCOME				
PLANNED EXPENDITURE				
Fixed				
Apartment rent	€400	€400	€400	1200
Insurance	€54	€54	€54	162
Subtotal	454	454	454	1362
Irregular				
Groceries	€125	€125	€125	375
Telephone	€165		€175	340
Subtotal	€290	125	€300	715
Discretionary				
Entertainment	€70	€70	€70	€210
Subtotal	70	70	€70	210
TOTAL EXPENDITURE	814	649	824	2287
NET CASH	= 286	451	276	1013
OPENING CASH	€100	386	837	100
CLOSING CASH	386	837	1,113	1213

I – E =

6. Prepare a simple budget for Elizabeth Dardis for the 3 months April to June using the information below. Opening cash on 1 April is €150.

Planned income:

- Elizabeth Dardis earns €1,250 per month

Planned expenditure:

- House mortgage is €560 per month
- Annual car tax is €140 and is due in May
- House insurance is €45 per month
- Groceries are usually €150 per month
- A gas bill is expected to be €100 in May

- Electricity bills are expected to be €65 in April and €80 in June
- Entertainment is expected to be €80 per month
- New clothes will cost €100 in June

ELIZABETH DARDIS	April	May	June	TOTAL
	€	€	€	€
PLANNED INCOME				
Salary	€1,250	€1,250	€1,250	3750
TOTAL INCOME				
PLANNED EXPENDITURE				
Fixed				
House mortgage	€560	€560	€560	1680
Car tax	€140	€140	€140	420
House insurance	€45	€45	€45	€135
Subtotal	€745	€745	€745	2235
Irregular				
Groceries	150	150	150	450
Electricity	€65		€80	€145
Gas	€100			100
Subtotal	315	150	230	695
Discretionary				
Entertainment	€80	€80	€80	€240
Clothes	€100			€100
Subtotal	€180	€80	€80	€340
TOTAL EXPENDITURE	1240	975	1055	3270
NET CASH	10	275	195	480
OPENING CASH	150	160	435	630
CLOSING CASH	160	435	630	€1,110

7. Prepare a simple budget for the O'Callaghan family for the 4 months July to October using the information below. Opening cash on 1 July is €200.

Planned income:

- Mark O'Callaghan earns €1,700 per month
- Rachel O'Callaghan earns €1,350 per month

Planned expenditure:

- House mortgage is €650 per month
- Car insurance will be €450 in July
- TV licence will cost €108 in August
- Groceries usually cost €170 per month
- Telephone bills are expected to be €100 in July and €150 in September
- Motor expenses are usually €65 per month and a car service in September will cost €120
- Entertainment is expected to be €80 per month
- A holiday will cost €1,800 in August

O'CALLAGHAN FAMILY	July	Aug	Sept	Oct	TOTAL
	€	€	€	€	€
PLANNED INCOME					
Salary – Mark	€1700	€1700	€1700	1700	
Salary – Rachel	€1350	€1350	1350	1350	
TOTAL INCOME					
PLANNED EXPENDITURE					
Fixed					
House mortgage	€650	€650	€65	€650	
Car insurance	€450				
TV licence	€108				
Subtotal					
Irregular					
Groceries	170	170	170	170	
Telephone					
Motor expenses					
Subtotal					
Discretionary					
Entertainment					
Holiday					
Subtotal					
TOTAL EXPENDITURE					
NET CASH					
OPENING CASH	200				
CLOSING CASH					

8. Prepare a simple budget for the Daly family for the 6 months January to June using the information below. Opening cash on 1 January is €300.

Planned income:
- Mark Daly earns €1,850 per month
- Elaine Daly earns €600 per month
- Child Benefit is €150 per month

Planned expenditure:
- House mortgage is €640 per month
- Insurance costs will be €80 per month
- TV costs will be €105 in February and €80 in May
- Groceries cost €175 per month
- Telephone bills are expected to be €85 in February, €70 in April and €100 in June
- Motor expenses are usually €120 per month plus a service in April costing €200
- Entertainment is expected to cost €75 per month
- A holiday will cost €1,500 in June
- Golf club subscription is due in February costing €1,400

DALY FAMILY	Jan	Feb	Mar	April	May	June	TOTAL
	€	€	€	€	€	€	€
PLANNED INCOME							
Salary – Mark							
Salary – Elaine							
Child Benefit							
TOTAL INCOME							
PLANNED EXPENDITURE							
Fixed							
House mortgage							
Insurance							
TV costs							
Subtotal							
Irregular							
Groceries							
Telephone							
Motor expenses							
Subtotal							
Discretionary							
Entertainment							
Holiday							
Golf club							
Subtotal							
TOTAL EXPENDITURE							
NET CASH							
OPENING CASH							
CLOSING CASH							

9. Prepare the household budget for the Caulwell family for the 4 months June to September using the information below. Opening cash on 1 June is €100.

Planned income:

- Simon Caulwell earns €1,300 net per month and gets a holiday bonus of an extra €150 net in July

- Eileen Caulwell earns €1,500 net per month

- Child Benefit is €150 per month

- Interest on savings is expected to be €50 in June

Planned expenditure:

- Apartment rent is €580 per month

- Repayments on Simon's car loan are €370 per month and will be fully paid by the end of July

- Car insurance premiums are €520 for Simon (due in June) and €285 for Eileen (due in August)

- House insurance of €360 per annum is payable monthly from June

- Household expenses are usually €480 per month except in July, when there will be a reduction of €150

- Car running costs are expected to be €80 per month for Simon and €150 per month for Eileen

- School uniforms and books will cost €340 in September

- Gas bills are expected to be €84 in June and €65 in August

- Telephone expenses are expected to be €90 in July and €110 in September

- Presents will cost €140 in September

- The Caulwell family has allocated €80 per month to entertainment

- A holiday in July will cost the Caulwells €1,650

CAULWELL FAMILY	June	July	Aug	Sept	TOTAL
PLANNED INCOME	€	€	€	€	€
Simon Caulwell – salary					
Eileen Caulwell – salary					
Child Benefit					
Interest on savings					
TOTAL INCOME					
PLANNED EXPENDITURE					
Fixed					
Apartment rent					
Car loan					
Car insurance					
House insurance					
Subtotal					
Irregular					
Household expenses					
Car running costs					
School uniforms and books					
Gas					
Telephone					
Subtotal					
Discretionary					
Presents					
Entertainment					
Holiday					
Subtotal					
TOTAL EXPENDITURE					
NET CASH					
OPENING CASH					
CLOSING CASH					

10. Prepare the household budget for Carole Sheridan for the 4 months September to December using the information below. Opening cash on 1 September is €120.

Planned income:

- Carole Sheridan earns €1,350 net per month and gets a bonus of an extra €3,000 net in December

- Child Benefit is €150 per month

- Interest on savings of €50 is expected in October

Planned expenditure:

- House mortgage is €340 per month

- Insurance payments of €540 per annum are payable monthly

- Childminding costs are €120 per month

- TV licence due in December will cost €62

- Household expenses are usually €220 per month

- Car running costs are expected to be petrol €80 per month; repairs and service €55 in November; car tax €180 in September

- Telephone bills are expected to be €80 in October and €72 in December

- Light and heating costs are estimated at €75 in September and €85 in November

- School uniforms and books will cost €110 in September

- Entertainment costs are expected to be €30 per month

- A party and presents for her daughter will cost €60 in November

- €120 will be spent on presents in December

- Carole hopes to go on a course in September costing €300

CAROLE SHERIDAN	Sept	Oct	Nov	Dec	TOTAL
	€	€	€	€	€
PLANNED INCOME					
Carole Sheridan – salary					
Child Benefit					
Interest on savings					
TOTAL INCOME					
PLANNED EXPENDITURE					
Fixed					
House mortgage					
Insurance					
Childminding					
TV licence					
Subtotal					
Irregular					
Household expenses					
Car running costs					
Telephone					
Light and heat					
School uniforms and books					
Subtotal					
Discretionary					
Entertainment					
Presents/party					
Course fees					
Subtotal					
TOTAL EXPENDITURE					
NET CASH					
OPENING CASH					
CLOSING CASH					

11. Prepare the household budget for the Gardiner family for the 4 months January to April using the information below. Opening cash on 1 January is €150.

Planned income:

- Alan Gardiner is unemployed and receives Jobseeker's Benefit of €560 per month
- Mary Gardiner earns €350 per month as a shop assistant
- The family receives rent allowance of €250 per month
- Child Benefit is €150 per month

Planned expenditure:

- House rent is €300 per month
- Repayments on a credit union loan are €80 per month
- Annual house insurance of €180 is payable monthly from January
- Groceries are usually €210 per month
- Telephone expenses are expected to be €55 in January and €60 in March
- Electricity charges will be €45 in February and €38 in April
- An oil refill in March will cost €108
- School expenses of €45 will be due in March
- Travel expenses are expected to be €35 per month
- €50 per month will be allocated to entertainment
- Painting and decoration will be necessary in April at a cost of €140

GARDINER FAMILY	Jan	Feb	Mar	Apr	TOTAL
	€	€	€	€	€
PLANNED INCOME					
Alan Gardiner – Job. Ben.					
Mary Gardiner – salary					
Rent allowance					
Child Benefit					
TOTAL INCOME					
PLANNED EXPENDITURE					
Fixed					
House rent					
Credit union loan					
House insurance					
Subtotal					
Irregular					
Groceries					
Telephone					
Electricity					
Oil					
School expenses					
Travel expenses					
Subtotal					
Discretionary					
Entertainment					
Painting and decoration					
Subtotal					
TOTAL EXPENDITURE					
NET CASH					
OPENING CASH					
CLOSING CASH					

12. The following is a budget for the Cuprial household for the 4 months September to December. Opening cash in hand is €325.

Planned income:

- Lucaz Cuprial earns €1,900 net per month and expects to receive a Christmas bonus of €700 net in December.

- Maria Cuprial earns €1,550 net per month and expects this to **decrease** by €400 per month from 1 November.

- Child Benefit is expected to be €300 per month.

Planned expenditure:

- The house mortgage of €860 per month will **increase** by €50 per month from 1 October.

- The house insurance premium is €600 per year, payable monthly from 1 September.

- The Cuprial household pays a health insurance premium of €165 per month, which will **increase** by €14 per month from 1 November.

- Household costs are €1,100 per month, except in December, when they will be €800 **extra**.

- The Cuprial household uses public transport to travel to work. Lucaz's bus ticket costs €126 per month and Maria's DART ticket costs €85 per month. They also expect to use taxis costing €60 for a concert in December.

- Bills for light and heat are expected to be €160 in September and €155 in November.

- Home heating oil is expected to cost €800 in October.

- Telephone bills for the landline are expected to be €120 in October and €94 in December. In addition, bills for mobile phones will cost the household €65 per month.

- Birthday presents will cost €100 in October and €120 in November, while Christmas presents will cost €850 in December.

- Entertainment will cost €320 each month, except in December, when concert tickets will cost an **extra** €180.

- The Cuprial family is going away for a weekend holiday in October at a cost of €900. They must pay a deposit of 20% of the total cost in September and the balance in October.

(a) Complete the blank household budget form using all the above figures.

(b) Name **one** company that provides health insurance to the general public in Ireland.

_____

(c) Explain the term 'discretionary expenditure'.

_____

_____

CUPRIAL FAMILY	Sept	Oct	Nov	Dec	Total
PLANNED INCOME	€	€	€	€	€
Lucaz Cuprial – salary					
Maria Cuprial – salary					
Child Benefit					
TOTAL INCOME					
PLANNED EXPENDITURE					
Fixed					
House mortgage					
House insurance					
Health insurance					
Subtotal					
Irregular					
Household costs					
Transport					
Light and heat					
Telephone					
Subtotal					
Discretionary					
Presents					
Entertainment					
Holiday					
Subtotal					
TOTAL EXPENDITURE					
NET CASH					
OPENING CASH					
CLOSING CASH					

13. The following is a budget for the Duffin family for the 4 months May to August. Opening cash in hand is €750.

Planned income:

- David Duffin earns €1,760 net per month.

- Lucile Duffin earns €2,600 net per month and expects to receive an extra €1,100 net in July as a holiday bonus.

- Child Benefit is €210 net per month.

Planned expenditure:

- The house mortgage of €709 per month will decrease to €700 per month from 1 June.

- The house insurance premium of €840 **per year** is payable **monthly** from 1 July.

- The Duffin family pays health insurance of €155 per month. This will increase by €15 per month from 1 August.

- Household expenses are usually €1,400 per month except in August, when they are €800 **less**.

- The Duffin family uses public transport to travel to work. David's train ticket costs €120 per month and Lucile's combined bus/Luas ticket costs €90 per month.

- Bills for light and heat are expected to amount to €240 in June and €289 in August.

- Telephone bills for the home are expected to be €195 in May and €180 in July. In addition, bills for mobile phones for all the family will be €150 per month.

- The family has booked a holiday costing €3,400. They must pay a deposit of €500 to the travel agent in June, a further instalment of €800 in July and the balance in August.

- Entertainment will cost €750 each month except in June, when it will cost an **extra** €600.

(a) Complete the blank household budget form using all the above figures.

(b) Apart from cash or cheque, name two other methods by which the Duffin family could pay their electricity bills.

_____

(c) The Duffin family intends to paint the living room in September at a cost of €850. State whether this expenditure will be fixed, irregular or discretionary.

_____

DUFFIN FAMILY	May	June	July	Aug	Total
PLANNED INCOME	€	€	€	€	€
David Duffin – salary					
Lucile Duffin – salary					
Child Benefit					
TOTAL INCOME					
PLANNED EXPENDITURE					
Fixed					
House mortgage					
House insurance					
Health insurance					
Subtotal					
Irregular					
Household expenses					
Transport					
Light and heat					
Telephone					
Subtotal					
Discretionary					
Holiday					
Entertainment					
Subtotal					
TOTAL EXPENDITURE					
NET CASH					
OPENING CASH					
CLOSING CASH					

Section A Questions

14. Lorna Doyle's wages are €950 net per month. She is expecting an increase of €45 net a month from 1 November. Write her wages into her budget for the 3 months October to December.

Planned Income	Oct	Nov	Dec	TOTAL
Wages				

Household Budgeting Revised (HL)

1. Study the completed budget form on p. 37 for the Nolan family for the 4 months January to April. Answer the questions below.

(a) Do John and Geraldine own the house in which they live? Give a reason for your answer.

_____

(b) Can they afford to pay for the redecorating planned for February out of net cash or savings?

_____

(c) Apart from cash or cheque, name one other way the Nolan family could pay their telephone bill. _____

(d) Child Benefit is €130 per month for each of the first two children and €140 for each additional child. How many children are in the Nolan family? _____

(e) In which months did deficits occur? Suggest ways these deficits could be avoided.

_____

_____

(f) Calculate the total amount spent on the car during the 4 months in question.

_____

(g) Can the Nolans really afford to go on their holiday in April? Give a reason for your answer.

_____

(h) Which type of expenditure would the purchase of lottery tickets be an example of?

_____

(i) One of the Nolan children, Linda, has asked for €180 to go on a school trip in April. Based on the budget, do you think her parents will be able to give her the money?

_____

(j) How much will the Nolans have saved during the 4 months if they do not go on the holiday? _____

(k) List four costs associated with running a car.

_____

(l) If the line rental for the telephone is €25 for 2 months and the calls cost 10c per unit, how many units did the Nolans use during the January/February period? _____

NOLAN FAMILY	Jan	Feb	Mar	April	TOTAL
	€	€	€	€	€
PLANNED INCOME					
John Nolan – salary	1,050	1,050	1,050	1,050	4,200
Geraldine Nolan – salary	950	950	950	950	3,800
Child Benefit	400	400	400	400	1,600
TOTAL INCOME	2,400	2,400	2,400	2,400	9,600
PLANNED EXPENDITURE					
Fixed					
House mortgage	760	760	760	760	3,040
Annual car tax			220		220
Car loan	225	225	225	225	900
House insurance	25	25	25	25	100
Annual car insurance	390				390
Health insurance		450			450
Subtotal	1,400	1,460	1,230	1,010	5,100
Irregular					
Household expenses	480	480	480	480	1,920
Car running costs	130	230	130	130	620
Telephone		105		120	225
Gas	45		60		105
School exam fees			420		420
Subtotal	655	815	1,090	730	3,290
Discretionary					
Entertainment	90	90	90	90	360
Holiday				470	470
Redecoration		325			325
Subtotal	90	415	90	560	1,155
TOTAL EXPENDITURE	2,145	2,690	2,410	2,300	9,545
NET CASH	255	−290	−10	100	55
OPENING CASH	100	355	65	55	100
CLOSING CASH	355	65	55	155	155

2. You are required to complete the personal budget form for the Hilliard family for the months of October, November and December as well as the Total column. The following information should be taken into account.

- Michael Hilliard expects to earn €160 per month extra in overtime in November and December

- Megan Hilliard is due a pay increase of 5% from 1 October

- Child Benefit is the same each month

- Due to an expected interest rate rise, the house mortgage will rise by 1%, beginning with the November payment

- The car loan will be fully repaid by the end of November

- Annual car insurance of €600 is payable quarterly (every 3 months)

- The annual house insurance premium is due for renewal on 1 October and the premium of €240 is payable monthly

- Household costs are estimated at €350 per month except in December, when there will be an increase of €150

- Car running costs per month from October onwards will be €120 per month, with an additional car service in November costing a further €90

- Electricity is estimated at €65 in October and €70 in December

- Telephone charges are usually €85 every 2 months

- €70 is allocated per month for entertainment except in December, when this will increase to €140

- Christmas presents in December will cost €120

- Home decoration will cost €440 in October

HILLIARD FAMILY	July	Aug	Sept	Oct	Nov	Dec	TOTAL
	€	€	€	€	€	€	€
PLANNED INCOME							
Michael Hilliard – salary	800	800	800				
Megan Hilliard – salary	1,000	1,000	1,000				
Child Benefit	60	60	60				
TOTAL INCOME	1,860	1,860	1,860				
PLANNED EXPENDITURE							
Fixed							
House mortgage	600	600	600				
Car loan	180	180	180				
Car insurance	150						
House insurance	18	18	18				
Subtotal	948	798	798				
Irregular							
Household costs	350	350	350				
Car running costs	110	110	150				
Electricity		60					
Telephone	85		85				
Subtotal	545	520	585				
Discretionary							
Entertainment	70	70	70				
Christmas presents							
Home decoration							
Holiday		750					
Subtotal	70	820	70				
TOTAL EXPENDITURE	1,563	2,138	1,453				
NET CASH	297	−278	407				
OPENING CASH	100	397	119	526			
CLOSING CASH	397	119	526				

3. You are required to complete the personal budget form for the Lawlor family for the months of April, May and June as well as the Total column. The following information should be taken into account.

- Kenneth Lawlor is due a salary increase of 10% from 1 April

- Sadie Lawlor expects to receive €120 overtime in May and June

- Child Benefit is the same each month

- The Lawlors expect to receive €600 from the sale of shares in May

- Due to an expected interest rate fall, the house mortgage will decrease by 4% beginning with the April payment

- Car loan repayments will continue until April, after which the loan will be fully repaid

- Insurance payments for the year total €648 and are paid monthly

- Groceries will cost €380 per month

- Car running costs are estimated as follows: April €85, May €105, June €85

- Gas bills are estimated at €45 in April and €30 in June

- €140 is allocated per month for entertainment

- Clothes expenditure is expected to be €230 in May

- A holiday in April will cost €650

- New furniture in April will cost €550

LAWLOR FAMILY	Jan	Feb	Mar	Apr	May	June	TOTAL
	€	€	€	€	€	€	€
PLANNED INCOME			~~2096~~				
Kenneth Lawlor – salary	750	750	750	810	810	810	4680 *4680*
Sadie Lawlor – salary	800	800	800	800	920	920	5040
Child Benefit	60	60	60	60	60	60	360
Sale of shares					600	1	600
TOTAL INCOME	1,610	1,610	1,610	1610	2,390	1790	
PLANNED EXPENDITURE							
Fixed							
House mortgage	525	525	525	504	504	504	3087
Car loan	145	145	145	145	145	145	725
Insurance	54	54	54	54	54	54	270
Subtotal	724	724	724	703	703	703	4281
Irregular							
Groceries	380	380	380	380	380	880	
Car running costs	70	85	150	85	105	85	
Gas		60	~~45~~	45		30	
Subtotal	450	525	530				
Discretionary							
Entertainment	140	140	140	140	140	140	
Clothes	160				230		
Holiday				650			
New furniture				550			
Subtotal	300	140	140				
TOTAL EXPENDITURE	1,474	1,389	1,394				
NET CASH	136	221	216				
OPENING CASH	50	186	407	623			
CLOSING CASH	186	407	623				

2250
+2430

4. You are required to complete the personal budget form for the Hammad family for the months of September to November as well as the Total column. The following information should be taken into account.

- Ahmed Hammad is due a salary increase of 15% from 1 October

- Aisha Hammad expects to receive €150 overtime in September and November

- Child Benefit is the same each month

- The Hammads expect to receive €2,000 from the sale of a second-hand car in October

- Due to an expected interest rate rise, the house mortgage will increase by 2% beginning with the October payment

- Car tax is due in October, costing €256

- House insurance costing €480, which is payable monthly, is due for renewal in September

- Groceries will cost €275 per month

- Telephone costs per month are expected to be €45 (mobile) and €70 (landline)

- Gas bills are estimated at €98 in September and €102 in November

- €120 is allocated per month for entertainment

- New clothes for the children in November will cost €320

- A holiday in October will cost €2,400

HAMMAD FAMILY	June	July	Aug	Sept	Oct	Nov	TOTAL
	€	€	€	€	€	€	€
PLANNED INCOME							
Ahmed Hammad – salary	1,700	1,700	1,700				
Aisha Hammad – salary	1,500	1,500	1,500				
Child Benefit	300	300	300				
Sale of car							
TOTAL INCOME							
PLANNED EXPENDITURE							
Fixed							
House mortgage	750	750	750				
Car tax							
House insurance	35	35	35				
Subtotal							
Irregular							
Groceries	275	275	275				
Telephone costs	95	95	95				
Gas		98					
Subtotal							
Discretionary							
Entertainment	120	120	120				
Clothes	189						
Holiday		500					
Subtotal							
TOTAL EXPENDITURE							
NET CASH							
OPENING CASH	250						
CLOSING CASH							

5. You are required to complete the personal budget form for the Rooney family for 2011 by filling in the figures for the Estimate May to December column and the Total for Year column. The following information should be taken into account.

- Gerard Rooney is due a salary increase of 10% from 1 May
- Elaine Rooney expects to earn an extra €150 per month from 1 October
- Child Benefit will continue each month as for the first 4 months of the year
- House mortgage is expected to decrease by €60 a month from 1 July
- House insurance costing €260 per annum is paid in 10 equal instalments between January and October
- Family car insurance is €740 per annum, payable in October
- Household costs are expected to remain the same for each month until September, but will increase by €30 per month from 1 October and by a further €200 in December
- Car running costs are expected to remain at €150 per month except for a car service costing €70 in July and car repairs costing €120 in December
- Electricity for the 12 months (January to December) is estimated at €450
- Birthday presents in July will cost €60 and Christmas presents in December will cost €150
- Entertainment is expected to continue to cost €45 per month except in December, when it will increase to €100
- The family holiday in July is expected to cost €1,500

ROONEY FAMILY	Jan	Feb	Mar	Apr	Total J–A	Estimate M–D	TOTAL FOR YEAR
	€	€	€	€	€	€	€
PLANNED INCOME							
Gerard Rooney – salary	900	900	900	900	3,600		
Elaine Rooney – salary	600	600	600	600	2,400		
Child Benefit	30	30	30	30	120		
TOTAL INCOME	1,530	1,530	1,530	1,530	6,120		
PLANNED EXPENDITURE							
Fixed							
Mortgage	380	380	380	380	1,520		
Annual car tax		320			320		
House insurance	26	26	26	26	104		
Annual car insurance							
Subtotal	406	726	406	406	1,944		
Irregular							
Household costs	350	350	350	350	1,400		
Car running costs	150	150	150	150	600		
Electricity		54		60	114		
Subtotal	500	554	500	560	2,114		
Discretionary							
Presents				20	20		
Entertainment	45	45	45	45	180		
Holiday		300			300		
Subtotal	45	345	45	65	500		
TOTAL EXPENDITURE	951	1,625	951	1,031	4,558		
NET CASH	579	–95	579	499	1,562		
OPENING CASH	100	679	584	1,163	100		
CLOSING CASH	679	584	1,163	1,662	1,662		

6. You are required to complete the personal budget form for Paul, Sinead and family for 2012 by filling in the figures for the Estimate April to December column and the Total for Year column. The following information should be taken into account.

- Paul O'Hara is due a salary increase of 5% from 1 August and a Christmas bonus of €500

- Sinead Scanlon expects to stay on €800 per month until the end of October but is due a rise of €110 per month from 1 November

- Child Benefit will continue each month as for the first 3 months of the year

- The house mortgage is expected to increase by €20 a month from 1 July

- Annual car tax of €440 is payable quarterly beginning in January

- The house insurance per month will continue as for the first 3 months of the year

- The car loan will be paid off at the end of October

- Household costs are expected to remain the same for each month until July but will increase by €40 per month from 1 August and by a further €120 in December

- There will be a car service in July costing €120 but otherwise car running costs are expected to remain at €150 per month

- Gas charges for the 12 months (January to December) are estimated at €570

- Telephone charges are expected to be €85 in May, €110 in July, €95 in September and €100 in December

- Presents for the remainder of the year will cost €240

- Entertainment is expected to continue as before with an additional €150 in December

- The family holiday in July is expected to cost €1,400

PAUL, SINEAD AND FAMILY	Jan	Feb	Mar	Total J–M	Estimate A–D	TOTAL FOR YEAR
	€	€	€	€	€	€
PLANNED INCOME						
Paul O'Hara – salary	660	660	660	1,980		
Sinead Scanlon – salary	800	600	800	2,200		
Child Benefit	30	30	30	90		
TOTAL INCOME	1,490	1,290	1,490	4,270		
PLANNED EXPENDITURE						
Fixed						
Mortgage	480	480	480	1,440		
Car tax	110			110		
House insurance	25	25	25	75		
Car loan	180	180	180	540		
Subtotal	795	685	685	2,165		
Irregular						
Household costs	420	420	420	1,260		
Car running costs	150	150	150	450		
Gas		80		80		
Telephone	70		85	155		
Subtotal	640	650	655	1,945		
Discretionary						
Presents		20		20		
Entertainment	80	80	80	240		
Holiday						
Subtotal	80	100	80	240		
TOTAL EXPENDITURE	1,515	1,435	1,420	4,370		
NET CASH	−25	−145	70	−100		
OPENING CASH	200	175	30	200		
CLOSING CASH	175	30	100	100		

7. After the Gleeson family had prepared their household budget for January to March, Mrs Gleeson decided to give up working outside the home to look after her children. This will result in a drop in the family's income. Consequently, the Gleesons decided to revise their budget in light of their changed circumstances.

(a) You are required to complete the revised budget form on p. 49 after taking the following into account.

- Mr Gleeson will do overtime, for which he will receive €120 per month from 1 January
- Mrs Gleeson's salary will stop at the end of January
- Child Benefit will double from 1 January
- Childminding costs will stop from 1 January
- Car running costs will be reduced by €30 per month
- The telephone expenses will be reduced to €50 per bill
- Entertainment expenses to be reduced by €25 per month
- The weekend away planned for March will not go ahead
- All other income and expenses to remain the same

(b) Do you think any further action is necessary by the Gleeson family?

_____

_____

8. After the Barnes family had prepared their household budget for October to December, Linda Barnes learned that she was to be put on a three-day week at work, which would result in a drop in the family's income. Consequently, the Barnes decided to revise their budget in light of their changed circumstances.

(a) You are required to complete the revised budget form on p. 50 after taking the following into account.

- Linda Barnes's wages will be reduced by 40% in each of the 3 months
- Brian Barnes will do some overtime in November and December for which he will earn €80 per month
- Childminding costs will be reduced by €30 per month from 1 October
- Linda Barnes decided to join a gym at an annual cost of €350 payable in October to occupy her spare time
- Car running costs will be reduced by €50 per month
- Using less light and heat will reduce electricity bills to €40 in October and €55 in December
- Linda Barnes will travel to work on public transport, which will cost €14 per month
- Entertainment expenses are to be reduced by €40 per month except in December, when they will remain as planned
- Planned expenditure on Christmas presents will be halved
- All other income and expenses to remain the same

(b) Do you think any further action is necessary by the Barnes family? If so, suggest two options available to them.

_____

_____

7.

GLEESON FAMILY	Jan	Feb	Mar	TOTAL	Jan	Feb	Mar	TOTAL
	€	€	€	€	€	€	€	€
PLANNED INCOME								
Jim Gleeson – salary	1,200	1,200	1,200	3,600				
Gail Gleeson – salary	850	850	850	2,550				
Child Benefit	30	30	30	90				
TOTAL INCOME	2,080	2,080	2,080	6,240				
PLANNED EXPENDITURE								
Fixed								
House mortgage	350	350	350	1050				
Car loan	120	120		240				
Childminding costs	90	90	90	270				
Car insurance		260		260				
House insurance	15	15	15	45				
Subtotal	575	835	455	1,865				
Irregular								
Household costs	280	280	280	840				
Car running costs	100	100	100	300				
Electricity		55		55				
Telephone	90		90	180				
Subtotal	470	435	470	1,375				
Discretionary								
Entertainment	70	70	70	210				
Presents		25		25				
Holiday			150	150				
Subtotal	70	95	220	385				
Savings	140	140	140	420				
TOTAL EXPENDITURE	1,255	1,505	1,285	4,045				
(including savings)								
NET CASH	825	575	795	2,195				
OPENING CASH	50	875	1,450	50				
CLOSING CASH	875	1,450	2,245	2,245				

8.

BARNES FAMILY	Oct	Nov	Dec	TOTAL	Oct	Nov	Dec	TOTAL
	€	€	€	€	€	€	€	€
PLANNED INCOME								
Linda Barnes – salary	700	700	700	2,100				
Brian Barnes – salary	500	500	500	1,500				
Child Benefit	60	60	60	180				
TOTAL INCOME	1,260	1,260	1,260	3,780				
PLANNED EXPENDITURE								
Fixed								
House mortgage	240	240	240	720				
Childminding costs	60	60	60	180				
Car insurance		240		240				
House insurance	25	25	25	75				
Gym membership								
Subtotal	325	565	325	1,215				
Irregular								
Household costs	290	290	290	870				
Car running costs	110	110	110	330				
Electricity	65		70	135				
Travel expenses								
Subtotal	465	400	470	1,335				
Discretionary								
Entertainment	80	80	120	280				
Presents			250	250				
Home decoration	460			460				
Subtotal	540	80	370	990				
Savings	80	80	80	240				
TOTAL EXPENDITURE (including savings)	1,410	1,125	1,245	3,780				
NET CASH	−150	135	15	0				
OPENING CASH	50	−100	35	50				
CLOSING CASH	−100	35	50	50				

Exam-style Questions

9. Roper Family

An original budget and a revised budget form for the Roper household from July to September is on the next page. After preparing the original budget, Mr Roper changed jobs and his salary increased. However, Mrs Roper lost her job in the local factory after it closed down in June. The Roper household decided to revise their budget due to their changed circumstances.

(A) You are required to complete the revised budget, taking the following into account.

- Mr Roper's annual salary will be €36,000 net, payable monthly. He also expects to receive a bonus of €1,000 net in September.

- Mrs Roper will receive €740 net monthly in Jobseeker's Benefit.

- The Ropers will sell one of their two cars and expect to receive €5,400 for it in August.

- Mortgage repayments will increase by 2% from 1 September.

- The Roper household will make one loan repayment in July and will repay the balance of the loan (€2,800) in August.

- Car insurance will decrease by €40 per month from 1 August.

- Household costs will decrease by 10% per month from 1 July.

- Car costs will decrease to €75 per month from 1 August.

- Entertainment costs will be reduced by 45%.

- Due to their changed circumstances, the holiday planned for August will be postponed.

- All other income and expenditure will remain the same.

(B) (i) In the original budget, name a month in which planned income is greater than planned expenditure.

_____

    (ii) In the original budget, by how much did the Roper household expect to overspend in the 3 months?

_____

    (iii) Give **one** reason why the repayments on the mortgage might increase.

_____

    (iv) Is the revised budget a good one? Give **two** reasons for your answer.

_____

_____

ROPER FAMILY	July	Aug	Sept	TOTAL	July	Aug	Sept	TOTAL
PLANNED INCOME	€	€	€	€	€	€	€	€
Mr Roper – salary	1,600	1,600	1,600	4,800				
Mrs Roper – salary	1,400	1,400	1,400	4,200				
Child Benefit	155	155	155	465				
Other								
TOTAL INCOME	3,155	3,155	3,155	9,465				
PLANNED EXPENDITURE								
Fixed								
House mortgage	900	900	900	2,700				
Loan repayments	450	450	450	1,350				
Car insurance	70	70	70	210				
Subtotal	1,420	1,420	1,420	4,260				
Irregular								
Household costs	800	800	800	2,400				
Car costs	165	165	165	495				
Light and heat	267		200	467				
Telephone	60	60	150	270				
Subtotal	1,292	1,025	1,315	3,632				
Discretionary								
Entertainment	220	220	220	660				
Presents	350		200	550				
Holiday		4,500		4,500				
Subtotal	570	4,720	420	5,710				
TOTAL EXPENDITURE	3,282	7,165	3,155	13,602				
NET CASH	−127	−4,010	0	−4,137				
OPENING CASH	500	373	−3,637	500				
CLOSING CASH	373	−3,637	−3,637	−3,637				

10. Pang Family

(A) A partially completed budget form for the Pang household is on the next page. You are required to complete this form by filling in the figures for the Estimate April to December column and the Total for Year column. The following information should be taken into account.

- Jack expects to get a promotion in July, which will result in a rise of 30% in salary from 1 July.

- Suelee expects to earn an extra €350 for overtime in August and will get a Christmas bonus of €500 in December.

- The Pang household expects to receive €2,000 in dividends in May.

- The house mortgage will increase by €27 per month from 1 June.

- The car loan will be fully paid off following the August payment.

- House insurance is payable monthly and will decrease by 20% from 1 June.

- Household costs will remain the same for the remainder of the year.

- Light and heat for the 12 months (January to December) is expected to be €850.

- Mobile phone costs are estimated to be €70 per month from 1 April and the house phone costs to be €100 every second month from 1 May.

- Car running costs are expected to remain at the same level each month.

- Jack and Suelee plan to go to France on a holiday which will cost €2,500. The balance must be paid in July.

- The household expects to spend €150 on presents in July and another €450 in December.

- There is no further household decoration planned for the year.

(B) Answer the following questions.

(i) Explain the term 'dividends' in the Pang household budget.

_____

(ii) At the end of March, what will the expected closing cash balance be for the Pang household?

_____

(iii) The expected closing cash balance has changed from February to March. Explain two major reasons for this change.

_____

_____

(iv) Identify one method of dealing with this temporary situation at the end of March.

_____

PANG FAMILY	Jan	Feb	Mar	Total J–M	Estimate A–D	TOTAL FOR YEAR
PLANNED INCOME	€	€	€	€	€	€
Jack Pang – salary	1,100	1,100	1,100	3,300		
Suelee Pang – salary	800	800	800	2,400		
Child Benefit	300	300	300	900		
Dividends						
TOTAL INCOME	2,200	2,200	2,200	6,600		
PLANNED EXPENDITURE						
Fixed						
Mortgage	450	450	450	1,350		
Car loan	325	325	325	975		
House insurance	30	30	30	90		
Subtotal	805	805	805	2,415		
Irregular						
Household costs	450	450	450	1,350		
Light and heat	100	78	90	268		
Telephone	140	95	170	405		
Car running costs	70	70	70	210		
Subtotal	760	693	780	2,233		
Discretionary						
France holiday deposit		700		700		
Presents	90			90		
Household decoration			2,000	2,000		
Subtotal	90	700	2,000	2,790		
TOTAL EXPENDITURE	1,655	2,198	3,585	7,438		
NET CASH	545	2	−1,385	−838		
OPENING CASH	175	720	722	175		
CLOSING CASH	720	722	−663	−663		

Household Accounts and Filing

In each of the following assignments, you are required to prepare an analysed cash book. Receipts should be analysed under the following headings: Wages; Child Benefit. Expenditure should be analysed under the headings indicated in each question.

Cash Transactions

1. From the following information, prepare an analysed cash book for Elaine Deasy. Use the following payment analysis columns: Groceries; Car; Light and heat; Other.

Jan 1	Opening cash	100
2	Received wages	250
3	Paid for groceries	85
5	Paid for petrol	20
6	Entertainment expenses	55
7	Paid electricity bill	48
7	Charity donation	5
7	New tyre	40

ANALYSED CASH BOOK

Dr

Date	Details	F	Total					
1/1/16	opening cash		£100					
2/1/16	receive wages		£250					
	to be		350					
	total		350					

Cr

Date	Details	F	Total	Groceries	Car	Light	Other
3/1/16	Paid for groceries		£85	£85			
5/1/16	paid for petrol expenses		£20		£20		
6/1/16	Entertainment		£55				£55
7/1/16	paid electricity bill		£48			£48	
7/1/16	charity donation		£5				£5
7/1/16	new tyre		£40		£40		
	total		253				
	total						
	Balance		97				
			350				

2. From the following information, prepare an analysed cash book for Liam Gahan. Use the following payment analysis columns: Groceries; Household bills; Car; Other.

Feb 1	Opening cash	80	Feb 8	Paid rent	115
2	Received wages	370	9	Petrol	22
4	Purchased groceries	110	10	Clothes and shoes	58
6	Paid house insurance	95	12	Chemist	16
7	Milk and bread	6	19	Received Child Benefit	90

ANALYSED CASH BOOK

Dr

Date	Details	F	Total
1/2/16	Opening Cash		80
2/2/16	Received		€390
19/2/16	child benifit		90
	total		540
	Balanced		450

Cr

Date	Details	F	Total	groceries/household	bills/Household	Car	other
4/2/16	Purchased groceries			€110			
6/2/16	Paid house insurance				€95		
7/2/16	Milk and bread			€6			
8/2/16	Paid rent				€115		
9/2/16	Petrol					22	
10/2/16	Clothes and shoes						€58
12/2/16	Chemist						€16
	Balance		€22				
			€28				
	459						

3. From the following information, prepare an analysed cash book for the Dunphy household. Use the following payment analysis columns: Groceries; Car; Entertainment; Telephone; Other.

Mar 1	Opening cash	210	
2	Received wages	1,250	
3	Received Child Benefit	60	
5	Purchased groceries	98	
6	Paid car insurance	367	
8	Petrol	21	
9	Paid telephone bill	65	

Mar 10	Entertainment	55
12	Purchased groceries	79
14	Car repairs	100
16	TV licence	68
18	Newspapers	12
20	Petrol	21

ANALYSED CASH BOOK

Dr

Date	Details	F	Total
1/3/16	Opening Cash		210
2/3/16	Received wages		1250
3/3/16	Received child benefit		60
	total		1520

Cr

Date	Details	F	Total	groceries	Car	enter	phone	other
5/3/16	Purchased groceries		98	60				
6/3/16	Paid car insurance				367			
8/3/16	Petrol				21			
9/3/16	Paid telephone bill						65	
10/3/16	Entertainment					55		
12/3/16	Purchased groceries			79				
14/3/16	Car repairs				100			
16/3/16	TV licence							68
18/3/16	Newspapers							12
20/3/16	Petrol				21			
	total		842					
	Balance		678					

(1520)
842 8 = 678

4. From the following information, prepare an analysed cash book for the Moffitt family. Use the following payment analysis columns: Groceries; Car; Entertainment; Household bills; Other.

May 1	Opening cash	250	May 11	Groceries	80
2	Received wages	1,100	13	Entertainment	45
3	Groceries	85	14	Received Child Benefit	90
4	Concert tickets	35	15	Petrol	25
7	Petrol	20	17	Gas	45
8	Mortgage	410	20	Clothes and shoes	82
9	Service charges	10	22	Entertainment	60

ANALYSED CASH BOOK

Dr

Date	Details	F	Total
1/5/16	Opening cash		250
2/5/16	Receiving wages		1,100
14/5/16	Receiving child benefit		90
	Balance		1449

Cr

Date	Details	F	Total	Groc	Car	Enter	bills	other
3/5/16	Groceries			85				
4/5/16	Concert tickets					35		
7/5/16	Petrol				20			
8/5/16	Mortgage						410	
9/5/16	Services charges							10
11/5/16	Groceries			80				
13/5/16	Entertainment					45		
15/5/16	Petrol				25			
17/5/16	Gas						45	
20/5/16	Clothes and shoes							82
22/5/16	Entertainment					60		
		total	897					
			542					

5. From the following information, prepare an analysed cash book for the Weldon family. Use the following payment analysis columns: Insurance; Household bills; Motor expenses; Other.

June	1	Opening cash	175
	3	Received wages	1,750
	4	Groceries	116
	7	House insurance	423
	9	Diesel	40
	12	Car service	149
	15	Cinema trip	45
June	19	Electricity bill	95
	23	Entertainment	76
	25	Diesel	40
	27	Mobile credit	30
	28	Travel insurance	68
	30	Groceries	120

ANALYSED CASH BOOK

Dr

Date	Details	F	Total
1/6/16	opening cash		£75
3/6/16	Receiving wages		1,750

Cr

Date	Details	F	Total	insurance	house bills	Motor expense	other
4/6/16	Groceries						£116
7/6/16	house insurance			423			
9/6/16	Disel Diesel		40			40	
12/6/16	car services		149			149	
15/6/16	Cinema trip						£45
19/6/16	Electricity bill				95		
23/6/16	Entertainment						76
25	Disel				40		30
27	Mobile credit						
28	Travel insurance		6°	68	40		
30	Groceries		£25				120

Bank Transactions Only

In each of the following assignments, you are required to prepare an analysed cash book.
Receipts should be analysed under the following headings: Wages; Child Benefit; Other.
Expenditure should be analysed under the headings indicated in each question.

6. From the following information, prepare an analysed cash book for David Dunne. Use the following payment analysis columns: Groceries; Car; Telephone; Mortgage.

Jan	1	Opening bank balance	1,650
	4	Paid for groceries with cheque no. 1	211
	6	Received wages and lodged cheque in bank	2,410
	8	Paid for petrol with cheque no. 2	40
	9	Paid telephone bill with cheque no. 3	87
	12	Sold old piano and lodged cheque	150
	14	Paid for groceries with cheque no. 4	242
	17	Paid mortgage with cheque no. 5	675
	24	Withdrew cash from ATM to pay for petrol	40

ANALYSED CASH BOOK

Dr

Date	Details	F	Total
1/1	opening bal		1650
6/1	Received wages		2410
12/1	sold piano		150
			4210

Cr

Date	Details	F	Total	Groc	car	Tel	Mort
4/1	Paid for groc		211	211			
8/1	petrol		40		40		
9/1	telephone bill		87			87	
14/1	sold piano		242	242			
	Paid for groc		40		40		
	Paid mortgage		675				675
	Bal c/d		1295				
	An z		2915				

7. From the following information, prepare an analysed cash book for Elaine Smith. Use the following payment analysis columns: Groceries; Entertainment; Light and heat; Education; Other.

Feb	1	Opening bank balance	475
	5	Purchased petrol and paid with cheque no. 7	50
	9	Paid for groceries with cheque no. 8	172
	11	Received wages and lodged cheque in bank	1,400
	14	Paid for a meal out with cheque no. 9	140
	21	Charity donation with cheque no. 10	100
	22	Paid for oil refill with cheque no. 11	245
	24	Paid for groceries with cheque no. 12	194
	27	Paid for school exams with cheque no. 13	180
	28	Paid electricity bill with cheque no. 14	140

ANALYSED CASH BOOK

Dr

Date	Details	F	Total
1/2	Opening Bank balance		£475
11/2	Received wages		£1,400
	total		1807
			1875

Cr

Date	Details	F	Total	Groc	Entertainment	Education	Other
5/2	Petrol		50				£50
9/2	Groceries		172	£172			
14/2	Paid for a meal		140				160
21/2	Charity donation		100				100
22/2	Oil		245				245
24/2	Groceries		194	194			
27/2	Paid school exams		160			180	
28/2	Paid electricity		140		140		
	Balance total		1221				
	Balance		654				
			1875				

8. From the following information, prepare an analysed cash book for Paul Palmer. Use the following payment analysis columns:
Transport; Gas; Rent; Groceries; Other.

Mar	1	Opening bank balance	845
	2	Paid for train fares with Laser card	50
	4	Paid gas bill with cheque no. 16	185
	7	Paid for groceries with cheque no. 17	125
	9	Received wages and lodged cheque in bank	1,470
	11	Paid rent with cheque no. 18	440
	15	Paid for taxi with cash	36
	18	Paid TV licence with cheque no. 19	145
	24	Paid for groceries with cheque no. 20	126
	27	Received Child Benefit directly into bank account	120
	30	Paid for train fares with Laser card	50

ANALYSED CASH BOOK

Dr

Date	Details	F	Total
1/3	Opening Bank Balance		845
9/3	Received wages		1470
27/3	Received child benefit		120

Cr

Date	Details	F	Total	Transport	Gas	Rent	Groceries	Other
2/3/16	Paid for train fares		£50	£50				
4/3/16	Paid gas bills		£185		£185			
9/3/16	Paid for groceries		£125				£125	
11/3/16	Paid rent		440			440		

9. From the following information, prepare an analysed cash book for Aarif Chopras. Use the following payment analysis columns: Insurance; Groceries; Light and heat; Car; Other.

May	1	Opening bank balance	1,200
	2	Paid for petrol with Laser card	45
	5	Paid electricity bill with cheque no. 2	146
	8	Paid for groceries with Laser card	210
	10	Received wages and lodged cheque in bank	1,250
	11	Paid insurance with cheque no. 3	550
	15	Paid for groceries with Laser card	220
	18	Paid gas bill through online banking	176
	24	Paid for car service with cheque no. 4	232
	27	Sold old furniture and lodged cheque to bank account	400
	30	Paid for entertainment with Laser card	120
	31	Paid for groceries with Laser card	220

ANALYSED CASH BOOK

Dr Date	Details	F	Total
1/5	Opening bank balance		1200
10/5	Recivd wages		1250
27/5	Sold old furniture		400

Cr Date	Details	F	Total	Groc	light heat	Car	other
2/5	petrol		45				45
5/5	paid electricity		146		146		
8/5	Groceries		210	210			245
10/5	paid insurance		550				550
15/5	groceries		220	220			
18/5	paid gas		176		176		
24/5	paid car services		232			232	
30/5	paid enter		120				120
31	groceries		220	220			

Cash and Bank Transactions

In each of the following assignments, receipts should be analysed under the following headings:
Wages; Child Benefit; Other.

11. From the following information, prepare an analysed cash book for the Spencer family. Use the following payment analysis columns: Groceries; Insurance; Telephone; Mortgage; Other.

Feb		
1	Opening cash balance	195
1	Opening bank balance	172
3	Received wages by cheque	1,350
5	Paid for groceries by cheque no. 1	80
6	Paid service charges by cheque no. 2	70
8	Paid mortgage by cheque no. 3	310
9	Paid for groceries by cash	65
11	Paid for car insurance by cheque no. 4	470
13	Paid telephone bill by cheque no. 5	85
15	Paid dentist in cash	18

Feb		
17	Family outing to cinema paid in cash	24
20	Paid mobile phone bill by cheque no. 6	31
22	Paid house insurance by cheque no. 7	210
24	Purchased groceries and paid by cheque no. 8	75
25	Pocket money for the children in cash	20
26	Received Child Benefit in cash	30
28	Paid monthly health insurance bill by cheque no. 9	62

ANALYSED CASH BOOK

Dr						Cr				
Date	Details	F	Cash	Bank		Date	Details	F	Cash	Bank

12. From the following information, prepare an analysed cash book for the Stanley family. Use the following payment analysis columns: Car; Light and heat; Clothes; Entertainment; Other.

Mar			
1	Opening balance	Cash 200, Bank 345	
4	Paid for petrol in cash		22
5	Paid gas bill by cheque no. 1		75
6	Entertainment expenses by cash		45
7	Purchased new football kit and paid by cheque no. 2		45
8	Received wages by cheque		1,420
9	Paid car tax by cheque no. 3		240
10	Paid for medicine in cash		20
11	Paid for groceries by cheque no. 4		250

Mar			
13	Paid electricity bill by cheque no. 5		70
15	Paid for newspapers in cash		10
17	Purchased new light bulbs with cash		10
20	Paid for petrol by cash		22
22	Paid mortgage by cheque no. 6		420
23	Family outing to café paid in cash		15
25	Entertainment expenses		55
27	Bought new clothes for Easter by cheque no. 7		250
28	Received Child Benefit in cash		60

ANALYSED CASH BOOK

Dr

Date	Details	F	Cash	Bank						

Cr

Date	Details	F	Cash	Bank						

13. From the following information, prepare an analysed cash book for the Maguire family. Use the following payment analysis columns: Groceries; Television; School; Mortgage; Other.

Sept	1	Opening cash balance	117
	1	Opening bank overdraft	240
	3	Paid for groceries by cheque no. 1	72
	4	Paid monthly TV subscription by cheque no. 2	24
	6	Received wages by cheque	1,250
	7	Cash win on the lottery	200
	8	Purchased wedding present and paid by cheque no. 3	100
	9	Bought meat and fish by cash	31

Sept	11	Paid for schoolbooks in cash	86
	12	Paid for groceries by cheque no. 4	84
	14	Purchased petrol in cash	24
	16	House decoration costs in cash	78
	18	Paid TV licence by cheque no. 5	68
	20	Paid mortgage by cheque no. 6	340
	22	Paid for groceries by cheque no. 7	70
	28	Received Child Benefit by cheque	60
	29	Paid for new school uniform in cash	48

ANALYSED CASH BOOK

Dr					
Date	Details	F	Cash	Bank	

Cr					
Date	Details	F	Cash	Bank	

14. From the following information, prepare an analysed cash book for the Doyle family. Use the following payment analysis columns: Insurance; Groceries; Clothes; Entertainment; Other.

May	1	Opening cash balance	112
	1	Opening bank balance	240
	3	Bought groceries and paid by cheque no. 1	92
	4	Withdrew cash from bank	100
	4	Received wages by cheque	1,200
	5	Paid car insurance by cheque no. 2	275
	7	Entertainment expenses in cash	40
	8	Purchased new clothes and paid by cheque no. 3	80
	9	Paid for car service by cheque no. 4	142
	10	Received Child Benefit in cash	90

May	11	Purchased groceries and paid by cheque no. 5	110
	13	Paid health insurance by cheque no. 6	150
	14	Paid telephone bill by cheque no. 7	92
	16	Outing to theatre paid by cash	40
	18	Paid mortgage by cheque no. 8	510
	20	Bought new shoes and paid by cheque no. 9	50
	22	Purchased groceries and paid in cash	55
	24	Entertainment expenses in cash	35
	26	Bought bread and milk	10
	27	Lodged cash in bank	90

ANALYSED CASH BOOK

Dr											
Date	Details	F	Cash	Bank							

Cr											
Date	Details	F	Cash	Bank							

15. From the following information, prepare an analysed cash book for the Dawodu family. Use the following payment analysis columns: Groceries; Television; School; Mortgage; Other.

July	1	Opening cash balance	510
	1	Opening bank overdraft	310
	4	Paid for groceries by cheque no. 1	120
	8	Received wages by cheque	2,420
	9	Cash win at bingo	140
	10	Purchased birthday present and paid by cheque no. 2	230
	13	Bought milk and bread in cash	22
	14	Paid for schoolbooks in cash	230
	15	Paid for groceries by cheque no. 3	156
	17	Purchased petrol in cash	45
	18	House decoration costs by cheque no. 4	320
	19	Paid TV licence by cheque no. 5	106
	21	Paid mortgage by cheque no. 6	700
	23	Paid for groceries by cheque no. 7	110
	25	Paid cable TV by cheque no. 8	140
	27	Received Child Benefit by cheque	300
	31	Paid for new school jacket in cash	55
	31	Purchased new fridge and paid by cheque no. 9	350

ANALYSED CASH BOOK

Dr										
Date	Details	F	Cash	Bank						

Cr										
Date	Details	F	Cash	Bank						

Comparing Actual with Budget

16. The following figures relate to the Deary family for the month of July. Complete the budget comparison statement below, then answer the questions that follow.

Budgeted: Income   Wages €1,644; Child Benefit €60.

                  Expenditure   Groceries €280; Car €80; Insurance €460; Mortgage €450; Light and heat €90; Entertainment €100.

Actual: Income   Wages €1,644; Child Benefit €60; Other €70 .

                  Expenditure   Groceries €310; Car €90; Insurance €450; Mortgage €450; Light and heat €78; Entertainment €150.

(a) How much had the Dearys intended to save in July?

_____

(b) By how much did the Dearys' actual income exceed their actual expenditure in July?

_____

(c) By how much did the Dearys' actual expenditure exceed their budgeted expenditure in July?

_____

(d) If the Dearys had €190 in their bank account at the end of June, how much money did they have in their bank account at the end of July?

_____

BUDGET COMPARISON STATEMENT			
INCOME	**Budgeted**	**Actual**	**Difference**
Wages			
Child Benefit			
Other			
TOTAL INCOME			
EXPENDITURE			
Groceries			
Car expenses			
Insurance			
Mortgage			
Light and heat			
Entertainment			
TOTAL EXPENDITURE			
NET CASH			

17. The following figures relate to the Daly family for the month of August. Complete the budget comparison statement below, then answer the questions that follow.

Budgeted: Income   Wages €2,200; Child Benefit €90.

Expenditure Telephone €80; Car tax €280; Groceries €350; Mortgage €570; Electricity €60; Entertainment €100; Petrol €180; Car insurance €460.

Actual: Income   Wages €2,200; Child Benefit €90.

Expenditure Telephone €90; Car tax €280; Groceries €455; Mortgage €570; Electricity €59; Entertainment €180; Petrol €180; Car insurance €488; House decoration €156.

(a) How much had the Dalys intended to save in August? _____

(b) What was the Dalys' net cash position at the end of August?

_____

(c) By how much did the Dalys' actual expenditure exceed their budgeted expenditure in August? _____

(d) In your opinion, what were the main causes of the Dalys' problems?

_____

(e) Suggest two ways the Dalys could solve their problems.

_____

_____

(f) Give one example of discretionary spending by the Dalys.

_____

(g) If the Dalys had €100 in their bank account at the end of July, how much money did they have in their bank account at the end of August?

_____

BUDGET COMPARISON STATEMENT			
INCOME	**Budgeted**	**Actual**	**Difference**
Wages			
Child Benefit			
TOTAL INCOME			
EXPENDITURE			
Telephone			
Car tax			
Groceries			
Mortgage			
Electricity			
Entertainment			
Petrol			
Car insurance			
House decoration			
TOTAL EXPENDITURE			
NET CASH			

Exam-style Questions

18. The Redmond family keeps a record of all financial transactions in an analysed cash book (bank columns only).
On 1 September they had €235 in the bank. During September they had the following transactions.

Sept 1   Paid car insurance by cheque no. 21   340
2   Withdrew cash from ATM for weekly shopping   55
4   Paid gas bill by cheque no. 22   66
6   Lodged wages cheque to bank   1,200
7   Paid for petrol by cheque no. 23   20
9   Paid credit card bill by cheque no. 24   120
11   Paid mortgage by cheque no. 25   330

Sept 13   Withdrew cash from ATM for weekly shopping   60
15   Lodged Child Benefit cheque to bank   60
17   Paid for petrol by cheque no. 26   20
22   Paid for new clothes by cheque no. 27   80
24   Paid electricity bill by cheque no. 28   45
25   Paid for weekly shopping by cheque no. 29   65

(A) Enter the above transactions in the analysed cash book (bank columns only) using the following money column headings.

Debit (receipts) side: Bank, Wages, Child Benefit.
Credit (payments) side: Bank, Car, Groceries, Light and heat, Mortgage, Other.

ANALYSED CASH BOOK

Dr					Cr				
Date	Details	F	Bank		Date	Details	F	Bank	

71

(B) Using the budget comparison statement below, enter the figures from the analysed cash book you have prepared into the Actual column. Show the difference between the actual and the budgeted figures in the Difference column and answer the questions that follow.

(i) How much had the Redmonds intended to save in September?

_____

(ii) By how much did the Redmonds' actual income exceed their actual expenditure in September?

_____

(iii) How much money did the Redmonds have in their bank account at the end of September?

_____

(iv) Suggest one reason why the Redmonds' car insurance was more than they budgeted for.

_____

BUDGET COMPARISON STATEMENT			
INCOME	**Budgeted**	**Actual**	**Difference**
Wages	1,235		
Child Benefit	60		
TOTAL INCOME	**1,295**		
EXPENDITURE			
Car expenses	290		
Groceries	170		
Light and heat	135		
Mortgage	330		
Other	175		
TOTAL EXPENDITURE	**1,100**		
NET CASH	195		

Section A Questions

19. Study the following meter readings taken from electricity bills. In each case calculate the number of units used and the total cost of the bill if electricity costs 9c per unit and there is a standing charge of €3.50 per bill. Ignore VAT.

(a) Present 22357; Previous 21089

Units used: _____

Total cost of bill: _____

(b) Present 34599; Previous 34001

Units used: _____

Total cost of bill: _____

(c) Present 44566; Previous 43889

Units used: _____

Total cost of bill: _____

20. Calculate the total cost of the following telephone bills. Assume a line rental of €26 per bill and VAT @ 10%. All units cost 10c.

(a) Local calls: 156 units _____

National calls: 66 units _____

International calls: 45 units _____

Mobile (calls to): 50 units _____

Total cost: _____

(b) Local calls: 278 units _____

National calls: 112 units _____

International calls: 68 units _____

Directory Enquiries: 8 units _____

Total cost: _____

21. Fill in the blanks.

(a) The debit side of the analysed cash book records money _____ .

(b) The credit side of the analysed cash book records money_____ .

22. From the following details for the O'Callaghan family, calculate the balance at the end of the month and state which side of the cash book it would be brought down on.

Opening bank balance   €120
Total receipts   €2,115
Total payments   €1,789

Balance: _____

Side: _____

Consumer Problems –
Sale of Goods and Supply of Services Act 1980

Study the situations below. From your knowledge of the Sale of Goods and Supply of Services Act 1980, answer the questions that follow.

1. Mr Smith purchased an iPod dock in his local electrical shop. When he got home he found it would not work. He returned it and was told he would have to accept a credit note in return.

   (a) Is Mr Smith entitled to a new iPod dock? Give a reason for your answer.

   _____

   _____

   (b) Does he have to accept the credit note?

   _____

   (c) Which other remedies may he choose from?

   _____

2. Ms Lawlor saw a microwave being demonstrated in McDonald's Electric, a shop in her local shopping centre. She ordered one but when it arrived she found that it did not have all the features that the one in the shop had.

   (a) Does Ms Lawlor have a valid complaint? Give a reason for your answer.

   _____

   _____

   _____

   (b) What remedies are available to Ms Lawlor in this case?

   _____

3. Mr Lyons went to his local hardware shop to purchase some glue to fix the ornament he had broken that day. He told the shopkeeper that he required glue that would stick to china. When he returned home he was unable to get the broken ornament to stay together and realised that the glue was only suitable for sticking to paper.

   (a) Explain why Mr Lyons has a valid complaint.

   _____

   _____

   (b) What remedies is Mr Lyons entitled to?

   _____

4. Miss Kennedy saw a roll of wallpaper in her local DIY centre that she thought would look very well in her sitting room. She asked the assistant for 10 rolls. When the decorators were in the middle of the job they noticed that four of the rolls were a slightly different shade and were in fact a different batch number.

(a) Explain why Miss Kennedy has a valid complaint.

_____

_____

(b) Is Miss Kennedy entitled to a refund or a credit note? Explain your answer.

_____

_____

5. Mr O'Reilly answered an advertisement in his local paper for an electrician. He needed his house rewired. The day after the job was completed, Mr O'Reilly switched on a light and all the fuses and sockets blew. The electrician had connected some wires incorrectly.

(a) What does the Sale of Goods and Supply of Services Act say about people who supply services?

_____

_____

(b) What remedies are available to Mr O'Reilly? Which should he choose in this case? Give a reason for your answer.

_____

_____

_____

6. Peter installed a satellite TV system 2 months ago but now realises that he does not watch TV enough to get full value from it. He wants to return it but the shop will not refund him his money. Is Peter entitled to get his money back? Give a reason for your answer.

_____

_____

_____

7. Catherine's new DVD recorder will not record properly, but when she returned it to the shop where she bought it she was told to return it to the manufacturer, as it was under guarantee. Catherine does not want to go to the expense of doing this. Was the shop correct in what they told Catherine? Explain your answer.

_____

_____

_____

Consumer Problems – The Consumer Protection Act 2007

Study the situations below. From your knowledge of the Consumer Protection Act 2007, answer the questions that follow.

8. The Murphy family booked a holiday from a tour brochure. The brochure said the hotel was just 5 minutes from the sea. When they arrived they found that the quickest way to the sea was by bus and took 25 minutes. What does the Consumer Protection Act 2007 say about situations like this?

_____

_____

_____

9. Paul saw a sign in a shop that said 'suits were €200, now €99'. Paul had been looking for a suit for some time and knew that these suits were never priced at €200. What does the Consumer Protection Act 2007 say about signs like this?

_____

_____

_____

10. Michelle Lyons saw a packet of cheese in her local store. The packet had a drawing of a harp and the words 'Best Irish Cheese'. However, when she brought the cheese home, she saw 'made in the United Kingdom' on the back of the packet. What does the Consumer Protection Act 2007 say about situations like this?

_____

_____

_____

11. Matching terms

Match the terms in column 1 with the correct explanation in column 2.

1. A person who buys goods and services	**A.** Impulse buying
2. A promise by a manufacturer to repair faults in a product or service	**B.** Loss leader
3. Proof of purchase	**C.** Ombudsman
4. Purchases made on the spur of the moment	**D.** Guarantee
5. Document allowing a consumer to purchase other goods in a shop up to the value of goods returned by them	**E.** Credit note
6. Any statements made about a good or service	**F.** Bar code
7. Goods sold below cost to attract customers into a shop	**G.** Trade association
8. A representative of the people	**H.** Unsolicited
9. An organisation set up under the Consumer Protection Act 2007	**I.** Trade description
10. The ITAA is an example of one	**J.** Receipt
11. A series of black and white lines and digits on the side of a product	**K.** National Consumer Agency
12. Goods sent to a customer which have not been ordered	**L.** Consumer

1. ☐   **2.** ☐   **3.** ☐   **4.** ☐   **5.** ☐   **6.** ☐

7. ☐   **8.** ☐   **9.** ☐   **10.** ☐   **11.** ☐   **12.** ☐

12. Word search

Solve the following clues, then locate and circle the answers in the grid below. The answers may read forwards, backwards or diagonally.

1. A person who buys goods or services (8) _____

2. A representative of the people (9) _____

3. Associations that look after the interests of retailers or manufacturers (5)

_____

4. A written promise to repair goods free of charge during a specified period (9)

_____

5. This is sometimes given in exchange for goods and allows you to purchase alternative goods in the same shop (6, 4) _____

6. A series of black and white lines on the side of a product (3, 4)

_____

7. Goods which, though cheaper, prove to be more expensive in the long run (5, 9)

_____

8. Written proof that a purchase has been made (7)_____

Q	C	A	W	E	D	S	R	S	B	N
W	O	S	Q	R	F	A	A	E	C	M
E	N	A	M	S	D	U	B	M	O	A
R	S	D	M	T	G	Z	A	R	D	E
T	U	R	E	C	E	I	P	T	E	C
Y	M	F	N	Y	H	X	M	T	R	O
U	E	G	B	N	O	T	E	E	C	N
F	R	H	V	U	J	C	D	U	L	O
A	P	J	C	I	K	I	A	I	K	M
L	O	K	X	O	T	V	R	O	H	I
S	G	U	A	R	A	N	T	E	E	E
E	I	L	Z	P	L	B	N	F	G	S

Section A Questions

13. Country Goodness sells frozen peas in three packet sizes, as indicated below. Tick the box corresponding to the size that represents the best value for money.

Size	Weight	Price	
Small	200 grams	€0.60	☐
Medium	500 grams	€1.25	☐
Large	1,000 grams	€2.60	☐

14. Name two laws or Acts that protect consumers' rights.

(a) _____

(b) _____

15. Which of the following would you complain to about a misleading advertisement?

(a) Ombudsman ☐

(b) National Consumer Agency ☐

(c) Consumer Association of Ireland ☐

(d) Your local TD ☐

16. Tick whether each of the following shop notices is legal or illegal.

	Legal	Illegal
(a) No Cash Refunds Under Any Circumstances	☐	☐
(b) Summer Sale Starts Tomorrow	☐	☐

17. You purchase a DVD player. After a while you realise that you do not make enough use of it. You bring it back to the shop but they refuse to refund you your money. Can you legally demand to get your money back? Give a reason for your answer. Yes ☐ No ☐

_____

_____

18. True or false

	True	False
(a) A student is a consumer when they purchase a new copybook in their local newsagent's shop	☐	☐
(b) The seller of the faulty goods decides which remedy the consumer should receive	☐	☐
(c) When a guarantee exists on a product, it is the manufacturer of the faulty goods who is responsible to the consumer and it is to the manufacturer that the goods must be returned	☐	☐
(d) If you receive goods that you did not order, you must keep them and pay for them if you do not return them within 30 days	☐	☐

19. Missing terms

Use the given letters to fill in the missing consumer words or phrases.

(a) `[_][R][A][_][D]  [N][_][M][_]`

(b) `[F][_][_][S][_]  [_][C][_][N][_][M][_]`

(c) `[_][A][V][_][_][T]  [E][_][P][_][_][R]`

(d) `[_][E][_][H][A][_][T][_][L][_]  [Q][_][A][_][I][_][_]`

(e) `[_][U][A][_][A][N][_][_][E]`

(f) `[C][_][E][_][I][_]  [N][_][_][E]`

(g) `[_][A][T][_][O][_][A][_]  [_][O][_][S][_][M][_][R][_][A][_][E][_][_][Y]`

(h) `[O][_][B][U][_][_][M][_][_]`

(i) `[_][O][_][S][_][M][_][_]  [A][_][_][O][_][I][A][_][I][_][N]`

(j) `[S][M][_][L][_]  [C][_][A][_][_]  [P][R][_][_][_][_][_][_][E]`

(k) `[_][A][_][C][O][_][E][_]`

(l) `[_][E][_][O][_][_]  [C][_][S][_]  [S][_][L][_][I][_][G]`

(m) `[_][E][_][E][I][_][_]`

1. Fill in the missing words to explain the main characteristics of money.

(a) Everyone has to _____ it as payment for goods and services.

(b) It has to be easy to _____, i.e. each note and coin has to be the same as other notes and coins of the same value.

(c) It has to be easy to _____ into smaller units, e.g. €1 = 100 cent.

(d) It has to be small and light and _____ to _____ around.

2. Use the letters below to help you identify the eurozone countries.

(a) | | U | | E | | | O | R | |
|---|---|---|---|---|---|---|---|---|

(b) | F | | N | | A | | |
|---|---|---|---|---|---|---|

(c) | | O | | | U | | | L |
|---|---|---|---|---|---|---|---|

(d) | B | | L | | I | | | |
|---|---|---|---|---|---|---|---|

(e) | | R | | | | N | |
|---|---|---|---|---|---|---|

(f) | | | A | | |
|---|---|---|---|---|

(g) | E | | T | | | | |
|---|---|---|---|---|---|---|

(h) | | T | | L | | |
|---|---|---|---|---|---|

(i) | | | | H | | | L | | N | | S |
|---|---|---|---|---|---|---|---|---|---|---|

(j) | | E | | M | | N | | |
|---|---|---|---|---|---|---|---|

(k) | A | | | | R | | A | |
|---|---|---|---|---|---|---|---|

(l) | | A | | | |
|---|---|---|---|---|

3. Word search

Locate the following terms associated with money in the grid below. The words may read forwards, backwards or diagonally.

Money	Barter	Euro	Cyprus	France	Greece	Slovakia	Slovenia

A	E	R	T	Y	U	I	O	P	Q	A
S	B	D	F	G	H	J	K	L	V	B
Z	X	A	V	B	N	N	M	K	L	H
Q	W	F	R	A	N	C	E	E	R	T
Y	U	I	O	T	P	O	I	U	Y	T
F	A	G	H	J	E	A	S	D	F	G
Z	S	C	V	B	U	R	N	A	M	E
T	U	Y	U	I	R	F	I	G	H	C
C	R	Z	X	M	O	N	E	Y	C	E
V	P	B	N	M	E	L	K	J	H	E
G	Y	F	D	V	S	A	Q	W	E	R
R	C	T	O	Y	U	I	O	P	P	G
A	S	L	D	F	G	H	J	K	L	N
C	S	L	O	V	A	K	I	A	V	B

Deposit Account Application Form

1. From the following details, you are required to complete the blank deposit account application form on p. 84.

Name:	Mr Kevin P. Conroy
Address:	27 Glendale Park, Rathdrum, Co. Wicklow
Previous address:	None, he has lived here since birth with his parents
Telephone:	022 1234567 (Home)
	01 7654321 (Work)
	089 3456789 (Mobile)
Date of birth:	16 March 1984
Marital status:	Single
No. of children:	None
Occupation:	Sales representative
Position:	Regional manager
Employer:	ALD Insurances Ltd, Insurance Brokers
Employment address:	288 Lower Baggott Street, Dublin 2
No. of years employed:	4
Annual gross pay:	€36,000
Monthly take-home pay:	€2,300
Existing bank accounts:	A deposit account with Dundrum Credit Union containing €4,000

Current Account Application Form

2. From the following details, you are required to complete the blank current account application form on p. 85.

Name:	Ms Elizabeth Pierce
Address:	45 St Mel's Park, Mullingar, Co. Westmeath
Previous address:	144 Mountain Close, Clonskeagh, Dublin 14
Telephone:	025 9876543 (Home)
	024 6574839 (Work)
	089 9182736 (Mobile)
Date of birth:	22 April 1972
Marital status:	Married
No. of children:	Two, ages 4 and 7
Occupation:	Accountant
Position:	Funds manager
Employer:	Alpha Financial Managers Ltd, Fund Managers
Employment address:	Unit 3, East Financial Services Centre, Mullingar, Co. Westmeath
No. of years employed:	10
Annual gross income:	€64,000
Monthly take-home pay:	€4,100
Existing bank accounts:	A deposit account with AIB containing €1,200

1.

DEPOSIT/CURRENT ACCOUNT APPLICATION FORM

1. Type of Account   Current ☐   Deposit ☐

2. Personal Details

Mr/Mrs/Ms/Other _____

Surname _____   First name(s) _____

Address _____

_____

Tel: Home _____ Work _____ Mobile _____

Date of birth ☐☐/☐☐/☐☐   Marital status Single ☐ Married ☐

No. of children _____   Ages _____

Residential Details

Are you Homeowner ☐ Tenant ☐ Living at home ☐ Other _____

3. Employment Details

Occupation _____ No. of years _____

Yearly gross pay _____

Employer's name _____

Address _____

_____

4. Account Details

Do you currently have any bank accounts?   Yes ☐   No ☐

Name of bank/financial institution _____

Current balance _____

5. Do you require (i) An ATM card   Yes ☐   No ☐

            (ii) A chequebook   Yes ☐   No ☐

2.

DEPOSIT/CURRENT ACCOUNT APPLICATION FORM

1. Type of Account   Current ☐   Deposit ☐

2. Personal Details

Mr/Mrs/Ms/Other _____

Surname _____   First name(s) _____

Address _____

_____

Tel: Home _____ Work _____ Mobile _____

Date of birth ☐☐ / ☐☐ / ☐☐   Marital status   Single ☐   Married ☐

No. of children _____   Ages _____

Residential Details

Are you   Homeowner ☐   Tenant ☐   Living at home ☐   Other _____

3. Employment Details

Occupation _____ No. of years _____

Yearly gross pay _____

Employer's name _____

Address _____

_____

4. Account Details

Do you currently have any bank accounts?   Yes ☐   No ☐

Name of bank/financial institution _____

Current balance _____

5. Do you require (i) An ATM card   Yes ☐   No ☐

(ii) A chequebook   Yes ☐   No ☐

Completing a Lodgement Slip

In each of the following, use the information given to complete the blank lodgement forms.

3. Mary O'Dwyer

Mary O'Dwyer, 213 Old Road, Salthill, Co. Galway, wishes to lodge €170 in notes to her current account number 87654321 on today's date. Her bank account is with AIB Salthill, sort code 677889.

4. Thomas Cooper

Thomas Cooper, 26 Iona Road, Killiney, Co. Dublin, wishes to lodge a cheque for €234.50 to his current account number 17392746 on today's date. His bank account is with AIB Killiney, sort code 122334.

5. Danielle Cullen

Danielle Cullen, 45 Heatherview Close, Clonmel, Co. Tipperary, wishes to make a lodgement consisting of €130 in notes, €45.40 in coins and €128 in cheques to her savings (deposit) account number 37498501 on today's date. Her bank account is with AIB Clonmel, sort code 344556.

6. Marcus Lennon

Marcus Lennon, 135 Ardmore Grove, Artane, Dublin 5, wishes to lodge €220 in notes, €32.50 in coins and two cheques for €50 and €35 to his deposit account number 28374659 on today's date. His bank account is with AIB Malahide Road, sort code 223344.

7. Alisha Jones

Alisha Jones, 45 Cedar Court, Shankill, Co. Dublin, wishes to lodge a cheque for €123.76 and €411.00 in notes to her current account number 94873628 on today's date. Her bank account is with AIB Bray, sort code 357913.

8. Grainne Taylor

Grainne Taylor, 73 Monroe Square, Rosslare, Co. Wexford, wishes to make a lodgement consisting of €214 in notes, €27.80 in coins and €239 in cheques to her savings (deposit) account number 12398773 on today's date. Her bank account is with AIB Rosslare, sort code 129845.

Completing a Withdrawal Slip

In each of the following, use the information given to complete the blank withdrawal forms below.

9. Anna Furey

Anna Furey, 25 Delcassion Place, Birr, Co. Offaly, wishes to withdraw €75 from her current account number 29873452 on today's date. Her account is with AIB Birr, sort code 935567.

10. Brendan Gray

Brendan Gray, 19 Templemore Gardens, Blackrock, Co. Cork, wishes to withdraw €156 from his deposit (savings) account number 34568922 on today's date. His account is with AIB Blackrock, sort code 936678.

11. Patricia Heary

Patricia Heary, 6 Bettystown Park, Ashford, Co. Wicklow, wishes to withdraw €56 from her current account number 18962355 on today's date. Her account is with AIB Ashford, sort code 937789.

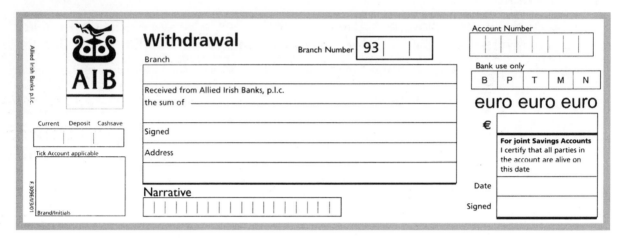

12. Jason Behan

Jason Behan, 11 Glenleigh Road, Mallow, Co. Cork, wishes to withdraw €95 from his current account number 12983756 on today's date. His account is with AIB Mallow, sort code 933847.

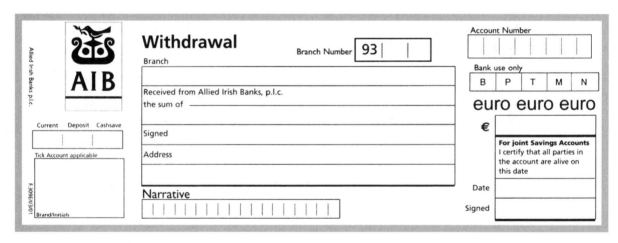

13. Bernadette Finn

Bernadette Finn, 26 Drumm Abbey, Ennis, Co. Clare, wishes to withdraw €278 from her deposit (savings) account number 87654321 on today's date. Her account is with AIB Ennis, sort code 936644.

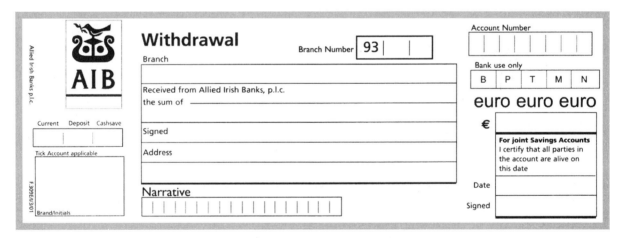

14. Shane Downes

Shane Downes, 18 Ledden Park, Balbriggan, Co. Dublin, wishes to withdraw €170 from his current account number 98765243 on today's date. His account is with AIB Balbriggan, sort code 939845.

Making Payments

Completing a Cheque

In each of the following, use the information given to complete the blank cheques below.

1. John Horton

John Horton wishes to pay Tesco Ltd the sum of €34 by cheque on today's date.

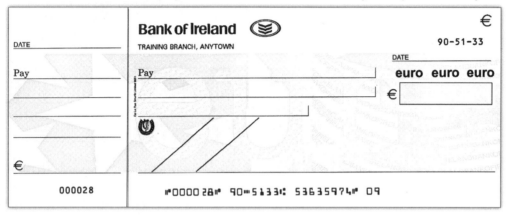

2. Martina Loughnane

Martina Loughnane wishes to write a cheque for €256.80 to the EBS. Use today's date.

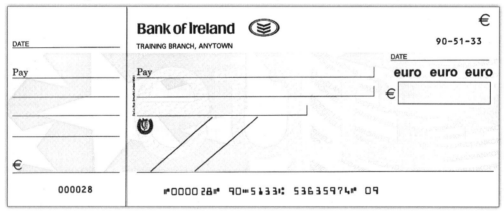

3. Roy Kane

Roy Kane wishes to pay €34.70 to O'Keeffe's Hardware by cheque on today's date.

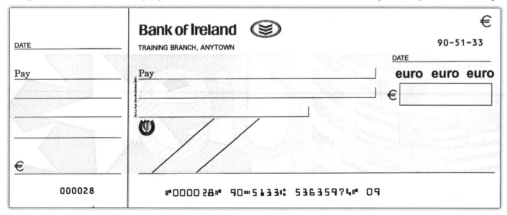

4. Josephine O'Leary

Josephine O'Leary wishes to pay her sister Elaine O'Leary €320.90 by cheque. Use today's date.

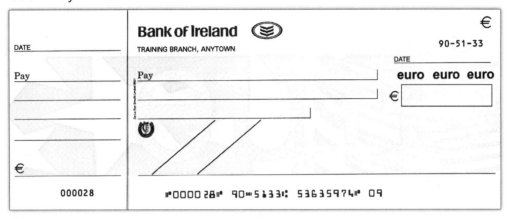

5. Dean O'Shaughnessy

Dean O'Shaughnessy wishes to write a cheque for €145.50 to Malden Motors. Use today's date.

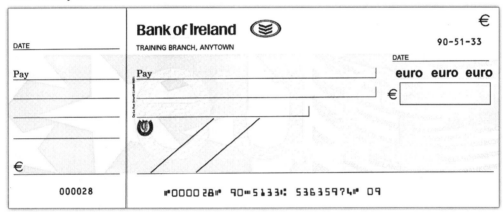

6. Lisa Rowland

Lisa Rowland wishes to pay €56.00 to PC World by cheque on today's date.

7. Word search

Solve the following clues and then locate and circle the answers in the grid. The answer may read forwards, backwards or diagonally in a straight line.

(a) A chequebook account (7) _____

(b) A method of paying regular bills of a fixed amount (8, 5) _____

(c) Banklink and Pass are examples of these cards (3) _____

(d) The person to whom a cheque is made payable (5) _____

(e) A cheque that has a date on it sometime in the future (9) _____

(f) The process of drawing two parallel lines across the face of a cheque (8) _____

(g) Permission to spend more than you have in your current account (9) _____

(h) A card that allows you to pay for goods and services from your current account (5)_____

(i) Having your wages paid directly into your bank account is known as this (7) _____

(j) A place where money can be stored safely after the bank has closed (5, 4)_____

Q	W	E	R	T	Y	U	I	O	P	P	L
J	C	R	O	S	S	I	N	G	A	O	K
A	U	S	D	F	G	H	J	Y	Y	S	M
M	R	D	E	B	I	T	E	V	P	T	N
Z	R	B	D	A	S	T	R	W	A	D	Y
C	E	V	N	O	M	K	L	Q	T	A	T
A	N	Q	P	R	U	I	O	L	H	T	U
S	T	A	N	D	I	N	G	M	J	E	I
S	D	T	K	E	Y	S	D	N	H	D	O
F	G	M	J	R	S	A	F	B	G	F	P
H	T	F	A	R	D	R	E	V	O	S	A
N	I	G	H	T	S	A	F	E	T	H	Y

8. Your employer has agreed to pay your salary directly into your bank account each month. List two advantages of this arrangement for your employer.

(a) _____

(b) _____

9. Name two ways of paying bills other than by cheque.

(a) _____

(b) _____

10. What do the following abbreviations stand for?

(a) ATM _____

(b) OD _____

(c) SO _____

(d) DD _____

(e) CT _____

(f) PIN _____

11. Match the terms in column 1 with the correct definitions from the list in column 2.

1. Post-dated cheque   **A.** The exchange of goods and services

2. Barter   **B.** A cheque that is more than 6 months old

3. Cheque   **C.** Has a date on it sometime in the future

4. Drawer   **D.** A written order to a bank to pay a sum of money to a named person

5. Stale cheque   **E.** The person who writes the cheque and from whose account the money will be taken

1. ☐   2. ☐   3. ☐   4. ☐   5. ☐

12. Melanie Staunton has her current account in the National Irish Bank, Artane. On 15 July she wrote a cheque for €45 to The Pizza House. Fill in the correct words from the list below.

| drawee | drawer | payee |

(a) Melanie Staunton is the _____ of the cheque.

(b) The Pizza House is the _____ of the cheque.

(c) National Irish Bank, Artane is the _____ of the cheque.

10 Saving and Investing

1. Calculate the following.

(a) Mr McHugh saves €15 per week for 3 years. _____

(b) Ms Walshe saves €12 per week for 5 years. _____

(c) Mr Dardis saves €5 per week for 2 years. _____

(d) Ms Wright saves €16 per week for 4 years. _____

(e) Mr Ward saves €4 per week for 10 years. _____

(f) Ms Barnes saves €6 per week for 7 years. _____

(g) Mr O'Driscoll saves €35 per week for 5 years. _____

(h) Ms Lehane saves €100 per month for 4 years. _____

(i) Mr Jones saves €250 per month for 3 years. _____

(j) Ms Costello saves €430 per month for 5 years. _____

(k) Mr Downes saves €325 per month for 8 years. _____

(l) Ms Campbell saves €237 per month for 6 years. _____

2. Calculate the balance in each of the following accounts after 1 year, 2 years and 5 years.

(a) Mrs McEvoy saved €1,200 at 8% simple interest.

   1 year: _____   2 years: _____   5 years: _____

(b) Mr Buchanan saved €1,700 at 6% simple interest.

   1 year: _____   2 years: _____   5 years: _____

(c) Ms Bruton saved €2,200 at 4% simple interest.

   1 year: _____   2 years: _____   5 years: _____

(d) Mrs Elders saved €3,400 at 5% simple interest.

   1 year: _____   2 years: _____   5 years: _____

(e) Mr Sherry saved €8,600 at 3.5% simple interest.

   1 year: _____   2 years: _____   5 years: _____

(f) Ms Denton saved €5,700 at 7.2% simple interest.

   1 year: _____   2 years: _____   5 years: _____

3. For each of the calculations in question 2 above, calculate the balance in the account after 1 year if DIRT is deducted from the interest received at the rate of 25%.

(a) _____   (b) _____   (c) _____

(d) _____   (e) _____   (f) _____

4. Calculate the balance in each account after 1 year, 2 years and 3 years. Make all answers correct to two decimal places.

(a) Mrs Dooley saved €1,000 at 8% compound interest.

1 year: _____   2 years: _____   3 years: _____

(b) Mr Geraghty saved €1,400 at 6% compound interest.

1 year: _____   2 years: _____   3 years: _____

(c) Ms Headon saved €2,400 at 4% compound interest.

1 year: _____   2 years: _____   3 years: _____

(d) Mrs Healy saved €1,200 at 11% compound interest.

1 year: _____   2 years: _____   3 years: _____

(e) Mr McGreevy saved €2,200 at 12% compound interest.

1 year: _____   2 years: _____   3 years: _____

(f) Ms Mooney saved €2,100 at 18% compound interest.

1 year: _____   2 years: _____   3 years: _____

(g) Mrs Cronin saved €2,400 at 7% compound interest.

1 year: _____   2 years: _____   3 years: _____

(h) Mr Neri saved €22,500 at 3.5% compound interest.

1 year: _____   2 years: _____   3 years: _____

5. (a) Aine had €5,000 invested at 6% simple interest for 2½ years in a special savings account that was subject to tax at 10%. Calculate the net interest earned.

_____

_____

_____

(b) Alan had €8,500 invested at 4% simple interest for 4½ years in a special savings account that was subject to tax at 10%. Calculate the net interest earned.

_____

_____

_____

(c) Jim had €22,000 invested at 8% simple interest for 3½ years in a special savings account that was subject to tax at 10%. Calculate the net interest earned.

_____

_____

_____

(d) Norin had €18,400 invested at 5% compound interest for 4 years in a special savings account that was subject to tax at 10%. Calculate the net interest earned to two decimal places.

_____

_____

_____

(e) Paulo had €12,250 invested at 4.5% compound interest for 3 years in a special savings account that was subject to tax at 10%. Calculate the net interest earned to 2 decimal places.

_____

_____

_____

6. Word search

Locate each of the following terms to do with saving and investing in the grid below.

Saving	
Investing	
Building society	
Credit union	
Simple interest	
Compound interest	
Compound annual rate (CAR)	
Deposit Interest Retention Tax (DIRT)	

T	I	S	O	P	E	D	Q	W	E	R	T
A	N	N	U	A	L	Y	U	I	R	O	A
A	S	D	F	G	H	J	K	L	A	Z	X
C	V	S	B	C	A	R	N	M	T	Q	W
E	B	U	I	L	D	I	N	G	E	E	R
T	Y	I	G	M	U	I	O	P	A	S	D
F	G	H	N	J	P	K	X	L	K	J	H
Z	X	C	I	V	V	L	B	A	N	M	L
K	N	J	V	H	E	G	E	F	T	D	S
Q	O	W	A	E	R	S	T	Y	S	R	U
I	I	O	S	P	O	A	T	S	E	E	D
F	N	G	H	C	J	K	L	M	R	T	Z
X	U	T	I	D	E	R	C	C	E	E	V
B	N	E	M	Z	X	C	V	B	T	N	N
Q	T	W	D	I	R	T	E	R	N	T	T
Y	U	I	O	P	A	S	D	F	I	I	G
H	J	K	L	Z	X	C	V	B	N	O	M
Q	C	O	M	P	O	U	N	D	W	N	E
R	G	N	I	T	S	E	V	N	I	Y	U

11 Borrowing

Calculating Repayments

[handwritten: € Month 3600 ÷ 36 = 100 (36)]

1. Mr Corcoran borrowed €3,600 repayable in equal monthly instalments over 3 years.

(a) What is his monthly repayment before interest? *[handwritten: 1896   616   100]*

(b) With interest at 6% per annum, how much will he have repaid at the end of 1 year?

[handwritten: 3600 × 6 ÷ 100 = 216 ÷ 36 = 6]
[handwritten: 100 + 6 = × 12 = 1272]

2. Ms Kealy borrowed €4,800 repayable in equal monthly instalments over 2 years.

(a) What is her monthly repayment before interest? *[handwritten: 1152]*

(b) With interest at 5% per annum, how much will she have repaid at the end of 1 year?

[handwritten: 20   1040]
[handwritten: 100 × 5 = 12]

3. Mr Hughes borrowed €2,400 repayable in equal monthly instalments over 2 years.

(a) What is his monthly repayment before interest? *[handwritten: 576]*

(b) With interest at 7% per annum, how much will he have repaid at the end of 1 year?

[handwritten: 168 or 14]
[handwritten: 100 × 7 =   × 12 =]

4. Ms Maguire borrowed €7,200 repayable in equal monthly instalments over 6 years.

(a) What is her monthly repayment before interest? *[handwritten: 12 384]*

(b) With interest at 6% per annum, flat rate, how much will she have repaid at the end of 2 years?

[handwritten: 734.72   18]
[handwritten: 100 × 6]

5. Mr Cummins borrowed €8,400 repayable in equal monthly instalments over 5 years.

(a) What is his monthly repayment before interest? *[handwritten: 16800]*

(b) With interest at 5% per annum, flat rate, how much will he have repaid at the end of 3 years?

[handwritten: 420   11.6666]

6. Ms Deans borrowed €7,200 repayable in equal monthly instalments over 3 years.

(a) What is her monthly repayment before interest? €770⁴

(b) With interest at 7% per annum, true rate (APR), how much will she have repaid at the end of the 3 years? _____

She will ~~get paid~~ have to pay €301 extra

7. Mr Leeson borrowed €5,000 repayable in equal monthly instalments over 5 years.

(a) What is his monthly repayment before interest? 5,500

(b) With interest at 4% per annum, true rate (APR), how much will he have repaid at the end of the 5 years? _____

8. Ms Denny borrowed €6,400 repayable in equal monthly instalments over 4 years.

(a) What is her monthly repayment before interest? _____

(b) With interest at 9% per annum, true rate (APR), how much will she have repaid at the end of 2 years? _____

Loan Application Forms

9. Michelle McCrone

Michelle McCrone lives at 72 St Stephen's Terrace, Tramore, Co. Waterford, in her own home, which she purchased with the help of a mortgage of €165,000 from the Educational Building Society. Her telephone number is 071-55677.

Michelle is a teacher and is employed by the Department of Education and Skills, Marlborough Street, Dublin 1. Her work telephone number is 01-1234567. She has been working as a teacher since 1995. She earns a salary of €3,220 per month. Her date of birth is 30/09/73 and she is married. Michelle has a bank account with the Bank of Ireland and the current balance is €1,140.

Michelle has decided to purchase a new car. To do this she needs to borrow €10,000, which she will repay in monthly instalments of €210 over the next 5 years.

Complete Michelle's loan application using the blank form on the next page.

LOAN APPLICATION FORM

1. Personal Details

Mr/Mrs/Ms/Other _Ms_

Surname _McCrone_ First name(s) _Michelle_

Address _Stephen's Terrance, Tramor Co. waterford_

Tel: Home _021-55677_ Work _01-1234567_

Date of birth $\boxed{3}\boxed{6}/\boxed{0}\boxed{9}/\boxed{7}\boxed{3}$ Marital status Single ☐ Married ☑

Residential Details

Are you Homeowner ☑ Tenant ☒ Living at home ☒ Other _____

2. Employment Details

Occupation _teacher_ No. of years _11_

Yearly gross pay _38640_

Employer's name _Department of education_

Address _Marlborough, Co. Dublin_

3. Loan Required

Amount required _10,000_

Purpose of loan _New car_

How long is the loan required for? _5 years_

How will the loan be repaid? _210 next 5 years every month_

4. Account Details

Do you currently have a bank account? Yes ☑ No ☐

Name of bank/financial Institution _Bank of Ireland_

Current balance _1,140_

Do you have any other loans at present? Yes ☐ No ☑

Details _Mortgage._

Signature _(signature)_ Date _28/1/16_

10. Mohsen Bernard

Mohsen Bernard lives at 14 Aranleigh Park, Walkinstown, Dublin 12 in a house he has rented for the past 2 years.

Mohsen works as a clerical officer with the Department of Social Protection, The Square, Tallaght, Dublin 24. His work telephone number is 01-1234567. He has been working as a clerical officer since 2000 and he earns a monthly salary of €2,670.

Mohsen has decided to purchase a new jet ski. To do this he needs to borrow €5,000, which he will repay in monthly instalments of €160 over the next 3 years.

Mohsen has a bank account with Ulster Bank and the current balance is €2,450. He also has a loan with the Greenhills Credit Union of €500.

Complete Mohsen's loan application using the blank form on the next page.

LOAN APPLICATION FORM

1. Personal Details

Mr/Mrs/Ms/Other _Mr_

Surname _Bernard_   First name(s) _moshen_

Address _16 Aranleigh park, walkinstown Dublin 12_

Tel: Home _____ Work _____

Date of birth ☐☐ / ☐☐ / ☐☐   Marital status   Single ☐   Married ☐

Residential Details

Are you   Homeowner ☐   Tenant ☐   Living at home ☐   Other _____

2. Employment Details

Occupation _____ No. of years _____

Yearly gross pay _____

Employer's name _____

Address _____

3. Loan Required

Amount required   _____

Purpose of loan   _____

How long is the loan required for?   _____

How will the loan be repaid?   _____

4. Account Details

Do you currently have a bank account?   Yes ☐   No ☐

Name of bank/financial Institution   _____

Current balance   _____

Do you have any other loans at present?   Yes ☐   No ☐

Details _____

Signature   Date

11. Word search

Locate the following terms from Chapter 11 in the word search below. The words may read forwards, backwards or diagonally.

| Borrowing | Interest | Overdraft | Term loan |
| Moneylender | Credit union | Mortgage | APR | Security |

Q	W	E	R	S	T	Y	U	U	I	O	P
A	S	D	F	E	G	A	G	T	R	O	M
G	H	J	K	C	L	K	J	H	G	F	D
Z	X	C	V	U	B	N	M	A	S	D	F
Q	B	O	R	R	O	W	I	N	G	W	E
R	T	Y	U	I	I	O	N	P	A	S	D
N	F	G	H	T	J	K	T	K	L	Z	X
O	X	C	V	Y	B	N	E	M	N	B	V
I	T	T	F	A	R	D	R	E	V	O	P
N	Q	E	W	E	R	T	E	Y	U	I	O
U	Z	X	R	A	S	D	S	F	G	H	J
T	Z	X	C	M	V	B	T	B	N	M	D
I	Q	W	E	R	L	T	Y	U	R	O	P
D	A	S	D	F	G	O	H	P	K	L	Z
E	Q	W	E	R	T	Y	A	Q	W	E	A
R	E	D	N	E	L	Y	E	N	O	M	B
C	A	S	D	F	G	H	J	K	L	C	D
E	W	Q	A	S	D	F	G	H	H	M	F

Section A Questions

12. Place a tick in the box beside the correct answer to indicate which of the following rates of interest charged on a loan is the most expensive.

    (a) 15% per annum flat rate ☐

    (b) 15% per annum APR ☑

13. Name two types of financial institution where a person could borrow money to purchase a private house.

    (a) _Borrowing_

    (b) _Loan_

14. What does APR stand for? _Annual precentace rate_

15. Name one type of security that each of the following may offer a bank.

    (a) Homeowner seeking a €25,000 loan _____

    (b) Student without any assets seeking a €2,000 loan _____

16. True or false

	True	False
(a) Term loans are usually repaid in one lump sum at the end of the term	☑	☐
(b) Overdrafts are usually repaid by fixed amounts and at regular intervals	☐	☑

17. A bank _Borrowed_ is a short-term loan.

18. List two rights a borrower has.

    (a) _____

    (b) _____

12 Household Purchases

1. Calculate the cost of each of the following.

(a) A weekly payment of €35 for 2 years _____ 3640

(b) A weekly payment of €44 for 4 years _____ 9152

(c) A weekly payment of €24 for 3 years _____ 3744

(d) A monthly payment of €125 for 3 years _____ 19500

(e) A monthly payment of €235 for 4 years _____ 68,880

(f) A monthly payment of €210 for 5 years _____ 54600

2. Calculate the cost of each of the following.

(a) A deposit of €100 plus 8 instalments of €150 each _____ 1300

(b) A deposit of €120 plus 15 instalments of €95 each _____ 1545

(c) A deposit of €50 plus 24 instalments of €211 each _____ 5114

(d) A deposit of €150 plus 36 instalments of €124 each _____ 4614

(e) A deposit of €60 plus 12 instalments of €255 each _____ 3120

(f) A deposit of €80 plus 48 instalments of €30 each _____ 1520

3. On 1 September, Maureen O'Dwyer got the following information about a Keep Cool fridge freezer priced at €550 from Ryan's Electrical Showrooms.

- **Rental:** €4.75 per week payable at the beginning of each week with no deposit.

- **Hire purchase:** €70 deposit plus €16 per month for 3 years with a final payment of €50.

- **Bank loan:** Maureen has saved €150 and has been told by her local bank that she can borrow €400 to be paid back over 3 years at the rate of €3.60 per month (including interest) for each €100 borrowed.

(a) Calculate the cost of each of the three methods (rental, HP and loan) for a 3-year period.

```
4.75              16                          3.60
x  52 x3          12                       x  12
741               3 t50+70                 x  3
         € 696.                               580
```

(b) Recommend one method to Maureen and give two reasons for your choice.

Bank loan because it cost less and it's Better

4. On 1 March, Patrick Lyons obtained the following information in respect of a Wash Well washing machine priced at €420 from Imelda's Electrical Showrooms.

- **Rental:** €3.80 per week.

- **Hire purchase:** €50 deposit plus €14.50 per month for 3 years with a final payment of €60.

- **Building society loan:** Patrick has saved €120 and has been told by his local building society that he can borrow €300 to be paid back over 3 years at the rate of €3.70 per month (including interest) for each €100 borrowed.

(a) Calculate the cost of each of the three methods (rental, hire purchase and loan) for a 3-year period.

Rental 3·80×52×3   Hire purchase 632   14·50×12 ×3 +50+60 =632

Ans €592.8

Building society loan

3·70 × 12 × 3 × 3 = 399·6 +120 = 519.6

(b) Rank them in order of cost, starting with the cheapest. State by how much each option is greater than the cash price.

The Building society loan because it is cheaper and it's more difficult But better

5. The Leopardstown Fitness Centre in Dublin is considering purchasing some new training equipment which has a retail price of €8,600. The club only has €600 available to fund the purchase at this time. Following discussions with their local bank as well as a sales representative from the suppliers, the centre is faced with the following options.

- **Rental:** Pay a monthly rental of €90 for 5 years plus an annual maintenance payment of €150.

- **Hire purchase:** Pay a deposit of €600 plus 60 monthly instalments of €150. A final payment of €480 must then be paid.

- **Bank loan:** Borrow the amount needed for 5 years, on which interest is charged at a flat rate of 7% per annum.

Calculate the total cost of each option for a 5-year period.

6. The Lakeside Community College in Kenmare is considering purchasing a new photocopier which has a retail price of €3,400. The school only has €800 available to fund the purchase at this time. Following discussions with their local bank as well as a sales representative from the suppliers, the school is faced with the following options.

- **Rental:** Pay a monthly rental of €80 each month for 3 years plus an annual maintenance payment of €140.

- **Hire purchase:** Pay a deposit of €800 plus 36 monthly instalments of €80. A final payment of €360 must then be paid.

- **Bank loan:** Borrow the amount needed for 3 years, on which interest is charged at a flat rate of 8% per annum.

Calculate the total cost of each option for a 3-year period.

_____

_____

_____

_____

_____

_____

7. On 1 November, Joshua Maguire got the following information about an Electra cooker priced at €800 from Iram's Electrical Distributers.

- **Rental:** €6.50 per week payable at the beginning of each week with no deposit.

- **Hire purchase:** €90 deposit plus €21 per month for 3 years with a final payment of €40.

- **Bank loan:** Joshua has saved €200 and has been told by his local bank that he can borrow €600 to be paid back over 3 years at the rate of €3.95 per month (including interest) for each €100 borrowed.

(a) Calculate the cost of each of the three methods (rental, HP and loan) for a 3-year period.

_____

_____

_____

_____

_____

_____

(b) Rank the three methods in order of cost, starting with the cheapest.

_____

8. On 1 April, Sonita Alenan obtained the following information about a new suite of furniture priced at €2,300 from Furniture World, Balbriggan.

   * **Rental:** €11.20 per week.
   * **Hire purchase:** €500 deposit plus €30 per month for 5 years with a final payment of €350.
   * **Credit union loan:** Sonita has saved €800 and has been told by her local credit union that she can borrow €1,500 to be paid back over 5 years at the rate of €2.50 per month (including interest) for each €100 borrowed.

   (a) Calculate the cost of each of the three methods (rental, hire purchase and loan) for a 5-year period.

   _____

   _____

   _____

   _____

   _____

   _____

   (b) Rank them in order of cost, starting with the cheapest. State by how much each option is greater than the cash price.

   _____

   _____

Section A Questions

9. State two pieces of information that should be included in a hire purchase agreement.

   (a) _____

   (b) _____

10. In hire purchase, the buyer does not become the owner until the last instalment is paid.

    True or false? _____

11. You are interested in purchasing a dishwasher by hire purchase. The shop quotes the following terms for the same machine.

    Deal A: €80 deposit plus 12 monthly instalments of €20
    Deal B: No deposit plus 12 monthly deposits of €30

    (a) Calculate and show the total cost of each deal.

    Deal A: _____ Deal B: _____

    (b) Suggest a reason for the difference in total cost between these two deals.

    _____

12. Write a brief explanation to show the main difference between a store card and a credit card.

    _____

    _____

Household and Business Insurance

1. Insurance proposal form

From the details below, complete the blank insurance proposal form for Mary O'Kane.

Mary O'Kane, born 31/1/76 and living at 24 Will Park Road, Finglas, Dublin 11, wishes to apply for motor insurance. She has 3 years no claims bonus and is looking for fully comprehensive cover. Her car is a five-door Renault Cruiser GTL with a 1600cc engine. The registration number is 10 D 12445. She will be the main driver and her husband, John, will be the named driver. She has a full licence, no previous accidents and no penalty points. In addition to the main cover, she wants windscreen cover and breakdown assistance. She is currently employed as a marketing executive and her vehicle has a market value of €21,000.

PROPOSAL FORM – MOTOR INSURANCE

Note: All questions must be answered truthfully and fully. Failure to do so could render the policy void.

1. The Proposer

Name: _____

Title: (Mr/Mrs/Ms) _____

Address: _____

_____

Occupation: _____

Date of birth: _____

2. The Vehicle

Make and model: _____ _____

Registration number: _____

Engine capacity: _____

Please outline any alterations which have been made to the vehicle _____

_____

Is the car normally kept in a garage?　　Yes ☐　　　No ☐

Address where the car is kept at night if different from above _____

_____

2. Additional Information

Type of insurance required
(Comprehensive/Third Party Fire and Theft)_____

Any additional cover required? _____

Do you have a full licence?　　　　Yes ☐　　　No ☐

Have you had any claims or accidents in the last five years?　　　　Yes ☐　No ☐

Have you ever been disqualified from driving or had your licence endorsed?　Yes ☐　No ☐

Do you wish to have any other persons named as co-drivers on the policy?

Name _____

Do you have a no claims bonus? Yes ☐　No ☐　How many years?_____

Do you have any penalty points? Yes ☐　No ☐　If yes, how many? _____

DECLARATION

I/We hereby declare that I/we am the owner of the vehicle, that all the above statements and particulars and other written statements made by me/us are true and complete and that they and this proposal form shall be the basis of the Contract between me/us and the Insurance Company.

Signature　　　　　　　　　　　　　　Date

2. Principles of insurance

Read the insurance mini case studies below. Use the principles of insurance to decide the answer in each case.

(a) Pauline Tighe insured the contents of her house for €30,000. When completing the proposal form, she indicated that she had installed special window locks on all the downstairs windows. As a result, her proposal was accepted and she was charged a special rate of €75. Later that year she had a burglary at her house and thieves stole €1,000 worth of property. The assessor noticed that the window locks had not been installed and the insurance company refused to pay the compensation. Explain why the company refused to pay.

_____

_____

_____

_____

_____

(b) Joe Walsh was not too upset when the car that he had owned for the last 3 years was stolen and found sometime later, crashed and burned out. It had cost him €15,000 and he had continued to insure it for that amount. For some time now he had had his eye on a new sports car and saw this as the ideal opportunity to get his dream car. The price of the new car was €25,000 and Joe had already saved the other €10,000. Therefore, he was very upset when the insurance company only offered him €9,000 and he has come to you for advice. Explain why the insurance company will only pay Joe €9,000.

_____

_____

_____

_____

_____

(c) Michael Maher insured his sports shop against fire with two different insurance companies for €165,000 each. Following a fire, the shop was completely destroyed and Michael made his two claims for compensation. Two months later, a cheque for €165,000 arrived by post, despite the fact that Michael had paid both premiums. Explain why Michael was only paid €165,000 and calculate how much each insurance company will pay.

_____

_____

_____

_____

_____

(d) Sarah Power insured her ten-speed racing bicycle against theft for €300. Sometime later it was stolen and Sarah received the insurance compensation of €300. Two months later, the bicycle was found along with other stolen property in the home of a local criminal. The bicycle was returned to Sarah and the following week the insurance company wrote asking Sarah to return the money to them. Explain why the insurance company did this.

_____

_____

_____

_____

_____

_____

_____

_____

_____

_____

(e) Daniel Murphy wrote to his insurance company to ask them if he could take out insurance on the following three items:

• His set of golf clubs, which he keeps in his house.

• His neighbour's car, which is always parked outside his house.

• His brother's antique table, which he is looking after while his brother is on holiday.

The insurance company wrote back saying he could insure two out of the three items. In the case of each of the items listed above, say if the insurance company would allow Daniel to insure them and give an explanation why in each case.

_____

_____

_____

_____

_____

_____

_____

_____

_____

_____

3. Word search

Solve the following clues, then locate and circle the answers in the grid. The answer may read forwards, backwards or diagonally in a straight line.

(a) A type of life assurance where the policy can be cashed by the insured person once they reach a certain age (9)

_____

(b) The term that describes the amount a life assurance policy is worth when it is cashed (9, 5)

_____

(c) The minimum car insurance policy required by law (5, 5)

_____

(d) The type of insurance provided by the VHI and Aviva (7)

_____

(e) The name of the insurance that is paid by all employees out of their income (4)

_____

(f) A reduction given to drivers by insurance companies as a reward for careful driving (2, 6, 5)

_____

(g) The type of insurance that covers injury to parts of your body (8)

_____

L	Q	W	E	Y	R	T	Y	U	I	O
N	O	Z	X	T	B	O	N	U	S	P
A	S	D	F	R	G	V	H	J	K	L
L	E	C	V	A	N	A	M	Q	W	A
A	N	B	N	P	M	L	L	M	E	L
N	D	C	V	D	P	U	K	E	R	L
O	O	S	U	R	R	E	N	D	E	R
S	W	G	V	I	S	J	K	I	T	I
R	M	F	B	H	E	A	L	T	H	S
E	E	Z	X	T	A	D	F	A	U	K
P	N	W	E	S	M	I	A	L	C	S
H	T	L	A	E	I	S	R	P	I	O

Insurance Premiums and Claims

1. Calculate the following life assurance premiums.

(a) Declan Gough, a teacher, wants to take out a life assurance policy on himself for €150,000 and has completed a proposal form that he received from LZ Insurances Ltd. Declan is a non-smoker and will be 27 on his next birthday. The basic yearly cost of the policy is €2.50 for every €1,000 insured. There is a 5% loading for people aged over 25 years and a 1% loading for smokers. All loadings are calculated as a percentage of the basic premium.

_____

_____

_____

(b) Elizabeth O'Carroll, a garda, wants to take out a life assurance policy on herself for €80,000 and has completed a proposal form that she received from GY Insurances Ltd. Elizabeth is a smoker and will be 36 on her next birthday. The basic yearly cost of the policy is €3.50 per €1,000 insured. There is a 5% loading for people aged over 30 years and a 1% loading for smokers. Dangerous occupations carry a loading of 5%. All loadings are calculated as a percentage of the basic premium.

_____

_____

_____

_____

_____

(c) Alex Doroz, an engineer, wants to take out a life assurance policy on himself for €260,000 and has completed a proposal form that he received from EF Insurances Ltd. Alex is a smoker and will be 43 on his next birthday. The basic yearly cost of the policy is €1.75 for every €1,000 insured. There is a 5% loading for people aged between 25 and 39 years and a 15% loading for people aged over 40 years. There is also a 2% loading for smokers. All loadings are calculated as a percentage of the basic premium.

_____

_____

_____

_____

2. Calculate the following motor insurance premiums using the schedule of charges below for Rest Easy Insurance Ltd.

- Basic premium: €30 per €1,000 value
- Comprehensive charge: €150
- Learner permit: 10% loading
- Under 25 years of age: 40% loading

- No claims bonus: 10% for each year up to 50% maximum
- Car alarm/immobiliser: 5% discount

In addition:

- All loadings are calculated as a percentage of the basic premium
- All reductions are calculated as a percentage of the basic premium
- No claims bonus is calculated as a percentage of the total cost of the policy after taking into account all loadings and reductions

(a) Helen Thompson wants to take out third party insurance on her car. She is 21 years old with a learner permit and this is her first time seeking insurance. Her car has a value of €5,500 and is fitted with an alarm.

_____

_____

_____

_____

(b) Karen Malone wants to take out comprehensive insurance on her 2-year-old car valued at €8,000. She is 24 years old and has had a full driving licence for the last 2 years. Those 2 years were claim free. Her car is alarmed.

_____

_____

_____

_____

(c) Harry O'Grady is a 31-year-old farmer living in Co. Meath. He wishes to take out comprehensive insurance on his new car valued at €24,000. He has a full driving licence and 4 years no claims bonus. The car is fitted with an alarm.

_____

_____

_____

_____

3. Calculate the following property insurance premiums.

(a) Pat and Fionnuala Healy wish to insure their house for €120,000 and contents for €35,000. They have received a quotation from Circle Insurances Ltd for buildings insurance at €2.50 per €1,000 value and contents insurance at €3 per €1,000 value. There is a discount of 10% of the basic premium for homes with an alarm and a further 5% for areas covered by a neighbourhood watch scheme. The Healys qualify for both reductions.

_____

_____

_____

_____

(b) Margaret and David Hanrahan wish to insure their house for €150,000 and contents for €30,000. They have received a quotation from Northern Insurances Ltd for buildings insurance at €3 per €1,000 value and contents insurance at €2 per €1,000 value. There is a discount of 10% of the basic premium for homes with an alarm and a further 5% for areas covered by a neighbourhood watch scheme. The Hanrahans have an alarm but do not live within a neighbourhood watch scheme.

_____

_____

_____

_____

_____

4. Calculate the following business insurance premiums.

(a) Arden Electronics Ltd is a small company with 10 employees. They wish to take out insurance and are seeking a quotation for the following: premises €80,000; three vehicles valued at €15,000 each; machinery worth €60,000; stock worth €10,000; and employer's liability insurance for their workforce.

Orchard Insurance Ltd supplied the following quotation for one year's insurance: premises €4.25 per €1,000 value; comprehensive motor insurance at €465 per vehicle; machinery insurance at €3.50 per €1,000 value; stock insurance at €12.50 per €1,000 value; employer's liability insurance €25 per employee. Arden Electronics would be given a 10% discount for having a security system in operation.
Calculate the amount of the premium paid by Arden Electronics for the above insurance.

_____

_____

_____

_____

_____

_____

(b) Echo Manufacturing Ltd has decided to change insurers and has asked Gis a Quote Ltd to give them a quotation for insuring the following: buildings €135,000; machinery €70,000; three delivery vans valued at €18,000 each; stock of equipment €85,000; and cash held in the office €1,250.

Gis a Quote Ltd supplied the following quotation for one year's insurance: insurance for buildings and machinery €3.50 per €1,000 value; motor van, third party fire and theft, €710 per van; stock insurance €11.50 per €1,000 value; cash insurance €12 per €500. They are also offering a new business introductory offer of a 20% discount off the total premium. Calculate the premium due.

_____

_____

_____

_____

_____

Calculating Compensation

5. Calculate the compensation payable in each of the following cases.

Indemnity

(a) Michael Connolly has his house insured for €185,000. The house is currently valued at €170,000. How much compensation will Michael receive if:

(i) A fire causes €20,000 worth of damage_____

(ii) His house is totally destroyed by fire _____

(b) Finbarr Dowling has his house valued at €160,000 and insured for €180,000. A fire occurred early last week. How much compensation will Finbarr receive if:

(i) Damage amounting to €25,000 was caused _____

(ii) The house was totally destroyed and total repair will cost €160,000 _____

(c) Elizabeth Larkin has her collection of French paintings insured for €190,000. Following a break-in at her home, she has made a claim to the insurance company for €230,000 – the current value of the paintings. How much compensation would she receive if the entire collection was stolen? _____

Average Clause

(d) Raymond O'Shea has his shop valued at €250,000 and insured for €200,000. A fire occurred early last week.

(i) Explain what is meant by average clause.

_____

_____

(ii) Using average clause, calculate how much compensation Raymond will receive if the fire causes €35,000 worth of damage._____

(e) Charles Guiney has his antique dining table valued at €12,000 insured for €10,000. How much compensation will Charles receive if:

(i) The table is totally destroyed by fire _____

(ii) A leaking tank causes €3,000 worth of damage to the table _____

(f) Peter King has his business stock valued at €120,000 and insured for €80,000 with Try Us for Price Ltd. Thieves broke in and stole goods valued at €30,000.

(i) How much compensation in total will Peter receive? _____

(ii) Explain why Peter cannot receive €30,000.

_____

_____

Contribution

(g) David O'Farrell has insured his stock valued at €30,000 for €30,000 with two insurance companies – Insure All Ltd and Protect All Ltd. How much compensation will David receive from each company if:

    (i) The stock is totally destroyed in a fire _____

    (ii) Stock valued at €10,000 is stolen _____

(h) Simon Sweeny has insured his Harley Davidson motorbike valued at €9,000 for €9,000 with three different insurance companies – New for Old Ltd, All Claims Ltd and Insure for Sure Ltd. How much compensation will he receive from each company if:

    (i) The bike is stolen and declared a write-off _____

    (ii) The bike is crashed and suffers €2,400 worth of damage _____

Exam-style Questions

6. Jim Kinsley had his house valued at €390,000 by a professional valuer. He insured the house and contents against fire only with his local insurance agent at an annual cost of €300. He insured the buildings for €330,000 and the contents for €50,000. The policy had an excess clause of €500. Last week, fire caused damage to the house (building) amounting to €26,000.

(A)   (i) What document should Jim complete when seeking compensation?

_____

    (ii) How much compensation will Jim receive? _____

(B) Before the next **renewal date**, Jim was approached by an **insurance broker** with a **proposal form** seeking Jim's insurance business. The broker offered Jim all risks cover on the house and its contents at the following rates: buildings €1.80 per €1,000 cover and contents €1.50 per €1,000 cover. Because the house would be unoccupied during the day, there was a **loading** on the **premium** for contents of €50 yearly.

    (i) Calculate the annual cost of the insurance quoted by the broker if Jim insured the house and contents for their full value.

_____

_____

_____

_____

    (ii) Explain the words in bold print.

_____

_____

_____

_____

_____

7. The Naughton family wishes to insure their house for €285,000 and their contents for €20,000. They received quotations from three different insurance companies. Calculate the total premium (buildings and contents) available from each of the three companies using the information below.

	Company A	Company B	Company C
Buildings	€2 per €1,000	€2.50 per €1,000	€3 per €1,000
Contents	€6.50 per €1,000	€5 per €1,000	€4 per €1,000

_____

_____

_____

_____

8. **Insurance claim form**

From the details below, complete the blank claim form for James O'Driscoll.

James O'Driscoll was involved in a road accident on 8 January 2011 at 8 p.m. when he reversed his car out of his driveway and accidentally crashed into the pillar. There was no other car involved. The registration number of his car is 10-G-2256 and his address is 32 Main Street, Oughterard, Co. Galway. He suffered no injuries, but an estimate from a local garage suggested that damage to the car and pillar amounted to €2,500. He has comprehensive car insurance and the policy number is P776334G.

ALL IN INSURANCE LTD
CLAIM FORM

1. Personal Details

Name: _____

Title: (Mr/Mrs/Ms) _____

Address: _____

_____

Occupation: _____

Date of birth: _____

Policy number: _____

2. Details of Loss or Damage

Please give a description of the loss or damage suffered.

_____

_____

_____

_____

Date and time of loss or damage: _____

Reported to gardaí at garda station: _____

3. Details of Claim

Description of item stolen or damaged: _____

Amount of claim: _____

Section A Questions

9. The fee paid to an insurance company for insurance is called the:

(a) Policy ☐

(b) Premium ☐

(c) Cover note ☐

(d) Tariff ☐

10. Which of the following are uninsurable risks?

(a) Your own house ☐

(b) Bankruptcy ☐

(c) Future hospital expenses ☐

(d) Your neighbour's house ☐

(e) Your football team losing their next match ☐

11. True or false

	True	False
(a) Comprehensive car insurance is required by law	☐	☐
(b) VHI is an example of medical insurance	☐	☐
(c) A premium is paid by the insurer to the insured	☐	☐
(d) Home insurance is required by law	☐	☐
(e) I can insure my own car and my neighbour's car	☐	☐
(f) Non-smokers receive a discount for life assurance	☐	☐

12. Match the terms in column 1 with the correct explanations in column 2.

1. Average clause	A. The person who calculates the premium
2. Loadings	B. The application form for insurance
3. Actuary	C. The fee paid to the insurance company
4. Contribution	D. Formula used to calculate compensation in the event of an item being underinsured
5. Proposal form	E. The value of a life assurance policy when it is cashed
6. Insurance policy	F. The person who calculates the amount of compensation
7. Premium	G. Additions to a premium for insurance
8. Surrender value	H. Decides compensation when an item is insured with more than one insurance company
9. Assessor	I. A legal document confirming that the insurance exists

1. ☐   2. ☐   3. ☐   4. ☐   5. ☐   6. ☐   7. ☐   8. ☐   9. ☐

15 Introduction to Economics

1. Calculate the rate of economic growth in the following situations.

Quantity of goods produced	(a)	(b)	(c)	(d)	(e)	(f)
Year 1	250,000	375,000	180,000	490,000	1,425,000	400,000
Year 2	300,000	431,250	196,200	524,300	1,596,000	392,000
Rate of economic growth						

2. Calculate the rate of inflation each year from the information given below.

Cost of living	(a)	(b)	(c)	(d)	(e)
Year 1	€5,600	€6,800	€8,200	€7,400	€6,350
Year 2	€5,824	€7,004	€8,405	€7,807	€6,477
Rate of inflation					

3. The following figures relate to the rate of inflation in Ireland and the United Kingdom over a 5-year period.

Ireland				
Year 1	Year 2	Year 3	Year 4	Year 5
3%	4%	3%	5%	3%

UK				
Year 1	Year 2	Year 3	Year 4	Year 5
4%	5%	5%	3%	4%

(a) What change occurred in Ireland's inflation rate in year 5 compared to year 4?

_____

(b) Calculate the average rate of inflation for Ireland over the 5-year period.

_____

(c) Calculate the average rate of inflation for the UK over the 5-year period.

_____

(d) Was the average inflation rate in Ireland in the 5-year period higher or lower than the average in the UK for the same period?

_____

4. Write down the elements of each factor of production that would be used to produce the following goods. In the case of enterprise, name an entrepreneur or company associated with that particular product. Use the example below as a guide.

Example:

Product: Oak kitchen

Land: Wood from the forest

Labour: Carpenter

Capital: Wood-cutting machine, wood-turning machine, tools, nails and screws

Enterprise: Rathcoole Kitchens Ltd

(a) Computer software

Sony, Microsoft and Toshiba

(b) Paper manufacturer

(c) Frozen fish meals

the birds eye

(d) School textbook

edco book learning

(e) Easter egg

More Malteasers

(f) Woollen jumpers

Nike

5. Word search

Locate and circle the following economic terms in the grid below. The answers may read forwards, backwards or diagonally.

Land	Labour	Capital	Enterprise	Mixed economy
Economic growth		Inflation	Gross National Product	

M	I	X	E	D	E	C	O	N	O	M	Y
Q	L	A	N	D	R	H	J	Z	D	F	H
W	A	F	T	A	H	G	K	X	S	G	E
E	B	G	E	E	T	F	P	C	A	N	C
R	O	H	R	W	W	I	R	V	P	O	O
T	U	J	P	Q	O	D	O	B	O	I	N
Y	R	K	R	M	R	S	D	N	I	T	O
U	A	L	I	S	G	A	U	N	A	A	M
I	S	Z	S	N	T	P	C	M	U	L	I
O	D	O	E	B	Y	O	T	Q	Y	F	C
P	R	X	C	V	U	I	L	W	T	N	J
G	C	A	P	I	T	A	L	E	R	I	K

Section A Questions

6. Each of the four factors of production gives some return. Fill in the correct return beside each of the factors of production listed below.

Land: _people rent land for money_

Labour: _is wages._

Capital: _The capital is the main_

Enterprise: _____

7. Write true or false beside each of the following statements. An increase in the rate of inflation with no change in our income will mean that:

(a) We can afford to buy more goods _~~too~~ true_

(b) We can afford to buy fewer goods _true_

(c) There will be no change in our purchasing power _____

8. An increase in the general level of prices in a country is called _____ .

9. List any two factors of production.

(a) _____

(b) _____

10. What do the initials GNP stand for? _____

11. Calculate the rate of inflation from the information given below.

- Cost of living year 1: €5,000
- Cost of living year 2: €5,250

_____

_____

_____

The National Budget

1. Study the following budgets. Calculate the balance on each budget. In each case, state whether each is a surplus, deficit or balanced budget.

	Income	Expenditure	Balance	Surplus, deficit or balanced?
(a)	€7,580 m	€6,560 m		
(b)	€9,800 m	€10,780 m		
(c)	€6,780 m	€5,500 m		
(d)	€8,945 m	€7,322 m		
(e)	€12,345 m	€13,987 m		
(f)	€8,880 m	€8,880 m		
(g)	€7,100 m	€9,250 m		
(h)	€6,440 m	€7,440 m		

2. In each of the following questions, use the information provided to prepare the national budget. In each case, state whether it is a surplus, deficit or balanced budget.

(a) **Income:**   Income tax €3,200 m; Corporation tax €1,700 m; VAT €890 m; DIRT €15 m; Customs and excise €570 m; Motor tax €180 m; Miscellaneous €1,200 m.

Expenditure: Health €1,300 m; Defence €1,100 m; Education and Skills; €1,800 m; Agriculture €2,300 m; Debt service €900 m; Other €315 m.

_____

_____

_____

_____

_____

_____

_____

_____

_____

_____

_____

_____

_____

_____

_____

(b) **Income:** Income tax €2,750 m; EU receipts €4,300 m; VAT €250 m; Profits from state-sponsored bodies €890 m; Travel tax €32 m; Corporation tax €1,750 m; Other €680 m.

Expenditure: Education and Skills €2,300 m; Administration €1,100 m; Security €1,550 m; Grants to business €430 m; Debt service €1,900 m; Agriculture €1,350 m; Social Protection €3,400 m.

(c) **Income:** Corporation tax €2,450 m; Capital tax €2,600 m; Customs and excise €1,200 m; EU receipts €1,200 m; DIRT €28 m; VAT €1,500 m; Other €700 m.

Expenditure: Defence €1,890 m; Agriculture €2,100 m; Employment programmes €250 m; Social Protection €3,680 m; Transport €1,650 m; Marine €900 m; Wages of state employees €4,500 m.

(d) **Income:** Income tax €2,340 m; VAT €1,100 m; Motor tax €260 m; Profits from
state-sponsored bodies €1,230 m; EU receipts €1,400 m; Customs
and excise €870 m; Capital tax €1,480 m.

Expenditure: Health €2,400 m; Defence €1,300 m; Grants to state bodies €1,100 m;
Social Protection €2,450 m; Security €890 m; Other €540 m.

(e) **Income:** Income tax €3,754 m; Excise duties €678 m; Profits from state-sponsored
bodies €126 m; Capital taxes €2,199 m; VAT €2,100 m;
EU receipts €900 m.

Expenditure: Education and Skills €4,500 m; Defence €700 m; Agriculture €1,100 m;
Enterprise and Innovation €2,340 m; Social Protection €3,560 m;
Environment €2,450 m.

(f) **Income:** Corporation tax €3,120 m; Capital tax €1,750 m; Customs and excise €1,870 m; EU receipts €120 m; DIRT €280 m; VAT €1,970 m; Other €650 m.

Expenditure: Defence €1,190 m; Agriculture €2,640 m; Employment programmes €1,250 m; Social Protection €4,120 m; Transport €1,150 m; Marine €800 m; Wages of state employees €2,500 m.

Income		
Corporation tax	3,120 m	
Capital tax	€ 1,750 m	
Custom and excise	€1,870 m	
Eu recipts	€120 m	
Dirt	€280 m	
VAT	€1,970 m	
Other	€650 m	
Expenditure		
Defence	€1,190 m	
Agriculture	€2,640 m	
Emplyomen prgrams	€1,250 m	
Social protection	€4,120 m	
Transport	€1,150 m	
Marine	€800 m	
wages of state employees	€2,500	€-3,870 m

3. From the following figures, prepare a national budget and answer the questions that follow.

Income: Income tax €2,325 m; VAT €1,750 m; Capital tax €1,840 m; Customs and excise €2,075 m; DIRT €45 m; Profits from state-sponsored bodies €920 m; Other €345 m.

Expenditure: Health €2,444 m; Education and Skills €1,656 m; Defence €900 m; Social Protection €2,750 m; Debt service €1,300 m; Agriculture €1,400 m; Administration €670 m; Miscellaneous €1,100 m.

Income tax	National budget 2015	2,325 m	
vat		€1,750 m	
capital tax		€1,840	
Customs and exercise		€2,075	
Dirt		€45 m	
Profits from states sponsored bodies		920 m	
Other		€345 m	€9300 m
Expenditure			
Education and skills		€1,656 m	
Defence		€900 m	
Social protection		€2,750	€12,020 m
Debt services		€1,300 m	
Agriculture		€1,400 m	
Administration		€670 m	9300) 12,220
Miscellanous		€1,100 m	12,020 9300
Health		€2,444 m	-2,920
			11,000

(a) Is there a budget surplus or a budget deficit? _Deposit_

(b) What was the government's main source of income? _-2720 Social protection_

(c) Which area accounted for the highest level of expenditure? _Health_

(d) What is meant by capital expenditure? _Long term spending goverment things_

(e) Suggest one item of capital expenditure that could be included in expenditure on health. _____

(f) List two examples of expenditure on defence. _army Security_

(g) List two examples of expenditure on education. _Schools and courses_

(h) Suggest two effects an increasing level of unemployment would have on the above budget. _because people will have social welfare_

(i) How would an increase in VAT of 10% affect the above budget? _____

(j) What percentage of total income was received from income tax? _45%_

(k) What percentage of total expenditure was spent on health? _38%_

4. From the following figures, prepare a national budget and answer the questions that follow.

Income: Income tax €2,700 m; Travel tax €250 m; Corporation tax €1,950 m; Customs and excise €1,300 m; DIRT €38 m; Proceeds from sale of semi-state company €1,750 m; Other €1,120 m.

Expenditure: Security €1,300 m; Education and Skills €2,100 m; Agriculture €1,400 m; Social Protection €3,150 m; Debt service €1,700 m; Grants to state bodies €1,250 m; Miscellaneous €1,100 m.

Income tax	€2,700 m	
Travel tax	€250 m	
Corporation tax	€1,950 m	
Custom and ~~exice~~ excise	€1,300 m	
Dirt	€38 m	
Proceeds from sale of semi state company	€1,750 m	9108 m
Other	€1,120 m	
Expenditure		
Security	€1,300 m	
Education and skills	€2,100 m	
Agriculture	€1,400 m	
Social Protection	€3,150 m	
Debt service	€1,700 m	€9108 m
Grants to state bodies	€1,250 m	€9110 m
Miscellanous	€1,100 m	€-2 m
		•2892 m

129

(a) Is there a budget surplus or a budget deficit? _____

(b) What was the government's main source of income? _€2,700_

(c) Which area accounted for the highest level of expenditure? _Social Protection_

(d) What is meant by capital income? _It's ment which gets the most_

(e) Suggest one item of capital income from the above list. _Income tax_

(f) List two examples of expenditure on security. _€890m and €1,300m_

_____

(g) List two examples of expenditure on social protection. _____

_____

(h) Suggest two effects a decreasing level of unemployment would have on the above budget.

People will get labour or be on ~~the~~

_____

(i) If inflation increased expenditure by 5%, what effect would it have on the above budget?

_____

(j) If you were Minister for Finance, suggest two changes you would make to the above budget.

_____

(k) What percentage of total expenditure was spent on education? _€2,100m_

5. The following is the national budget for Lambia (figures are in millions).

Income

Income tax	€2,300	
VAT	€1,700	
Capital tax	€1,500	
Customs and excise	€ 800	
Other	€1,100	€7,400

Expenditure

Education	€2,400	
Health	€1,500	
Security	€ 900	
Social Protection	€3,400	
Miscellaneous	€1,100	€9,300
Budget deficit		€1,900

(a)   (i) Redraft the above budget after taking the following into account:

- Income tax increased by 5%
- Health increased by 2%
- VAT reduced by 3%
- Social Protection decreased by 8%
- Customs and excise increased by 4%

_____

(ii) How have the changes affected the budget deficit?

_____

(b)   (i) Redraft the above budget after taking the following into account.

- Income tax decreased by 2%
- Education increased by 10%
- VAT increased by 1%
- Social protection increased by 4%
- Capital taxes increased by 5%
- Miscellaneous decreased by 6%

_____

(ii) How have the changes affected the budget deficit?

_____

6. Study the budget below for the Department of Education and Skills.

Income		Expenditure	
Allocation from the national budget	€2,300 m	Teachers' salaries	€350 m
ESF grant	€500 m	Grants to schools	€128 m
Exam fees	€1 m	New buildings	€1,400 m
		Exam costs	€3 m
		Sports facilities	€150 m
		Administration	€260 m
		PLC courses	€125 m
		Third level	€275 m
		School secretarial and maintenance	€78 m
		Miscellaneous	€32 m

(a) Prepare the budget for the Department of Education and Skills.

Income		
Allocation from the national budget	2,300m	
E.S.F grant	€500m	2801m
Exams Fees	€1m	
Expenditure		
Teachers salaries	350m	
Grants to schools	128m	
New building	1,400 m	
Exam costs	3m	
Sport facilities	150m	
Administration	260 m	
Plc courses	125m	
Third level	275m	
school secretarial and maintenance	78m	
miscelous	38m	2608

(b) What economic term is used to describe this budget? _____

(c) Explain why this budget can never be a deficit budget.

_____

7. Cross-grid

Solve the clues and complete the cross-grid below.

1. Purchasing stationery for government departments is an example of _____ expenditure (7) *current*

2. Building a new motorway is an example of _____ expenditure (7) *Capital*

3. The state company responsible for broadcasting is called ~~esb~~ (3) *RTe* ~~tax~~

4. Services provided by the state for the citizens of a country are called public _____ (9) ~~ESB~~ *utilities*

5. The tax paid by companies on their profits is called _____ tax (11) *expenditure*

6. A budget where income is equal to expenditure is called a _____ budget (8) *balanced*

7. A budget where income is greater than expenditure is called a _____ budget (7)

8. The state company responsible for the generation of electricity is called _____ (3)

9. The government department responsible for the building of schools is the Department of _____ and Skills (9) *education*

10. An economy where the provision of goods and services is shared by government and private enterprise is called a _____ economy (5)

11. The state company responsible for the supply of natural gas is called An Bord _____ (4)

12. A budget where income is less than expenditure is called a _____ budget (7) ~~surplus~~

1. c u r r e n t
2. c a p i t a l
3. R T E
4. u t i l i t i e s
5. e x p e n d i t u r e
6. b a l a n c e d
7. s u r p l u s
8. E S B
9.
10. M i x e d
   G a i s
12. d e f i c i t

8. Fill in the gaps

Fill in the gaps in the following paragraph using the words below.

Finance	current	FÁS	Justice and Law Reform
deficit	surplus	public	national borrowing
semi-state	utilities	income	ESB
capital	Education and Skills		

The ___National___ budget is prepared each year by the Minister for ___Finance___. It consists of a list of planned ___income___ and planned expenditure for the coming 12 months. Usually, the expenditure will be greater than the income and if this is the case the difference is called a budget ___Surplus deficit___. If income exceeded expenditure, however, there would be a budget ___Surplus___. Any deficit will be made up by ___borrowing___.

The national budget shows the amount of money that is being allocated to each of the services that the state wishes to provide. Services provided by the state for the citizens of a country are known as ___Semi public state utilities___. Examples of government expenditure include the building of schools and the payment of teachers by the Department of ___Education and skills___ and the provision of gardaí and prison officers by the Department of _____. Some essential services in Ireland are provided by _____ bodies. These include the generation and supply of electricity by the ___ESb___ and the provision of training services for the unemployed by ___Fás___.

Government spending can be divided into two groups – current and capital. _____ refers to day-to-day spending, while _____ expenditure refers to spending on long-term projects such as building a new motorway.

9. Word search

Write a short explanation of each of the following terms and locate each term in the word search below. The answers may read forwards, backwards or diagonally.

(a) Public utilities _____

(b) National budget _____

(c) Current income _____

(d) Local authority _____

(e) Capital expenditure _____

(f) Surplus _____

(g) Deficit _____

(h) Taxation _____

Y	T	I	R	O	H	T	U	A	E
Q	P	W	E	R	T	Y	U	I	X
A	U	C	A	P	I	T	A	L	P
D	B	S	D	F	G	H	O	J	E
E	L	K	L	Z	X	C	C	V	N
F	I	M	N	B	A	U	V	C	D
I	C	Z	E	L	Q	R	W	E	I
C	U	R	M	T	Y	R	U	I	T
I	T	O	O	P	A	E	S	D	U
T	I	F	C	G	H	N	J	K	R
L	L	A	N	O	I	T	A	N	E
Q	I	A	I	Z	X	C	V	B	N
R	T	A	X	A	T	I	O	N	G
R	I	S	U	L	P	R	U	S	T
T	E	G	D	U	B	Y	U	I	O
X	S	V	B	N	M	L	K	J	G

Section A Questions

10. True or false

	True	False
(a) A budget where income exceeds expenditure is called a deficit budget	~~☑~~	☑
(b) Garda wages is an example of government current expenditure	☑	☐
(c) Building a new hospital is part of government capital expenditure	☑	☐

11. Match the terms in column 1 with the correct example from column 2.

1. A public utility   A. RTÉ

2. A semi-state company   B. Education and Skills

3. A government department   C. Water supply system

1. C   2. A   3. B

12. Match the terms in column 1 with the correct example from column 2.

1. A balanced budget   A. Income €4,000 m; Expenditure €8,500 m

2. A surplus budget   B. Income €6,500 m: Expenditure €1,400 m

3. A deficit budget   C. Income €9,500 m; Expenditure €9,500 m

1. C   2. B   3. A

13. Classify the following items of expenditure under capital expenditure or current expenditure for a delivery van manufacturing business.

		Capital expenditure	Current expenditure
(a)	Purchase of heating oil		✓
(b)	Machinery	✓	
(c)	Wages		✓
(d)	Repairs to machinery		✓
(e)	Delivery vans for resale		✓
(f)	Repayment of bank term loan	✓	✗
(g)	Carriage outwards	✓	✗
(h)	Factory extension	✓	

14. Place a tick beside the items of government expenditure that you consider to be current (revenue).

(a) Wages for hospital workers ☐

(b) Building a new school ☐

(c) Purchase of new garda cars ☐

(d) Stationery for government departments ☐

(e) Airfares for senior public servants ☐

(f) Pensions for retired people ☐

15. List four examples of government spending on social protection.

(a) _____

(b) _____

(c) _____

(d) _____

16. The estimated government current budget for next year is as follows:

• Government current income: €9,796 m

• Government current expenditure: €10,366 m

(a) What is the amount of the difference in the two figures given? _____

(b) What is the economic term used to describe this difference? _____

17. Which of the following would a household regard as capital expenditure?

(a) Repairs ☐   (b) A new bathroom ☐   (c) Petrol expenses ☐

18. Which of the following state companies is involved in training people who are unemployed?

(a) An Post ☐   (b) Coillte ☐   (c) FÁS ☐   (d) BIM ☐

19. The government of Newland had the following budget for last year:

• Income: €960 m

• Expenditure: €995 m

Is the budget showing a surplus or a deficit? _____

20. Match the semi-state body in column 1 with the correct business activity in column 2.

1. ESB   **A.** Supply and distribution of natural gas

2. Bord Gáis   **B.** Operates the postal service

3. VHI   **C.** Provides medical insurance

4. An Post   **D.** Generates and supplies electricity

1. ☐   2. ☐   3. ☐   4. ☐

17 Foreign Trade

Balance of Trade/Balance of Payments Calculations

1. In each of the following, calculate the balance of trade and state whether each is a surplus or a deficit.

	Year 1	Year 2	Year 3	Year 4	Year 5
Visible imports (€)	2,000 m	6,734 m	4,222 m	3,472 m	6,123 m
Visible exports (€)	2,150 m	5,977 m	5,111 m	3,471 m	6,211 m
Balance of trade	150	757	889	1	88
Surplus or deficit	deficit / Surplus	Surplus / Deficit	Deficit / Surplus	Surplus / Deficit	Deficit / Surplus

2. In each of the following, calculate the balance of payments and state whether each is a surplus or a deficit.

	Year 1	Year 2	Year 3	Year 4	Year 5
Visible imports (€)	1,842 m	4,243 m	2,642 m	3,124 m	4,142 m
Invisible imports (€)	1,900 m	1,799 m	2,432 m	3,100 m	3,444 m
Visible exports (€)	1,643 m	3,892 m	2,800 m	2,744 m	4,624 m
Invisible exports (€)	1,792 m	3,712 m	2,140 m	2,892 m	3,142 m
Balance of trade	-307			588	5108
Surplus or deficit	Deficits			Deficit	surplus

3. For each of the following, calculate the:

(a) Balance of trade

(b) Net earnings from invisible trade

(c) Balance of payments on current account

	Year 1	Year 2	Year 3	Year 4	Year 5
Visible imports (€)	10,642 m	19,721 m	21,642 m	32,641 m	13,743 m
Invisible imports (€)	7,932 m	10,427 m	8,632 m	3,423 m	11,412 m
Visible exports (€)	14,711 m	26,429 m	14,721 m	21,722 m	8,417 m
Invisible exports (€)	6,422 m	2,173 m	4,279 m	19,714 m	3,419 m
Balance of trade					
Net earnings					
Balance of payments					

Exchange Rate Calculations

Use the exchange rate table below to calculate the answer to questions 4 to 14.

United Kingdom	0.90	Switzerland	2
United States	1.40	South Africa	10.5
Japan	170	Denmark	9

4. Calculate each of the following.

(a) John Corrigan wants to exchange €570 for Japanese yen _____96,900_____

(b) Fergus Flood wants to exchange €270 for Swiss francs _____540_____

(c) Olive Kelleher wants to exchange €185 for South African rand _____1850_____

(d) Jason Looby wants to exchange €340 for Danish kroner _____3060_____

(e) Robert McShane wants to exchange €1,456 for US dollars _____2038.4_____

(f) Carmel O'Dowd wants to exchange €460 for sterling _____464_____

5. Christopher Shannon wants to send €30 as a present to each of his two nieces – one in America and one in Japan. How much will each get in their own currency?

_____Japan = 5,100   America 42_____

6. Michael Andrews has booked a hotel for a holiday in Switzerland. The total cost of the hotel is €245, which he has paid by credit card.

(a) Calculate how much the hotel is owed in Swiss francs. _____490_____

(b) What is the nightly charge in Swiss francs if Michael is staying for 7 nights? _____17(5_____

7. Mary Jones is going on a school tour to London and has saved €150 for spending money. How many pounds sterling will she receive when she goes to the bank to change her money?

_____135_____

8. Calculate each of the following.

(a) Niall Downes wants to exchange £450 sterling for euro _____€500_____

(b) Eva Fagan wants to exchange $91 US dollars for euro _____€65_____

(c) Thelma Fitzpatrick wants to exchange 840 South African rand for euro _____80_____

(d) Graham Tyrrell wants to exchange 9,860 Japanese yen for euro _____58_____

(e) Jane Breslin wants to exchange 4,800 Swiss francs for euro _____2400_____

9. Ann Devlin wants to purchase some items from a British mail order catalogue. The prices are quoted in sterling and are as follows.

- Set of CDs: £50
- Set of golf clubs: £480
- CD storage rack: £39

(a) How much is each article in euro? _____

(b) What is the total cost in euro? _____

10. Mathew Delaney wants to check the cost of hotel rooms in England, New York and Denmark for a weekend stay. The rates per night he was quoted were as follows:

- England: £58.50

- New York: $100.80

- Copenhagen: 540 kroner

Calculate the price in euro for each of the rates above. Which rate is the cheapest and which is the most expensive?

£ 65.00

$ 72

kroner 90

11. Students of St Paul's Secondary School returned from their educational tour of Copenhagen and combined all their remaining currency. It amounted to 546 Danish kroner. How much is this in euro? 60.07

12. David Hayes purchased an air trip as follows:

- Dublin to London with Aer Lingus: €80

- London to Zurich with British Midland: £144 sterling

- Zurich to Dublin with Swissair: 320 Swiss francs

What is the total cost of the round trip in euro?

£ 65.88   €100 Sterling

288

640   400

13. A Japanese student arrived in Ireland to study English for 4 weeks. The cost of the English course was ¥110,500 and she brought spending money of ¥139,400. Calculate the cost of the course in euro and the euro amount she will receive when she exchanges her spending money in the bank.

14. Aidan Macken saw a car advertised in England for £6,750. If Aidan wants to bring the car to Ireland he will have to pay tax of €1,500. If Aidan decides to go ahead with the deal, what will the total cost of the car be in euro?

15. Invisible trade

Tick to indicate whether each of the following are invisible imports or invisible exports.

	Invisible import	Invisible export
(a) Dutch tourists take their holidays in Clare		✓
(b) American company located in Dublin sends profits back to the US	✓	
(c) Irish band performs concerts in Russia		✓
(d) British band performs concerts in Dublin	✓	
(e) Irish author writes a world bestseller		✓
(f) Irish emigrants save their money in an Irish bank		✓
(g) Aer Lingus service a Jamaican aircraft		✓
(h) Ryanair charter a French aircraft	✓	
(i) Irish dance school takes out insurance with a British insurer	✓	
(j) Irish school on an educational trip to Switzerland	✓	
(k) The Irish soccer team qualifying for the World Cup finals		✓
(l) Riverdance profits brought back to Ireland		✓
(m) Irish people investing their money in foreign banks	✓	
(n) An Irish-owned and bred horse wins the Aintree Grand National in England		✓
(o) Irish golfers win the World Cup		✓
(p) Irish holidaymakers travel to the UK with British Airways	✓	

16. Cross-grid

Solve the clues below to complete the cross-grid.

1. Foreign tourists holidaying in Ireland is an example of an ____ export (9) *invisible*

2. When total exports are less than total imports, the result is a ____ (7) *deficit*

3. Buying Irish goods in place of foreign imports is called ____ (6, 12) *import substitution*

4. Selling Irish goods to foreign countries is called ____ (9) *exporting*

5. A statement of visible imports and visible exports is called the ____ of trade (7) *balance*

6. When total exports are greater than total imports, the result is a ____ (7) *surplus*

7. The quantity of a foreign currency which can be purchased for one euro is called the ____ (8, 4) *exchange rate*

8. The job of ____ Ireland is to promote exports (10)

9. Bringing foreign goods into Ireland is called ____ (9) *importing*

10. A statement of total imports and total exports is called the balance of ____ (8) *payments*

11. Ireland's biggest trading partner is the ____ (6, 7) *uk*

12. There are currently 27 members of this group (8, 5) *europe union*

						1. I	N	**V**	I	S	I	B	L	**e**					
				2. **d**	**e**	**f**	**I**	**c**	**i**	**t**									
		3.					**S**												
		4.					**I**												
					5. **B**														
		6.				**L**													
7.						**E**													
		8.			**T**														
		9.			**R**														
			10.		**A**														
	11.				**D**														
	12.				**E**														

17. Word search

Write a short explanation of each of the terms below in the space provided. Locate each of the words in italics in the word search below. The answers may read forwards, backwards or diagonally.

(a) *Importing* _____

(b) *Exporting* _____

(c) *Visible* trade _____

(d) *Invisible* trade _____

(e) *Balance* of trade _____

(f) *Import substitution* _____

(g) *European Union* _____

(h) *Exchange rate* _____

(i) *Enterprise Ireland* _____

E	U	R	O	P	E	A	N	Q	W	E	R	T	Y	U
X	N	N	A	S	E	S	I	R	P	R	E	T	N	E
C	O	Z	I	N	V	I	S	I	B	L	E	X	C	V
H	I	Q	M	O	W	M	E	R	T	T	Y	U	I	O
A	T	A	P	S	N	P	D	F	A	G	H	J	K	L
N	U	Z	O	F	X	O	C	R	V	E	B	N	M	M
G	T	Q	R	W	E	R	R	T	L	Y	T	U	I	O
E	I	A	T	S	D	T	F	B	G	H	R	J	K	L
Z	T	X	I	C	V	B	I	R	E	L	A	N	D	B
N	S	M	N	Q	W	S	E	R	T	Y	D	U	I	O
P	B	A	G	N	I	T	R	O	P	X	E	S	D	F
Z	U	X	C	V	V	B	N	M	A	S	D	F	G	H
Q	S	W	N	E	R	T	Y	U	I	O	P	A	S	D
F	G	B	A	L	A	N	C	E	H	J	K	L	Z	X
C	V	B	N	M	Q	W	E	R	T	Y	I	O	P	A

Section A Questions

18. Complete the table below for any four non-EMU member countries.

	Country	Currency
(a)	~~France~~ Nigeria	Nira
(b)	~~Germany~~ USA	dollars
(c)	~~Italy~~ ~~Greece~~ Russia	Ruble
(d)	Romania	Lei

19. You are going on holidays to the US. You wish to change €450 into dollars to bring with you. Your local bank has the following information on display in the foreign exchange section:

	We Buy	We Sell
US Dollars	1.48	1.44

Calculate how much you will receive in dollars for your €450. _____ we sell _____

20. The figures below relate to a country's international trade for a given year.
- Visible imports €21 m; Visible exports €16 m
- Invisible imports €34 m; Invisible exports €22 m

Tick the correct figure for the balance of trade.

(a) €17 m ☒   (b) €7 m ☐   (c) €5 m ☑   (d) €12 m ☐

21. American tourists using Aer Lingus to travel to Ireland is an example of:

(a) Invisible import ☐   (b) Visible import ☐   (c) Invisible export ☑

22. An Irish-made product sells in Ireland and the UK. In Ireland the selling price is €24. If the exchange rate is €1 = £0.90, what should the price of the product be in sterling?

_____ 21 60 _____

23. What do the following letters stand for?

(a) BOP _____

(b) EU _Euro_ _____

24. From Ireland's point of view, which of the following is an invisible export?

(a) Irish tourists going on holiday to Germany ☒

(b) Irish meat sold in France ☑

(c) English tourists coming to Ireland on holiday ☑

25. Which of the following countries are in the European Union?

(a) Denmark ☐   (b) Norway ☑   (c) Sweden ☐

26. Which of the following countries are not in the European Union?

(a) Belgium ☐   (b) Switzerland ☑   (c) Luxembourg ☐

Forms of Business

1. On 8 March 2011, Lorraine Nolan of 6 Merchant Row, Westport, Co. Mayo and Maurice Walshe of 16 Main Street, Boyle, Co. Roscommon formed a private limited company called NW Marketing and Design Ltd. The objectives of the company are to provide marketing, advertising and design services to businesses in the West of Ireland. The authorised share capital of NW Marketing and Design Ltd is 50,000 €1 ordinary shares. On 8 March 2011, Lorraine Nolan purchased 15,000 shares and Maurice Walshe purchased 8,000 shares. The registered office is Unit 3, The Business Centre, Westport, Co. Mayo. Complete the memorandum of association below.

MEMORANDUM OF ASSOCIATION

1. The name of the company is: _____

2. The objectives for which the company is established are:

_____

_____

_____

3. The liablility of the members is: _____

4. The authorised share capital of the company is:

_____

We, the several persons whose names, addresses and descriptions are subscribed, wish to be formed into a Company in pursuance of the memorandum of association and we agree to take the number of shares in the capital of the Company set opposite our respective names.

Name, Address and Description	Number of Shares Taken
_____	_____
_____	_____
_____	_____
_____	_____

Dated: _____

Registered Office: _____

---

2. On 6 April 2011, Brandon Maguire of 8 Limekiln Park, Ennis, Co. Clare and Gina Morales of 23 Raglin Street, Tralee, Co. Kerry formed a private limited company called BG Software Solutions Ltd. The objectives of the company are to develop computer software for use by schools and other educational establishments throughout Ireland and abroad. The authorised share capital of BG Software Solutions Ltd is €250,000. On 6 April 2011, Brandon Maguire purchased 25,000 shares and Gina Morales purchased 38,000 shares. The registered office is 67 O'Malley Place, Limerick. Complete the memorandum of association below.

MEMORANDUM OF ASSOCIATION

1. The name of the company is: _____

2. The objectives for which the company is established are:

_____

_____

_____

3. The liablility of the members is: _____

4. The authorised share capital of the company is:

_____

We, the several persons whose names, addresses and descriptions are subscribed, wish to be formed into a Company in pursuance of the memorandum of association and we agree to take the number of shares in the capital of the Company set opposite our respective names.

Name, Address and Description	Number of Shares Taken
_____	_____
_____	_____
_____	_____
_____	_____

Dated: _____

Registered Office: _____

---

3. Business project

Make contact with a sole trader or small private limited company in your area. Do an individual or group project on your chosen business. You could use the following headings:

Name	Owners/shareholders	Limited liability
Finance	Setting up	Growth and development
Main customers	Main suppliers	Marketing and advertising
Problems encountered	Employees	Benefits of being self-employed
Products/services supplied		

4. Cross-grid

Use the clues below to complete the cross-grid.

1. The document that sets out the internal rules of a company is called the articles of _____ (11)

2. and 3. The document that must be received before a company can commence trading is the _____ (11) of _____ (13)

4. and 5. Having this means that the owners of the business will only lose the amount of their investment in the event of bankruptcy (7, 9)

6. and 7. A person who owns and runs his or her own business (4, 6)

8. The document that contains the objectives of a company is called the _____ (10) of association

9. The minimum number of people necessary to form a private limited company (3)

10. The meeting of shareholders which must be held every year (3)

11. The term that describes the selling off of a state company (13)

5. Word search

Locate the following terms from Chapter 18 – Forms of Business in the grid below. The answers may read forwards, backwards or diagonally.

| Limited liability | Sole trader | Ltd | Co-operative | Incorporation |
| Semi-state company | Privatisation | Memorandum | Articles | AGM |

I	Q	W	E	R	T	Y	U	I	M	O
N	L	I	M	I	T	E	D	P	E	Q
C	I	A	S	D	R	L	F	G	M	H
O	A	Z	X	Y	A	O	V	B	O	N
R	B	Z	D	A	D	S	E	T	R	Z
P	I	T	A	S	E	O	D	F	A	H
O	L	Z	X	C	R	V	B	B	N	N
R	I	Q	W	E	R	E	T	Y	D	U
A	T	A	G	M	A	T	S	D	U	F
T	Y	Q	W	E	R	A	T	Y	M	O
I	P	A	S	D	F	T	G	H	J	K
O	Z	X	C	V	B	S	A	S	D	F
N	Q	W	A	R	T	I	C	L	E	S
Q	W	E	R	T	Y	M	U	I	O	P
E	V	I	T	A	R	E	P	O	O	C
A	S	D	F	G	H	S	L	K	J	H

Section A Questions

6. In business, a sole trader is one of the following.

(a) A person who checks the quality of new shoes ☐

(b) A person who receives dividends ☐

(c) A person who sells fish for a company ☐

(d) A business run by its owner ☐

(e) A business that is always losing money ☐

7. State two advantages of a sole trader as a form of business.

(a) _____

(b) _____

8. How many people are necessary to form a private limited company?

(a) Between 1 and 10 ☐

(b) Between 1 and 30 ☐

(c) Between 1 and 50 ☐

(d) None of the above ☐

9. Tick the appropriate box in each of the following.

(a) A private limited company has the following letters after its name.

Co. ☐   Plc ☐   Ltd ☐   Inc. ☐

(b) The document that gives information about a company to the general public is the:

Articles of association ☐

Memorandum of association ☐

10. Name the document that is often referred to as the birth certificate of a company.

_____

11. True or false

	True	False
(a) The minimum number of shareholders in a private company is 3	☐	☐
(b) The maximum number of shareholders in a private company is 50	☐	☐
(c) The maximum number of shareholders in a sole trader is 2	☐	☐
(d) A shareholder owning 100 shares in a company has 100 votes	☐	☐
(e) A private company has the word 'Ltd' after its name	☐	☐

Business Finance

1. Word search

Locate and list three short-, medium- and long-term sources of finance in the word search.

Short term	Medium term	Long term
_____	_____	_____
_____	_____	_____
_____	_____	_____

```
Q   H   V   B   N   C   M   G   K   L   K
E   I   O   V   E   R   D   R   A   F   T
R   R   Z   L   U   E   H   A   J   J   E
T   E   X   K   D   D   G   N   H   L   R
Y   P   G   J   S   I   F   T   A   G   M
U   U   N   H   E   T   D   S   O   F   L
I   R   I   G   S   O   S   I   P   D   O
O   C   S   F   N   R   A   U   M   S   A
S   H   A   R   E   S   Q   Y   N   A   N
P   A   E   D   P   W   D   T   B   Z   L
A   S   L   S   X   E   N   R   V   X   O
L   E   A   S   E   B   A   C   K   C   I
```

Section A Questions

2. Tick the most suitable source of finance for each of the following items required by Smith & Sons Motors Ltd.

Items	Short term	Medium term	Long term
(a) Buildings	☐	☐	☐
(b) Computer	☐	☐	☐
(c) Cars for resale	☐	☐	☐
(d) Advertising	☐	☐	☐

3. Which of the following is not a short-term source of finance?

(a) Factoring ☐

(b) Bank overdraft ☐

(c) Term loan ☐

(d) Accrued expenses ☐

(e) Trade creditors ☐

4. Tick the most suitable source of finance for each of the following items required by L. O'Kelly, a dairy farmer.

Items	Short term	Medium term	Long term
(a) Animal feed	☐	☐	☐
(b) Land	☐	☐	☐
(c) Machinery	☐	☐	☐
(d) Electricity	☐	☐	☐
(e) Diesel	☐	☐	☐

5. Explain the main difference between a grant and a loan.

_____

_____

6. Tick the most suitable source of finance for the Boswell family, who wish to purchase €300 worth of home heating oil.

(a) Short term ☐

(b) Medium term ☐

(c) Long term ☐

Planning the Business

Cash Flow Forecasts

1. Complete the following three cash flow forecast extracts.

(a)

DETAILS	Jan	Feb	Mar	Apr	TOTAL
Total receipts	34,500	44,000	39,500	42,000	
Total payments	22,000	34,000	31,500	28,000	
Net cash					
Opening cash	3,500				
Closing cash					

(b)

DETAILS	Jan	Feb	Mar	Apr	TOTAL
Total receipts	67,000	58,500	76,500	71,000	
Total payments	62,000	61,000	90,000	46,000	
Net cash					
Opening cash	5,000				
Closing cash					

(c)

DETAILS	Jan	Feb	Mar	Apr	TOTAL
Total receipts	49,500	51,000	34,000	62,900	
Total payments	40,000	56,000	45,000	60,500	
Net cash					
Opening cash	3,700				
Closing cash					

2. From the following information relating to Simon & Co. Ltd, prepare a cash flow forecast for the 4 months January to April. Opening cash on 1 January is €4,700.

Estimated income:

* Sales: January €9,500; February €10,700; March €12,600; April €15,700
* Capital introduced by owner in February €6,000

Estimated expenditure:

* Purchases: January €5,400; February €9,200; March €7,000; April €8,400
* Electricity: February €600; April €500
* Telephone: February €250; April €250
* Wages: €2,000 per month
* Rent: €500 per month

DETAILS	Jan	Feb	Mar	Apr	TOTAL
Receipts					
Sales					
Capital					
Total receipts					
Payments					
Purchases					
Electricity					
Telephone					
Wages					
Rent					
Total payments					
NET CASH					
OPENING CASH					
CLOSING CASH					

3. From the following information relating to D & M Ltd, prepare a cash flow forecast for the 4 months March to June. Opening cash on 1 March is €1,500.

Estimated income:

- Sales: March €28,400; April €37,000; May €42,800; June €57,600
- Receipts from debtors: March €19,100; April €20,200; May €24,600; June €23,600
- Rent received: €2,000 per month

Estimated expenditure:

- Purchase of materials: March €17,800; April €22,600; May €29,200; June €36,000
- Payments to creditors: March €10,000; April €18,400; May €20,700; June €28,200
- Electricity: March €800; May €1,000
- Telephone: March €250; May €500
- Insurance: €5,600 in April
- Advertising: €1,300 per month
- Purchase of new machine: May €15,000
- Purchase of new vehicle: June €12,000

DETAILS	Mar	Apr	May	June	TOTAL
Receipts					
Sales					
Debtors					
Rent received					
Total receipts					
Payments					
Purchases					
Creditors					
Electricity					
Telephone					
Insurance					
Advertising					
Machinery					
Vehicle					
Total payments					
NET CASH					
OPENING CASH					
CLOSING CASH					

4. From the following information relating to Heatco Ltd, prepare a cash flow forecast for the 4 months March to June. Opening cash on 1 March is €2,000.

Estimated income:

* Sales: March €30,600; April €35,400; May €33,100; June €40,200
* Receipts from debtors: March €12,100; April €14,700; May €15,100; June €18,200
* Rent received: €600 per month

Estimated expenditure:

* Purchase of materials: March €16,700; April €22,400; May €21,000; June €19,100
* Payments to creditors: March €10,300; April €12,600; May €14,800; June €22,600
* Wages: €6,000 per month
* Insurance: €5,000 in March
* Electricity: April €700; June €600
* Advertising: €1,700 per month
* Purchase of new computer: April €10,000
* Purchase of new vehicle: May €12,000

DETAILS	Mar	Apr	May	June	TOTAL
Receipts					
Sales					
Debtors					
Rent received					
Total receipts					
Payments					
Purchases					
Creditors					
Wages					
Insurance					
Electricity					
Advertising					
Computer					
Vehicle					
Total payments					
NET CASH					
OPENING CASH					
CLOSING CASH					

5. From the following information relating to Kielty & Sons Ltd, prepare a cash flow forecast for the 4 months January to April. Opening cash on 1 January is €2,500.

Estimated income:

- Sales: January €15,000; February €18,400; March €22,000; April €19,100
- Receipts from debtors: January €12,400; February €14,700; March €8,300; April €15,600
- Government grant: April €5,000

Estimated expenditure:

- Purchase of materials: January €10,400; February €27,000; March €14,600; April €26,200
- Payments to creditors: January €8,000; February €14,600; March €12,700; April €15,000
- Purchase of new machinery: January €12,000
- Wages: €2,300 per month
- Electricity: February €170; April €250
- Telephone: January €250; March €220
- Motor expenses: €210 per month plus fleet service in April costing €650
- Advertising and marketing: €270 per month
- Insurance: €1,200 in January

DETAILS	Jan	Feb	Mar	Apr	TOTAL
Receipts					
Sales					
Debtors					
Government grant					
Total receipts					
Payments					
Purchases					
Creditors					
Machinery					
Wages					
Electricity					
Telephone					
Motor expenses					
Advertising					
Insurance					
Total payments					
NET CASH					
OPENING CASH					
CLOSING CASH					

6. (a) Study the partially completed cash flow forecast below. You are required to complete this statement for the months of March, April, May and June as well as the Total column. The following information should be taken into account.

- Monthly receipts from cash sales are expected to increase by 25% beginning in May
- A European Union grant of €50,000 is expected in April
- The shareholders are to invest an additional €60,000 in the business in June
- Increases in material costs will mean that purchases will increase by 20% beginning in March
- Wages and advertising will remain unchanged
- A rent increase is due from May of 15%
- Insurance for the year is due in June and will cost €8,500
- New equipment costing €100,000 will be purchased in April

(b) State two important pieces of information that can be obtained from this cash flow forecast.

_____

_____

(c) The firm forgot to allow for overtime payments of €6,000 for the 4-month period. If these had been included, show how they would have affected the net cash position at the end of June.

_____

DETAILS	Jan	Feb	Mar	Apr	May	June	TOTAL
Receipts							
Sales	44,000	44,000					
EU grant							
Share capital							
Total receipts	44,000	44000					
Payments							
Purchases	15,000	15,000					
Advertising	1,600	1,600					
Wages	2,000	2,000					
Rent	1,500	1,500					
Insurance							
Motor vehicles		25,000					
Equipment							
Total payments	20,100	45,100					
NET CASH	23,900	−1,100					
OPENING CASH	5,000	28,900	27,800				
CLOSING CASH	28,900	27,800					

7. (a) Study the partially completed cash flow forecast below. You are required to complete this statement for the months of September, October, November and December as well as the Total column. The following information should be taken into account.

- Monthly receipts from cash sales are expected to increase by 30% beginning in October
- An Enterprise Ireland grant of €40,000 is expected in November
- The firm will sell off some surplus warehouse space in October, which is expected to raise €15,500
- Increases in material costs will mean that purchases will increase by 25% beginning in October
- Telephone bills in September and November will be €550 and €580, respectively
- An additional employee will be taken on in December, causing the wages bill to rise by €350 per month
- Advertising costs will remain unchanged
- A rent increase is due from September of 10%
- The loan repayments will end after the October payment
- New vehicles costing €60,000 will be purchased in November

(b) The firm forgot to allow for a special advertising campaign that was brought out in December costing €3,000. If this had been included, show how it would have affected the net cash position at the end of June.

DETAILS	July	Aug	Sept	Oct	Nov	Dec	TOTAL
Receipts							
Sales	50,000	60,000					
Grant							
Sale of warehouse							
Total receipts	50,000	60,000					
Payments							
Purchases	35,000	35,000					
Telephone	450						
Wages	4,500	4,500					
Advertising	1,300	1,300					
Rent	5,000	5,000					
Loan repayments	6,500	6,500					
Vehicles							
Total payments	52,750	52,300					
NET CASH	−2,750	7,700					
OPENING CASH	3,000	250	7,950				
CLOSING CASH	250	7,950					

21 ★ Communications

1. Graph and chart work

Display the following sets of information on pie charts.

(a) S. Ryan, grocer, projects his first year costs as follows:

Rent €10,000; Wages €15,000; Light and heat €10,000; General expenses €5,000.

(b) The 5 Star Hotel Chain reports that their guests over the last 12 months fell into five main categories as follows:

Business travellers 105,000; Holidaymakers 90,000; Conference delegates 45,000; Weekend breaks 90,000; Miscellaneous 30,000.

2. Display the following sets of information on trend graphs.

(a) Happyflyer recorded the following passenger numbers for the last 2 years.

2011: Jan–Feb 14,000; Mar–Apr 25,000; May–June 46,000; July–Aug 54,000; Sept–Oct 42,000; Nov–Dec 20,000.

2012: Jan–Feb 18,000; Mar–Apr 31,000; May–June 40,000; July–Aug 62,000; Sept–Oct 55,000; Nov–Dec 32,000.

(b) Hyland's Co-op wants to compare their sales and profit figures for the last 5 months.

Sales: January €120,000; February €90,000; March €65,000; April €57,000; May €105,000

Profits: January €35,000; February €30,000; March €25,000; April €28,000; May €35,000

3. Display the following sets of information on bar charts.

(a) The Green Glens 9 Hole P&P Club recorded the following holes-in-one last year.

5 on the 1st; 2 on the 2nd; 8 on the 3rd; 4 on the 4th; 11 on the 5th; 1 on the 6th; 9 on the 7th; 6 on the 8th; and 5 on the 9th.

(b) The Motor Industry Trade Association reports the following car sales for last year.

Fiat 12,000 cars; Renault 15,000 cars; Ford 20,000 cars; Citroën 3,000 cars; Toyota 15,000 cars; Nissan 18,000 cars; BMW 2,000 cars; Mercedes 2,500 cars.

4. Cross-grid

Complete the communications cross-grid from the clues below.

1. The transfer of information between two people is called _____ (13)

2. Communication within an organisation is called _____ communication (8)

3. Communication between a firm and people outside is called _____ communication (8)

4. Transferring messages by computer is known as _____ (1, 4)

5. Telephone, intercom and radio are examples of _____ communication (4)

6. The person in a firm responsible for communications is the public _____ officer (9)

7. Letters, fax and memos are examples of _____ communication (7)

8. This organisation provides the state broadcasting service (3)

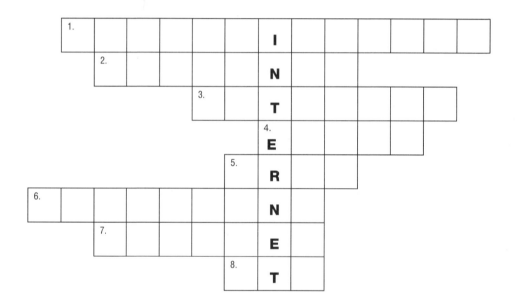

5. Word search

Locate the following communications terms in the word search below. The answers may read forwards, backwards or diagonally.

Oral	Written	Visual	Internal	External
Public relations officer	Internet	Email	Text	RTE
An Post	Eircom	Bar chart	Pictogram	Trend graph

A	T	T	Q	G	M	G	V	E	R	Q	Q
Q	E	E	P	U	B	L	I	C	E	L	W
I	N	X	R	F	N	H	S	W	L	K	T
N	R	T	T	D	B	J	U	Q	A	J	R
T	E	X	E	E	W	K	A	L	T	H	E
E	T	T	W	O	R	A	L	K	I	G	N
R	N	S	E	F	I	N	Q	J	O	F	D
N	I	O	R	F	T	L	A	H	N	D	G
A	J	P	T	I	T	M	W	L	S	S	R
L	H	N	Y	C	E	N	E	G	R	A	A
L	I	A	M	E	N	B	R	F	T	B	P
S	G	C	T	R	A	H	C	R	A	B	H
R	F	V	U	S	V	V	T	D	Y	V	R
E	I	R	C	O	M	C	Y	S	U	C	T
T	D	B	I	A	C	X	G	A	I	X	Y
Y	S	N	P	I	C	T	O	G	R	A	M
U	Z	M	O	P	X	Z	U	Z	O	Z	U

Section A Questions

6. Divide the following methods of communication into three groups: internal, external and both.

| Intercom | Television | Canteen notice board | E-mail | Telephone | Staff newsletter |
| Memo | Newspaper | Letter | Fax machine | Meetings | Report |

Internal	**External**	**Both**
_____	_____	_____
_____	_____	_____
_____	_____	_____
_____	_____	_____

7. Communication between a business and the outside world is called _____ communication.

8. Communication within a business is called _____ communication.

9. Match the terms in column 1 with the explanations in column 2.

1. Eircom	**A.** Form of visual communication
2. E-mail	**B.** Form of written communication
3. Trend/line graph	**C.** Telecommunications company
4. Fax machine	**D.** Mobile phone operator
5. Meteor	**E.** Method of communicating with computer users

1. ☐   **2.** ☐   **3.** ☐   **4.** ☐   **5.** ☐

10. Tick the appropriate box to indicate if each of the following is an example of oral, written or visual communication.

	Oral	**Written**	**Visual**
(a) Telephone	☐	☐	☐
(b) Notice board	☐	☐	☐
(c) Fax	☐	☐	☐
(d) Pictogram	☐	☐	☐
(e) Internet	☐	☐	☐

11. Give two examples of internal communication in a hospital.

(a) _____

(b) _____

12. Give two examples of external communication in a taxi firm.

(a) _____

(b) _____

13. Write down two duties of a public relations officer.

(a) _____

(b) _____

Letter and Report Writing

Letter Writing

Write the letter referred to in each of the following. Use today's date in each case.

1. Stephen O'Brien, 22 Ardmore Park, Artane, Dublin 5, wants to write a letter to Mr Lynch, St Gerard's CBS, Coolock, Dublin 5, explaining why his son Neil was absent from school for the previous two days and requesting a meeting to be arranged with the Year Head to discuss Neil's progress at school.

2. Geraldine Moronney, 12 Forest Hills, Dundalk, Co. Louth, wrote a letter to the Slieve Mor Hotel, Castleblaney, Co. Monaghan, booking a reservation for herself, her husband and their two children for the week of 4 July to 11 July. In the letter she stated that she wanted a double and a twin room with a sea view and that she was enclosing a cheque for €200 as a deposit. She also requested a receipt and confirmation of the booking from the hotel.

3. John Lynch of 18 New Street, Mullingar, Co. Westmeath, bought a new JSS colour television set, model no. 77Y, from June Tapley, manager of Boyle's Electrical Store, Bells Shopping Mall, Mullingar, Co. Westmeath, on Saturday, 9 March. He paid €560 by cheque. When he brought it home, he discovered that the sound was not working on the television set and has decided to write a letter of complaint.

4. Fatima Amer of 191 Lincoln Park, Dunmore East, Co. Waterford, wants to write a letter to her local councillor, Mr Frank O'Regan, complaining about the state of the footpath outside her house and asking when the council will be able to carry out the necessary repairs. Mr O'Regan has an office in City Hall, Kilkenny.

Report Writing

5. Prepare the report compiled by Eleanor Fanning, The High School, Kildare, for Ms Browne, her Media Studies teacher, outlining the most popular radio stations among the students in second year.

6. Prepare the report compiled by Maria O'Dwyer and Eamon Shanahan from your school for the CSPE teacher on the different activities that students in the school are involved with in the local community.

7. Prepare the report sent by Michel Sangana, an LCA student in your school, to the career guidance teacher outlining the different nationalities represented among the students in the school. Include a section on what the school could do to fully involve all students in school life.

8. Prepare the report sent by Peter Fielding, marketing executive with Global Researchers Ltd, Dublin Road, Wexford, to the marketing manager of Selby's Soft Drinks outlining the results of research carried out into the new soft drink being produced by Selby's. Use the following headings:

   - Current market leaders
   - Recommended price
   - Suitable methods of advertising
   - Sales promotion techniques

23 Chain of Production

1. Chain of production

Describe the chain of production applying to the following goods. The first one has been done for you. When you have finished, think of five products and complete the chain of production in the space provided.

Product	Primary	Secondary	Tertiary
(a) Oak fitted kitchen	Forest/tree	Carpenter/cabinet maker	Transport
(b) Vegetable soup	Farm	Factory	Shop
(c) Calendar	trees/forest	Factory	Shop
(d) Southern fried chicken	Farm	Factory	Shop
(e) Diamond necklace	Mine	Factory	shop
(f) CD	mine	Factory	shop
(g) Cream cake	farm	Factory	Shop
(h) Hanging basket	tree	Factory	shop
(i) Textbook	tree/forest	Factory	shop
(j) Cardboard box	tree/forest	Factory	Shop
(k) Book	tree	factory	Shop
(l) wardrobe	tree	factory	Shop
(m) Marble floor			
(n)			
(o)			

2. Channel of distribution

Illustrate an appropriate channel of distribution for the following goods and services. The first one has been done for you.

(a) Compact disc

Manufacturer ⟶ Retailer ⟶ Consumer

(b) Package holiday

Tour operator ⟶ retailer ⟶ Consumer

(c) Biscuit

Baker ⟶ _____ ⟶ Consumer

(d) Schoolbook

Manufactor ⟶ _____ ⟶ _____

(e) Electrical appliance

_____   _____   _____

(f) Designer clothes

_____   _____   _____

(g) Soft drinks

_____   _____   _____

(h) Motor car

_____   _____   _____

(i) Commercial aeroplane

_____   _____   _____

(j) Landscape gardening service

_____   _____   _____

3. Word search

Locate and circle the following types of retailer in the grid below. The answers may read forwards, backwards or diagonally.

Supermarket	Mail order	Discount	Department	Automatic
Multiple	Chain	Independent	Voluntary	

```
E  S  R  T  Y  C  U  I  O  P  V
T  U  F  H  J  I  G  J  L  D  O
N  P  M  U  L  T  I  P  L  E  L
E  E  C  B  N  A  M  W  E  P  U
D  R  I  D  U  M  Y  T  R  A  N
N  M  A  I  L  O  R  D  E  R  T
E  A  O  S  P  T  G  F  D  T  A
P  R  C  C  L  U  B  A  S  M  R
E  K  H  O  H  A  H  G  N  E  Y
D  E  W  U  T  A  L  S  E  N  M
N  T  R  N  R  E  I  L  A  T  H
I  I  O  T  C  B  N  N  E  R  T
```

24 People at Work

1. The public and private sectors

Tick whether each of the following work in the Public Sector or Private Sector.

	Public sector	Private sector
(a) Technician with Bord Gáis	✓	☐
(b) Restaurant owner	☐	✓
(c) Insurance consultant with Zurich Insurance	☐	✓
(d) Professional golfer	☐	✓
(e) HSE nurse	✓	☐
(f) Electrician with the ESB	✓	☐
(g) Electrician with ElectroServices Ltd	✓	☐

2. Organisational charts

Using the information below, draw organisational charts for each of the following.

(a) Your school.

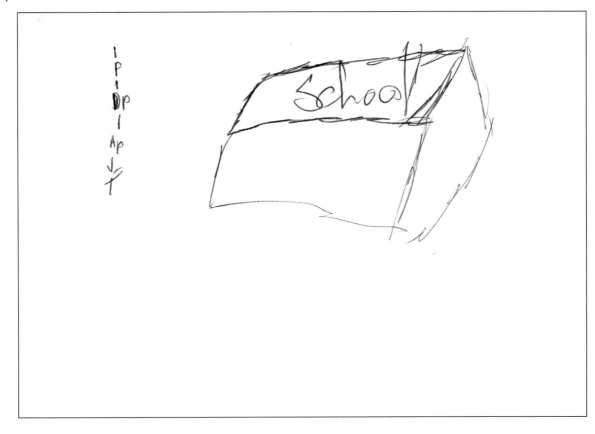

(b) A large manufacturing company with five departments.

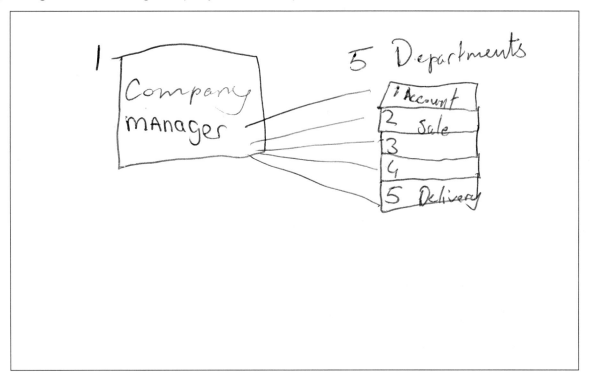

(c) Lacey's Department Store is owned by Mr and Mrs Lacey and has a board of directors, a managing director and six departments (clothing, electrical, toys, hardware, perfume and furniture). Each department has a manager, an assistant manager and 10 sales assistants. In addition, the furniture department has a delivery department with two drivers.

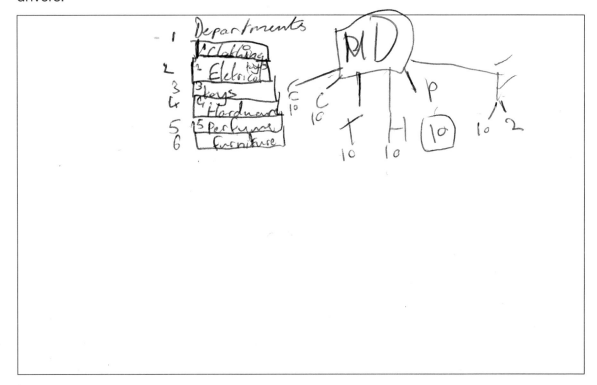

(d) The National Hospital is owned by the Department of Health and Children and run by a board of management. There is a chief executive and five departments (maternity, children's, adults, accident and emergency, and outpatients). Each department has a consultant, three doctors and 10 nurses.

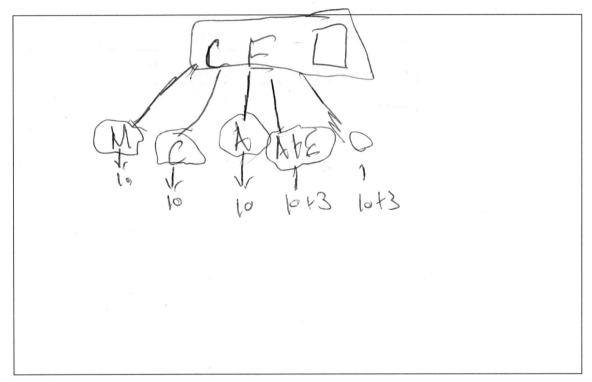

3. Word search

Solve the clues below and then find each correct term in the word search. The answers may read forwards, backwards or diagonally.

(a) Anything that requires effort (4) _work_

(b) Work for which payment is received (10) _Employment_

(c) A person who works for others (8) _Employee_

(d) Those who are available for work (6, 5) _Unemployed_

(e) Those who are unable to find employment (10) _unemployed_

(f) Those who work for themselves are _self_ -employed (4).

(g) The chain of authority in a business is called the _____ structure (12)

(h) The person who runs the business on a daily basis is the _____ director (8)

W	E	R	O	T	M	Y	E	U	T	I
S	W	O	R	K	A	H	E	L	N	O
U	D	F	G	G	N	J	Y	K	E	P
N	A	S	A	D	A	F	O	G	M	H
E	B	N	N	M	G	L	L	K	Y	J
M	V	C	I	A	I	S	P	S	O	F
P	R	E	S	K	N	J	M	E	L	G
L	T	Y	A	U	G	I	E	L	P	O
O	K	G	T	F	D	C	B	F	M	P
Y	J	H	I	A	S	V	N	M	E	L
E	C	R	O	F	R	U	O	B	A	L
D	L	C	N	N	M	E	R	T	Y	U

Section A Questions

4. The labour force includes (tick the correct box/boxes):

(a) Old-age pensioners ☐

(b) University students ☐

(c) Unemployed people seeking employment ☐

(d) All employed people ☐

5. List two rewards of becoming self-employed.

(a) _____

(b) _____

6. List two risks of becoming self-employed.

(a) _____

(b) _____

7. 'The unemployment rate is now 10%.' Does this mean that 10% of the population is unemployed? Explain your answer briefly.

_____

_____

8. Fill in the blanks in the paragraph below using the following words.

employment	payment	employer	employees	work

_____ is defined as any activity that requires effort, e.g. doing your homework. Having a job in a petrol station is also work because it too requires effort. The difference is that _____ is received for working in the petrol station but not for doing your homework. Work that is carried out for payment is called _____. People who work for others in return for payment are called _____. The person who employs others and pays them for work is called the _____.

9. List two rights of an employee.

(a) _____

(b) _____

10. List two responsibilities of an employee.

(a) _____

(b) _____

Calculating Gross Wages

1. Use the following information to calculate basic pay for each employee.

(a) Michael works a basic week of 39 hours at €18.60 per hour. _____

(b) Ruth works a basic week of 35 hours at €10.50 per hour. _____

(c) Anthony works a basic week of 45 hours at €14.65 per hour. _____

(d) Linda works a basic week of 40 hours at €11.20 per hour. _____

(e) Edward produced 500 wire hangers this week, for which he is paid 25c per hanger.

_____

(f) Barry made 72 visits last week to prospective customers and 18 resulted in a sale. He is paid €18 for each successful sale. _____

(g) Ingrid, a telesales agent with Cityair, received 156 telephone enquires last Wednesday, from which 68 adult and 16 child air tickets were sold. She is paid €2.20 per adult ticket sold and €1.20 per child ticket sold. _____

_____

(h) Dave repaired eight washing machines, four fridges and six dishwashers this week. He is paid €8 per washing machine, €10 per fridge and €12 per dishwasher. _____

_____

2. Use the following information to calculate overtime/bonus pay for each employee.

(a) Neil has a basic wage of €9.50 per hour. This week he worked 12 hours overtime, for which he received double pay. _____

_____

(b) Collin has a basic wage of €12.80 per hour. This week he worked 8 hours overtime, for which he received time and a half. _____

_____

(c) Fiona has a basic wage of €9 per hour. This week she worked 16 hours overtime, for which she received time and one-third _____

_____

(d) Ross has a basic wage of €8.20 per hour. This week he worked 14 hours overtime. Overtime is paid at the rate of time and a half for the first 8 hours and double time thereafter. _____

_____

(e) Siobhan has a basic wage of €11.50 per hour. This week she worked 12 hours overtime. Overtime is paid at the rate of time and one-fifth for the first 4 hours and double time thereafter. _____

_____

(f) Liam is paid a bonus of €2.40 per unit produced in excess of 300 in any one week. This week he produced 375 units. Calculate his bonus. _____

_____

(g) Olivia is paid a bonus of €45.50 for every insurance sale she makes in excess of three in any one week. Last week she successfully negotiated seven sales. Calculate her bonus.

_____

_____

(h) Terry receives a bonus of 4% of all gift shop sales made by him on cross-Channel trips with East Coast Ferries. Last week he sold €1,230 worth of goods. _____

_____

3. Joseph Garvey works a basic 39-hour week, for which he is paid €12 per hour. Overtime is paid at time and a half. Calculate Joseph's gross wage during a week when he worked 50 hours. _____

_____

4. Marina McKnight works a basic 39-hour week, for which she is paid €15 per hour. Overtime is paid at time and two-thirds. Calculate Marina's gross wage during a week when she worked 54 hours. _____

_____

5. Martina O'Reilly works a basic 38-hour week, for which she is paid €12 per hour. Overtime is paid at double time. Calculate Martina's gross wage during a week when she worked 48 hours. _____

_____

6. Germaine Day works at Casey's Lights producing battery-operated torches. She is paid €2 for every torch produced. If she produces more than 60 torches in a week she is paid a bonus of €2 for every extra torch produced. Calculate Germaine's gross wage during a week when she produced 72 torches. _____

_____

7. James Mulvey works at Roscommon Crystal producing high-quality wineglasses for the export market. He is paid €12 for every glass produced. If he produces more than 25 glasses in a week he is paid €15 for every additional glass produced. Calculate James's gross wage during a week when he produced 31 glasses. _____

_____

8. Josephine O'Driscoll is a car saleswoman. She is paid a basic salary of €700 per month. In addition, she is paid a commission of 2% on every car she sells. Last month she sold cars to the value of €125,000. Calculate her gross wage for last month. _____

9. Jack O'Rourke sells life assurance door to door. He is paid a basic monthly salary of €800 to cover his expenses. In addition, he is paid a commission of 10% of sales made. Last month his insurance sales were €13,400. Calculate his gross wage for last month.

10. Sam Nealon works at McCann's Fruit Market, where he picks and packs strawberries into punnets. He is paid €0.50 for every punnet he fills and this rises to €0.80 per punnet after he fills 300. Calculate Sam's gross wage in a week when he fills 375 punnets.

11. Patricia O'Neill is an author and is paid a 10% commission on all copies of her book sold. Calculate her commission in a month when 1,400 copies were sold at €15.50 each.

Payslips

12. Understanding payslips

Payslips can come in many different forms, but they all contain the same information. Study the payslips below and answer the questions that follow each one. In each case, the normal working week is 39 hours.

(a) **Michael McGrath**

EMPLOYEE: MICHAEL MCGRATH			Week 11	16 May 2011
PAY	**€**	**DEDUCTIONS**	**€**	
BASIC	975.00	PAYE	245.60	
OVERTIME	100.00	PRSI/USC	76.59	
		SAVINGS	100.00	**NET PAY**
GROSS PAY	1,075.00	TOTAL DEDUCTIONS	364.00	711.00

(i) What is Michael's basic pay per hour? _____

(ii) Calculate how much Michael earns for one hour's overtime if he is paid double time.

(iii) How many hours overtime did Michael work in the week? _____

(iv) The following week, Michael worked 47 hours. His PAYE was €345.65 and his PRSI/USC was €95.95. There was no change in his basic pay or savings. Using this information, complete his payslip for week 12, dated 23 May.

EMPLOYEE:			Week		
PAY	€	DEDUCTIONS	€	
BASIC		PAYE		
OVERTIME		PRSI/USC		
		SAVINGS		NET PAY
GROSS PAY		TOTAL DEDUCTIONS		

(b) **Orla McGuinness**

EMPLOYEE: ORLA MCGUINNESS			Week 12	10 April 2011	
PAY	€	DEDUCTIONS	€	
BASIC	1,170.00	PAYE	276.56	
OVERTIME	180.00	PRSI/USC	81.25	
		SAVINGS	120.00	NET PAY
GROSS PAY	1,350.00	TOTAL DEDUCTIONS	477.81	872.19

(i) What is Orla's basic pay per hour? _____

(ii) Calculate how much Orla earns for one hour's overtime if she is paid time and a half.

_____

(iii) How many hours overtime did Orla work in the week? _____

(iv) The following week, Orla worked 45 hours. Her PAYE was €288.50 and her PRSI/USC was €86.78. There was no change in her basic pay or savings. Using this information, complete her payslip for week 13, dated 17 April.

EMPLOYEE:			Week		
PAY	€	DEDUCTIONS	€	
BASIC		PAYE		
OVERTIME		PRSI/USC		
		SAVINGS		NET PAY
GROSS PAY		TOTAL DEDUCTIONS		

(c) **Harry Daly**

EMPLOYEE: HARRY DALY			Week 31	17 July 2011
PAY	€	DEDUCTIONS	€	
BASIC	702.00	PAYE	154.65	
OVERTIME	108.00	PRSI/USC	46.79	
		TRADE UNION	15.00	NET PAY
GROSS PAY	810.00	TOTAL DEDUCTIONS	216.44	593.56

(i) What is Harry's basic pay per hour? _____

(ii) Calculate how much Harry earns for one hour's overtime if he is paid double time.

_____

(iii) How many hours overtime did Harry work in the week? _____

(iv) The following week, Harry worked 49 hours. His PAYE was €179.78 and his PRSI/ USC was €56.32. There was no change in his basic pay or trade union. Using this information, complete his payslip for week 32, dated 24 July.

EMPLOYEE:			Week	
PAY	€	DEDUCTIONS	€	
BASIC		PAYE		
OVERTIME		PRSI/USC		
		TRADE UNION		NET PAY
GROSS PAY		TOTAL DEDUCTIONS		

(d) **Nicola McCourtney**

EMPLOYEE: NICOLA MCCOURTNEY			Week 44	13 Nov 2011
PAY	€	DEDUCTIONS	€	
BASIC	468.00	PAYE	40.56	
OVERTIME	96.00	PRSI/USC	16.98	
		SAVINGS	10.00	NET PAY
GROSS PAY	564.00	TOTAL DEDUCTIONS	67.54	496.46

(i) What is Nicola's basic pay per hour? _____

(ii) Calculate how much Nicola earns for one hour's overtime if she is paid time and one-third. _____

(iii) How many hours overtime did Nicola work in the week? _____

(iv) The following week, Nicola worked 45 hours. Her PAYE was €44.97 and her PRSI/USC was €19.86. There was no change in her basic pay or savings. Using this information, complete her payslip for week 45, dated 20 November.

EMPLOYEE:				Week	
PAY	**€**	**DEDUCTIONS**	**€**		
BASIC		PAYE			
OVERTIME		PRSI/USC			
		SAVINGS			**NET PAY**
GROSS PAY		TOTAL DEDUCTIONS			

Complete the following payslips using the information in the assignments below and today's date.

13. (a) Cathal Burns works 39 hours in a standard week, for which he is paid €8.50 per hour. Overtime this week is 8 hours at double time. PAYE is €45, PRSI/USC is €14, medical insurance is €7, union dues are €2 and pension is €8.

EMPLOYEE: CATHAL BURNS				Week 11	
PAY	**€**	**DEDUCTIONS**	**€**		
Basic		PAYE			
Overtime		PRSI/USC			
		Pension			
		Health			
		Union			**NET PAY**
GROSS PAY		TOTAL DEDUCTIONS			

(b) Rachel Canning works 40 hours in a standard week, for which she receives €16.40 per hour. Overtime this week is 10 hours at time and a half. PAYE is €70, PRSI/USC is €18, union dues are €3, pension is €10 and savings club is €3.

EMPLOYEE: RACHEL CANNING				Week 11	
PAY	**€**	**DEDUCTIONS**	**€**		
Basic		PAYE			
Overtime		PRSI/USC			
		Pension			
		Savings			
		Union			**NET PAY**
GROSS PAY		TOTAL DEDUCTIONS			

(c) Kevin Clarke produced 3,500 nametags last week, for which he receives 5c per tag. The firm also offers a bonus payment of €10 for every 50 tags produced in excess of 3,200. PAYE is €50, PRSI/USC is €12, union dues are €2, medical insurance is €4 and pension is €6.

EMPLOYEE: KEVIN CLARKE			Week 11		
PAY	**€**	**DEDUCTIONS**	**€**	
Basic		PAYE		
Bonus		PRSI/USC		
		Pension		
		Health		
		Union		NET PAY
GROSS PAY		TOTAL DEDUCTIONS		

(d) Jennifer Dowdall sold 24 sets of encyclopedias last week at a total price of €4,800. Her commission is 8%. She also did 8 hours overtime in the office, for which she is paid €10 per hour. PAYE is €80, PRSI/USC is €18, medical insurance is €8, pension is €10 and savings club is €5.

EMPLOYEE: JENNIFER DOWDALL			Week 11		
PAY	**€**	**DEDUCTIONS**	**€**	
Commission		PAYE		
Overtime		PRSI/USC		
		Pension		
		Health		
		Savings		NET PAY
GROSS PAY		TOTAL DEDUCTIONS		

(e) Peter Farrell worked 150 hours last month, for which he was paid €12 per hour. Overtime during the month amounted to 20 hours, for which he was paid double time. PAYE was €640, PRSI/USC was €140, union dues were €12, medical insurance was €45 and pension was €80.

EMPLOYEE: PETER FARRELL			Week 11		
PAY	**€**	**DEDUCTIONS**	**€**	
Basic		PAYE		
Overtime		PRSI/USC		
		Pension		
		Health		
		Union		NET PAY
GROSS PAY		TOTAL DEDUCTIONS		

(f) Lorraine Rice, a vet, attended to 15 animals at her surgery last week at a fixed charge of €35 each. There were seven house calls during the same week at a fixed charge of €42 each. PAYE was €70, PRSI/USC was €10, medical insurance was €12 and pension was €8.

EMPLOYEE: LORRAINE RICE				Week 11	
PAY	€	DEDUCTIONS	€	
Surgery		PAYE		
House calls		PRSI/USC		
		Pension		
		Health		NET PAY
GROSS PAY		TOTAL DEDUCTIONS		

14. Elaine Fitzgerald is employed in an electronics factory. Her normal working week is 39 hours. Any additional hours worked are overtime and are paid at time and a half. Elaine's payslip for week 10 was as follows.

EMPLOYEE: ELAINE FITZGERALD			Week 10	6 May
PAY	€	DEDUCTIONS	€	
Basic	195.00	PAYE	64.25	
Overtime	7.50	PRSI/USC	16.50	
		Union	7.00	NET PAY
GROSS PAY	202.50	TOTAL DEDUCTIONS	87.75	114.75

(a) What is Elaine's basic pay per hour? _____

(b) How many hours overtime did she work in week 10? _____

(c) Elaine worked 2 hours overtime the following week. Her PAYE was €66.50 and her PRSI/USC was €17. There was no change in her basic pay or her trade union deduction. Using this information, complete her payslip for week 11 on the blank payslip supplied below.

EMPLOYEE: ELAINE FITZGERALD			Week 11	
PAY	€	DEDUCTIONS	€	
Basic		PAYE		
Overtime		PRSI/USC		
		Union		NET PAY
GROSS PAY		TOTAL DEDUCTIONS		

15. Ken Moloney works a 35-hour week at Rigney's Butchers and is paid €9.40 per hour. During the week ending 26 October, he worked 8 hours overtime in addition to his standard hours, for which he is paid time and a half. His tax credit is €24 per week and he pays a €3 union subscription and medical insurance of €24 per week. He pays tax at 20% and PRSI/USC at 7.5%.

EMPLOYEE: KEN MOLONEY			Week		
PAY	€	**DEDUCTIONS**	€	
Basic		PAYE		
Overtime		PRSI/USC		
		Health		
		Union		NET PAY
GROSS PAY		**TOTAL DEDUCTIONS**		

16. Ronan Quinn works a 40-hour week at Oliver Computers and is paid €18.50 per hour. During the week ending 8 November, he worked a late shift, for which he received an additional payment of 10% of basic pay. He also worked 6 hours overtime in addition to his standard hours, for which he is paid double time. His tax credit is €35 per week and he pays a pension contribution of 5% of gross pay and medical insurance of €30 per week. He also pays €25 per week into a savings fund. He pays tax at 20% and PRSI/USC at 6%.

EMPLOYEE: RONAN QUINN			Week		
PAY	€	**DEDUCTIONS**	€	
Basic		PAYE		
Overtime		PRSI/USC		
Shift		Pension		
		Medical		
		Saving		NET PAY
GROSS PAY		**TOTAL DEDUCTIONS**		

17. Lisa Shannon works a 48-hour week at Cork Airport and is paid €9.60 per hour. During the week ending 29 January, she worked 16 hours overtime in addition to her standard hours, for which she is paid time and one-third. She is also due a productivity bonus payment of €35. Her tax credit is €30 per week and she pays a €3 union subscription and a pension contribution of 5% of gross wage. She pays tax at 20% and PRSI/USC at 6%.

EMPLOYEE: LISA SHANNON			Week		
PAY	€	**DEDUCTIONS**	€	
Basic		PAYE		
Overtime		PRSI/USC		
Bonus		Union		
		Pension		NET PAY
GROSS PAY		**TOTAL DEDUCTIONS**		

18. Study the payslip below and answer the questions that follow.

EMPLOYEE: JUSTIN MORAN			Week 11	7 Jan	
PAY	**€**	**DEDUCTIONS**	**€**		
Basic	430.00	PAYE	138.00		
Overtime	?	PRSI/USC	34.02		
		Pension	43.74		
		Health	7.00		
		Union	3.00		**NET PAY**
GROSS PAY	486.00	**TOTAL DEDUCTIONS**	?		260.24

(a) Complete the payslip by filling in the missing figures.

(b) If Justin's basic pay is calculated as a piece rate at €5 per unit, calculate how many units he produced this week. _____

(c) How many hours overtime did Justin work this week if the overtime rate is €7 per hour?

_____

(d) If PRSI/USC is calculated on total gross pay, what percentage PRSI/USC is Justin paying? _____

Wages Book

19. Calculate the total wages bill for each of the following firms.

(a) **Firm A – Basic week of 38 hours**

1. Peter   38 hours   Basic rate: €9 per hour

2. Paul   42 hours   Overtime rate: Time and one-third

3. Michael   46 hours   Employer's PRSI: 10%

4. Simon   44 hours

Total wages bill: _____

_____

_____

_____

_____

_____

_____

_____

(b) **Firm B – Basic week of 39 hours**

1. Joan	39 hours	Basic rate:	€10.50 per hour
2. Elaine	42 hours	Overtime rate:	Double
3. John	44 hours	Employer's PRSI:	10%
4. Peter	50 hours		
5. Hugh	46 hours		

Total wages bill: _____

_____

_____

_____

_____

_____

_____

_____

20. Elcando Ltd has three employees who are paid on a monthly basis. Each employee pays income tax (PAYE) at the rate of 20% of gross pay. The employer's rate of PRSI is 13% of gross pay.

(a) What is a wages book? _____

_____

(b) Complete the wages book for the month of April using the partially completed wages book below.

(c) Calculate the total cost of wages for Elcando Ltd for the month of April. _____

WAGES BOOK								
Date	**Employee name**	**Gross wage**	**Deductions**				**Net wages**	**Employer PRSI**
			PAYE	**PRSI/USC**	**Pension**	**Total**		
Apr 30	S. Byrne	1,300		108	92			
Apr 30	P. McDonald	1,500		124	108			
Apr 30	J. Kelly	1,700		142	120			
	TOTAL							

21. Merrille Ltd has three employees who are paid on a monthly basis. Each employee pays income tax (PAYE) at the rate of 20% of gross pay, PRSI/USC at the rate of 6% of gross pay and union subscription of €5. The employer's rate of PRSI is 12% of gross pay.

(a) Complete the wages book for the month of May using the partially completed wages book below.

(b) Calculate the total cost of wages for Merrille Ltd for the month of May. _____

			WAGES BOOK					
Date	Employee name	Gross wage	Deductions				Net wages	Employer PRSI
			PAYE	PRSI/USC	Union	Total		
May 31	L. Dervan	1,600						
May 31	K. Murray	1,200						
May 31	M. Twomey	1,400						
	TOTAL							

22. Prepare a cash analysis statement to calculate the least number of each note and coin that will be needed to pay wages at the end of the week.

		CASH ANALYSIS STATEMENT											
Employee name	Total wage	50	20	10	5	2	1	50	20	10	5	2	1
A. Adlum	367.98												
B. Barker	466.37												
C. Coyne	245.76												
D. Davis	388.56												
E. Edwards	157.46												
F. Feeley	369.36												
G. Graham	298.57												
H. Harris	577.65												
TOTAL	2,871.70												

23. Complete the table below by working out the missing figures in each line.

Basic pay	Overtime	Total pay	PAYE	PRSI	Union	Pension	Total	Net pay
160		200	45		4	6	67	133
	55	295		23	3	8	122	173
360	120		105	35		12		324
258		302	76	18	5		109	193
399	0		144	62	0	15		178
146	24	170		16	4	0	58	

Section A Questions

24. Write out the following abbreviations in full.

(a) PAYE _____

(b) PRSI _____

(c) USC _____

25. Match the terms on the left with the explanations from the list on the right.

1. Gross pay		**A.** A form of additional income
2. Net pay		**B.** Deductions from income required by law
3. Overtime		**C.** The untaxed part of income
4. Statutory deduction		**D.** Total pay before deductions
5. Non-statutory deduction		**E.** Gross pay minus deductions
6. Tax credit		**F.** Medical insurance is an example of this

1. ☐   **2.** ☐   **3.** ☐   **4.** ☐   **5.** ☐   **6.** ☐

26. Name two voluntary and two statutory deductions from wages.

(a) Voluntary _____

(b) Statutory _____

27. State two benefits an employee could receive from paying PRSI/USC.

(a) _____

(b) _____

28. State two methods other than time basis by which an employee can be paid.

(a) _____

(b) _____

26 Industrial Relations

1. Industrial relations case study

Michael Lynch has been running his small clothing business, ML Fashions Ltd, for 10 years. He is assisted by four managers – Marketing, Finance, Office and Production. Over that time his workforce has grown to 32 people, made up of 16 machinists, two designers, eight administrative staff, four marketing and selling, and two finance. Last year the machinists joined a trade union which specialises in representing workers in the clothing industry and elected Sharon Treacy as their shop steward. In July the machinists went on official strike for three days over their claim for a pay rise.

(a) Outline three reasons for joining a trade union.

_____

_____

_____

(b) List three functions of a shop steward.

_____

_____

_____

(c) What is meant by an official dispute?

_____

_____

(d) What two things is the union required to do before an official strike can take place?

_____

_____

(e) Other than a pay claim, name five causes of industrial disputes.

_____

_____

_____

_____

_____

2. Word search

Solve the clues below, write the answer in the space provided and then locate each one in the word search. The answers may read forwards, backwards or diagonally.

(a) This term describes the situation where men and women are not treated equally

_____

(b) Another name for a 'work to rule' _____

(c) The Irish Congress of Trade Unions _____

(d) A strike in support of others _____

(e) Sometimes called a 'who does what' dispute _____

(f) A process of discussion and compromise offered by the LRC _____

(g) The union representative on the shop floor _____

(h) The officer who investigates complaints of unfair treatment _____

(i) When a third party tries to solve a dispute _____

(j) A strike that has not been sanctioned by the ICTU _____

Q	D	E	M	A	R	C	A	T	I	O	N
W	O	I	D	D	N	Y	H	P	C	N	O
E	P	U	F	I	G	T	B	O	O	B	I
R	A	Y	G	S	M	I	G	I	N	V	T
T	S	T	H	C	Q	L	F	U	C	C	A
Y	C	R	J	R	W	A	D	Y	I	Z	R
U	I	E	K	I	E	U	L	T	L	L	T
I	T	W	L	M	R	Q	A	R	I	K	I
O	E	Q	Z	I	T	E	I	E	A	J	B
P	H	M	X	N	Y	J	C	W	T	H	R
A	T	N	C	A	U	K	I	Q	I	G	A
S	A	B	V	T	I	L	F	A	O	F	X
D	P	V	B	I	O	P	F	S	N	D	I
F	M	C	G	O	S	L	O	W	A	C	A
G	Y	X	Z	N	L	L	N	P	T	G	F
H	S	A	F	P	I	O	U	U	O	S	D
J	S	T	E	W	A	R	D	U	Y	H	R
K	L	Z	X	C	V	B	N	M	Q	W	S

Section A Questions

3. Insert the words *redundant* and *dismissed* in the correct place in the sentence below.

Mary was _____ because she was caught stealing from her employer, but John was made _____ because there was no work for him to do.

4. What do the following initials stand for?

(a) ICTU _____

(b) IBEC _____

5. Write a short explanation of each of the following terms used in industrial relations.

(a) Work to rule _____

_____

(b) Arbitration _____

_____

6. Name one trade union and one employer organisation.

(a) Trade union _____

(b) Employer organisation _____

7. Write down four possible causes of trade dispute.

_____

_____

_____

_____

27 Marketing

1. Word search

Solve the clues below and then find each correct term in the word search. The answers may read forwards, backwards or diagonally.

(a) The process of getting your product from the producer to the consumer
_____ (9)

(b) The market for your product or service is known as the _____ market (6)

(c) The four Ps of marketing are _____ , _____ ,
_____ and _____ (7, 5, 5, 9)

(d) Using existing reports, articles and surveys to research a market is called
_____ research (4)

(e) Launching a product on a small scale to check public reaction is called
_____ marketing (4)

(f) The part of the population whose views and opinions are sought regarding a product or service is called the _____ (6)

W	E	R	T	Y	U	I	O	P	P	O
Y	M	T	R	E	Q	R	J	H	R	I
T	A	R	G	E	T	E	K	G	O	J
U	R	H	J	R	E	W	L	F	D	K
I	K	G	F	T	W	Q	H	E	U	L
O	E	C	I	R	P	T	S	D	C	H
P	T	D	S	Y	L	K	A	S	T	G
A	I	E	A	U	A	Y	M	A	M	F
S	N	K	S	K	C	U	P	B	F	D
D	G	J	L	T	E	S	L	N	D	S
F	G	H	Q	I	O	I	E	G	S	A
P	R	O	M	O	T	I	O	N	A	A

2. Case study. Read the passage below and then answer the questions that follow.

The staff of the marketing department at Leemar Publications are having their weekly meeting to discuss progress on preparations for the publication of their new magazine aimed at teenagers between the ages of 14 and 18. The areas being discussed are research, advertising, content and launch.

The marketing manager stressed the importance of going through each element of the marketing mix before making any final decisions. The market research carried out so far was outlined and conclusions were drawn from the information received. The sales manager said that they would be using a variety of techniques to promote the magazine.

The advertising manager went through the various ideas for advertising the magazine and the team discussed which ones would be most effective. They also suggested firms that may be interested in advertising in the magazine, thereby providing additional income for Leemar and allowing them to sell the magazine at a cheaper price than their competitors.

(a) List the four elements of the marketing mix.

_____

(b) State four aims of market research.

_____

_____

_____

_____

(c) What method of market research would be most suitable in this situation?

_____

(d) Suggest two suitable means of advertising a magazine aimed at the 14–18 age group.

_____

_____

(e) Suggest two methods of sales promotion suitable for this type of publication.

_____

_____

(f) Suggest two types of firm that might advertise in a magazine aimed at the 14–18 age group.

_____

_____

(g) Write five questions for a questionnaire that might be used during the research for this magazine.

_____

_____

_____

_____

_____

Section A Questions

3. Fill in the blanks in the following sentences using the words provided.

market research	product	target market	market	price

(a) The part of the population our product is aimed at is called the _____ _____.

(b) _____ and _____ are two elements of the marketing mix.

(c) Gathering, recording and analysing all the information relating to a product and its market is known as _____ _____.

(d) The place where goods and services are bought and sold is called the _____.

4. What are the four Ps of marketing?

(a) _____

(b) _____

(c) _____

(d) _____

5. List three pieces of information a firm might try to find out using market research.

(a) _____

(b) _____

(c) _____

6. List three methods of collecting information for market research.

(a) _____

(b) _____

(c) _____

7. In each case below, name an organisation that provides the following services.

(a) Local advertising service _____

(b) National advertising service _____

8. How would you best advertise a concert to be given by a local band in your town centre next month? Give one reason for your answer.

Television ☐   Local radio ☐   National radio ☐

Reason: _____

9. List two examples of sales promotion methods other than advertising.

(a) _____

(b) _____

Delivery Systems

1. Use the grid below to calculate the following distances.

(a) Belfast to Rosslare _____

(b) Cork to Sligo _____

(c) Athlone to Donegal _____

(d) Carlow to Tralee _____

(e) Dublin to Rosslare _____

(f) Dundalk to Galway _____

(g) Cork to Dublin _____

(h) Dundalk to Tralee _____

(i) Belfast to Waterford _____

(j) Galway to Dublin _____

(k) Cork to Waterford _____

(l) Cork to Rosslare _____

(m) Athlone to Tralee _____

(n) Cork to Limerick _____

(o) Limerick to Mullingar _____

Athlone

225	**Belfast**															
115	250	**Carlow**														
85	140	172	**Cavan**													
220	425	188	300	**Cork**												
185	180	296	110	400	**Donegal**											
125	167	84	112	260	222	**Dublin**										
145	85	172	82	325	158	85	**Dundalk**									
110	340	178	200	142	260	232	256	**Ennis**								
87	305	178	166	210	205	216	238	70	**Galway**							
120	325	142	206	105	296	198	240	37	105	**Limerick**						
48	180	100	64	236	172	82	92	164	144	148	**Mullingar**					
210	330	98	275	208	390	164	246	246	274	210	204	**Rosslare**				
118	205	230	126	336	66	216	168	195	138	232	135	326	**Sligo**			
188	430	252	312	120	350	303	346	94	162	105	254	290	288	**Tralee**		
175	332	74	235	126	356	158	242	164	220	130	170	82	292	210	**Waterford**	
190	310	76	256	188	372	142	228	228	254	190	185	19	306	275	62	**Wexford**

2. Journey and arrival times

Use the grid on p. 192 and the following information to calculate the journey time and arrival time in each case.

	Journey departure time	Speed (km/hr)	Journey time	Arrival time
(a) Dublin to Cork	9.00 a.m.	65		
(b) Cork to Limerick	11.15 a.m.	60		
(c) Donegal to Waterford	2.20 p.m.	89		
(d) Dundalk to Sligo	1.17 p.m.	56		
(e) Galway to Rosslare	4.24 p.m.	68.5		
(f) Athlone to Dublin	2.45 p.m.	50		
(g) Belfast to Rosslare	1.15 p.m.	60		
(h) Cavan to Sligo	3.10 p.m.	42		

3. Calculating total journey costs

(a) Calculate the cost of delivery from the following information assuming 250 working days per year. Give your answer correct to two decimal places.

- Distance 275 km per day
- Average speed 55 kph
- Fuel consumption 20 km per litre
- Fuel costs €1.25 per litre
- Driver's wages €15 per hour

- Loading and unloading 2 hours
- Annual insurance €600
- Annual tax €350
- Annual repairs and maintenance €800

Total cost of delivery: _____

_____

_____

_____

_____

(b) Calculate the cost of delivery from the following information assuming 250 working days per year.

- Distance 360 km per day
- Average speed 45 kph
- Fuel consumption 20 km per litre
- Fuel costs €1.14 per litre
- Driver's wages €16.50 per hour

- Loading and unloading 3 hours
- Annual insurance €1,200
- Annual tax €280
- Annual maintenance €1,800

Total cost of delivery: _____

_____

_____

_____

_____

(c) Calculate the cost of delivery from the following information assuming 280 working days per year.

- Distance 428 km per day
- Average speed 53.5 kph
- Fuel consumption 20 km per litre
- Fuel costs €1.16 per litre
- Driver's wages €16 per hour up to 5 p.m. and €18 per hour after 5 p.m.

- Loading and unloading 2 hours
- Annual insurance €1,736
- Annual tax €280
- Annual maintenance €728
- Departure time 9.30 a.m.

Total cost of delivery: _____

_____

_____

_____

_____

(d) Calculate the cost of delivery from the following information assuming 300 working days per year.

- Distance 520 km per day
- Average speed 40 kph
- Fuel consumption 13 km per litre
- Fuel costs 51c per litre
- Driver's wages €17.40 per hour up to 4 p.m. and €19.50 per hour after 4 p.m.

- Loading and unloading 2.5 hours
- Annual insurance €780
- Annual tax €330
- Annual repairs and maintenance €810
- Departure time 10 a.m.

Total cost of delivery: _____

_____

_____

_____

_____

(e) Calculate the cost of delivery from the following information assuming 260 working days per year.

- Distance 420 km per day
- Average speed 80 kph
- Fuel consumption 35 km per litre
- Fuel costs €1.20 per litre
- Driver's wages €21 per hour up to 4 p.m. and €26 per hour after 4 p.m.

- Loading and unloading 3 hours
- Annual insurance €1,950
- Annual tax €312
- Annual maintenance €1,040
- Departure time 9 a.m.

Total cost of delivery: _____

_____

_____

_____

_____

(f) Calculate the cost of delivery from the following information assuming 280 working days per year.

- Distance 275 km per day
- Average speed 55 kph
- Fuel consumption 25 km per litre
- Fuel costs €1.23 per litre
- Driver's wages €22.60 per hour up to 4 p.m. and €30 per hour after 4 p.m.

- Loading and unloading 3.5 hours
- Annual insurance €924
- Annual tax €196
- Annual repairs and maintenance €700
- Departure time 11 a.m.

Total cost of delivery: _____

_____

_____

_____

_____

_____

_____

4. The following information relates to Talbot Coaches, a company specialising in coach hire services. Assume 350 working days per year.

- Daily hire rate – €320 (53-seater coach); €240 (35-seater coach)
- Overnight allowance for driver €35 per night

- Annual insurance €1,470
- Annual tax €560
- Annual maintenance €770
- Guide is €40 per day

Using the above information, calculate the following.

(a) The Maryfield Ladies Club wants to hire a 53-seater coach for a trip to Galway departing on Friday and returning on Sunday. They do not require a guide.

_____

_____

_____

_____

_____

(b) The Wicklow Harriers Athletic Club wants to hire a 35-seater coach to take them to a meet in Cork. They will depart on Friday and return on Saturday. No guide is required.

_____

_____

_____

_____

_____

_____

(c) The Ennis Military History Society wants to hire a 53-seater coach to bring a group of 42 members on a tour of Ireland. They will depart on Monday and return on the following Saturday. They will require a guide. How much will this trip cost per person?

_____

_____

_____

_____

_____

_____

_____

_____

5. Citylink Air offers the following charter rates to the travel business. Assume 250 flying days per annum.

- Within Europe €35,000; Europe to US €96,000
- Annual insurance €15,000

- Take-off charges €100 per flight
- Servicing €100,000 per annum

(a) (i) How much will it cost Sunfly Travel to charter a plane from Shannon to Majorca?

_____

_____

_____

_____

_____

(ii) If Sunfly can fill all 140 seats on the plane, how much will they have to charge each of their customers if they just cover their costs? _____

(b) (i) How much will it cost Maurice Carlyle to charter a plane to bring 380 of his customers to the US on a sales mission? _____

_____

_____

_____

_____

(ii) How much is the cost of the trip per person to the nearest euro? _____

6. X-PRESS Couriers offers the following rates to its business customers.

- Within Dublin €18
- Rest of Ireland €28
- Within Leinster €22
- Plus 50c per kg weight

Using the above information, calculate the cost of the following deliveries by courier.

(a) A package weighing 3 kg from Dublin to Cork   _____

(b) A package weighing 6 kg from Bantry to Kinsale   _____

(c) A package weighing 0.5 kg from Dublin to Galway   _____

(d) A package weighing 1.5 kg from Wicklow to Wexford _____

7. Word search

Locate the following words associated with transport in the grid below. The answers may read forwards, backwards or diagonally.

Rail	Road	Sea	Air
Luas	DART	Irish Rail	Pipeline
Eurotunnel	Container	Courier	Common carrier

Q	R	E	N	I	A	T	N	O	C	U	H
W	R	O	A	D	D	A	I	P	O	I	G
E	A	C	S	A	F	S	Y	O	M	O	F
R	I	I	A	R	G	D	T	I	M	P	D
T	L	V	R	T	H	F	R	C	O	R	S
Y	G	B	M	L	K	G	W	A	N	T	A
U	H	N	I	R	I	S	H	R	A	I	L
L	L	E	N	N	U	T	O	R	U	E	Y
I	U	M	N	Y	U	H	Q	I	E	J	I
O	J	A	B	P	S	J	X	E	F	A	P
A	E	Q	S	O	C	O	U	R	I	E	R
S	K	A	V	I	E	L	X	L	G	C	N
D	L	S	C	O	N	T	A	I	N	E	R
F	Z	E	N	I	L	E	P	I	P	B	M
G	X	Z	X	Y	T	N	V	B	C	Z	X

Section A Questions

8. Choose a suitable delivery system (road, rail, sea, air or pipeline) for each of the following and give one reason for your choice in each case.

(a) Fresh vegetables from Meath to Wicklow

_____

(b) Liquid chemicals from Dublin to Cork

_____

(c) Tour operator bringing holidaymakers from Ireland to Spanish resorts

_____

(d) Urgent medical supplies from London to Sligo

_____

(e) Gas from Scotland to Ireland

_____

(f) Frozen foods from a manufacturer in Athlone to supermarkets throughout Ireland

_____

9. List four airports in Ireland.

(a) _____

(b) _____

(c) _____

(d) _____

10. List three ports in Ireland.

(a) _____

(b) _____

(c) _____

11. Choose a suitable form of transport for each of the following.

(a) Cars from Japan to Ireland _____

(b) Post from Ireland to the US _____

(c) Famine relief from Ireland to Africa _____

(d) Drinks from a brewery in Cork to pubs throughout Ireland _____

(e) Fresh salmon from Ireland to Britain _____

(f) Oil from the Middle East to Ireland _____

(g) The day's takings from a large supermarket to the bank _____

(h) Newspapers from Dublin to Kerry _____

Completing Documents

Use the blank documents below to complete the following assignments. Ordinary Level students should ignore terms of sale.

Orders

1. Delaney Golf Shop, Tralee, Co. Kerry, ordered the following goods from Golfing Needs Ltd, Westport, Co. Mayo, on 9 October 2011.

   - 6 starter sets @ €190 each

   - 8 superlong drivers @ €270 each

   - 16 XD putters @ €35 each

   - 100 XD golf balls @ €1 each

   - 8 golf bags @ €80 each

ORDER

I would we sent you our goods in a pacaging.

No. _087335412_

VAT No. IE_123456_

TO _Golfing needs_
ltd westport
Co mayo

Date _11/11/11_

Please supply the following as per quotation no. _____

Quantity	Description		Unit Price
6	Starter sets	for each	€190
8	super long drivers		€270
16	XD putters		€35
100	xd golf balls		€1
8	golf bags		€80

Comments: _Thanks for your delivery._

Signature: _Cian Delaney Delaney_

Position: _Purchasing manager_

---

2. Lincolns Restaurant, The Mall, Athlone, Co. Westmeath, ordered the following supplies from LNN Food Supplies, Athlone, Co. Westmeath, on 20 May 2011.

- 12 frozen turkeys @ €8 each

- 3 bags of potatoes @ €1.50 each

- 14 bags of assorted vegetables @ €0.80 each

- 120 bread rolls @ €0.10 each

ORDER

12 that you ordered
mostly food and
you will have everything
down in the description

No. 085216789

VAT No. 1556943

Date 11/6/11

TO Lincolns resturant
the mall
Athlone

Please supply the following as per quotation no. _____

Quantity	Description	Unit Price
12	frozen turkeys	€8
3	bags of potatoes	€1.50
14	Bags of assorted vegetables	0.80e
120	Bread rolls	for each 10c each

Comments: thanks for your delivery

Signature: Nicholas Danca

Position: Purchasing manager

Invoices

3. McGuire Ltd, 96 Main Street, Urlingford, Co. Kilkenny, sent an invoice on 3 March 2011 for the following goods to Smith Brothers Hardware, Northside Shopping Centre, Coolock, Dublin 5.

- 5 B&D electric saws @ €65 each
- 10 B&D electric hammer drills @ €45 each
- 50 assorted screwdrivers @ €4 each
- VAT is to be charged at 20% and there is a trade discount of 10%
- The terms of sale are 5% cash discount for accounts settled within 1 month

INVOICE

I would like to order some tools

No. _655679_
VAT No. IE 214137
Date 3/3/11

Order No. _____
TO *Smith Brothers Hardware Northside Shopping center*

Quantity	Description	Unit Price	Total (Ex. VAT)
5	B and D electric saws	€65	€325
10	B and d hammer drills	€45	€450
50	assorted screwdrivers	€4	€200
		Total (Ex. VAT)	1075 975
	−10%	Less Trade Discount	97.50
	+20%	Add VAT	215
		Total	1215

E&OE

1075 ?

1. 107.5
2. 967.5
3 193.4
total 4. 1,160.9

Math is Wrong do again please

975 = Total   *24/1*

X

4. J. Murphy, Unit 6B, Limerick Business Park, received an invoice dated 4 October 2011 from Electrical Distributors Ltd, Bluebell Industrial Estate, Dublin 24, for the following goods.

- 10 Electro fridge-freezers @ €320 each
- 8 Electro range cookers @ €450 each
- 15 Heatwell microwave ovens @ €80 each
- VAT is to be charged at 20% and there is a trade discount of 25%
- The terms of sale are 5% cash discount for accounts settled within 1 month

Complete

INVOICE

I would like to order some kitchen material

Order No. 217436

TO _____

No. 0873621337

VAT No. IE567921

Date 4/10/2011

Quantity	Description	Unit Price	Total (Ex. VAT)
10	Electro fridge Freezers	€320	€3200
8	Electro range cookers	€450	€3600
15	Heatwell microwaves	€80	€1200
	Total (Ex. VAT)		8000
	−25 Less Trade Discount		2000
	=		6000
	+20% Add VAT		1200
	Total		7200

E&OE

Check the maths!

Do again here :

5. Study the document below and answer the questions that follow.

Fine Foods Ltd		No.	12
37A Bakers Enterprise Park		VAT No.	IE124784
Wexford		Date	3 March 2011
Tel: (053) 1234567; Fax: (053) 7654321		Order No.	71

Email: info@finefoods.ie
Website: www.finefoods.ie

To   Mr Charles Dowdall
AB Wholesalers Ltd
Eastern Road
Laois

Terms: 5% Cash Discount – 1 month

Quantity	Description	Unit Price	Total (Ex. VAT)
4	Sanyo Televisions Model RT	700	2,800
6	Mitsubishi Hi Fi Model TY	300	1,800
5	HP Printers Model YU	200	1,000
	Total (Ex. VAT)		5,600
	Less Trade Discount 20%		1,120
			4,480
	Add VAT 10%		448
	Total		4,928

E&OE

(a) What name is given to this document? _Charels Dowdall invoice_

(b) Who is the sender of this document? _37A Bakers Enterprise park_

(c) Who is the receiver of this document? _Charels Dowdall_

(d) What steps should the buyer take after receiving this document?
He should say thank you for listening tell me when it will be brought check everything if it was delivered

(e) Explain the term '5% cash discount – 1 month'.
it take 5% off

(f) Explain what is meant by 'less trade discount 20%'.
you will get a 20% because of the trading

(g) Explain what is meant by the abbreviation E&OE.
ERROR + OMMISSION Excluded

6. Study the document below and answer the questions that follow.

Treble Base Productions Ltd				No.	67
Music House				VAT No.	IE972343
Kenmare				Date	27 June 2011
Co. Kerry				Order No.	124

Tel: (052) 7345767; Fax: (052) 4794520
administration@treblebase.com

To   Ms Elaine Garvey
Sounds Good Music Store
23 Abbey Street
Athlone

Terms: Carriage paid by seller

Quantity	Description	Unit Price	Total (Ex. VAT)
12	Sony MP3 Players	100	1,200
10	Apple iPods	150	1,500
20	Docking stations	40	800
	Total (Ex. VAT)		3,500
	Less Trade Discount 20%		700
			2,800
	Add VAT 10%		280
	Total		3,080

E&OE

(a) What name is given to this document? _Ms Elaine Invoice garvey_

(b) Who is the sender of this document? _Music house trebel base production_

(c) Who is the receiver of this document? _Elaine garvey_

(d) What steps should the seller of the goods take before sending this document?

Thank you for listening & to can you please send us a date of when the equipments are coming check everything ✓

(e) Explain the term 'carriage paid by seller'.

✓   _Transport is paid by the seller_

Credit Notes

7. Max Fashions, 72 Leinster Terrace, Dalkey, Co. Dublin, received a credit note dated 20 March 2011 from The Clothes Warehouse, Dunboyne, Co. Meath, for the following goods which had been returned:

- 6 two-piece suits @ €150 each
- 4 Galleon shirts @ €45 each

VAT had been charged at 10% and there was a trade discount of 20%.

Complete the blank credit note below.

CREDIT NOTE

Max Fashion 72
Leinster Terrance,
Dalkey co. Dublin

Order No. 554311

TO The Clothes
warehouse,
Dunboyne
Co. meath

No. 9855311
VAT No. Ei8566722
Date _____

Quantity	Description	Unit Price	Total (Ex. VAT)
6	two piece suit	€150	€900
4	galleon shirts	€45	€180

Total (Ex. VAT)	1,080
Less Trade Discount	€216
	874
Add VAT €87.40	€87.40
Total	961.4

10%

✓
✓
✗
✗
✗

E&OE

---

again Maths is Wrong.
Do again.

1080

✗ 20

÷ 100

=

Then take away from 1080
− 216
=

8. Hadleigh Toy Importers, Longlea Business Park, Middleton, Co. Cork, sent a credit note dated 12 September 2011 to Daly's Toy Emporium, Main Street, Drogheda, Co. Louth, for the following goods which had been returned marked damaged:

- 3 Monopoly sets @ €19 each

- 2 Baby All Gone dolls @ €30 each

VAT had been charged at 20% and there was a trade discount of 25%.

Complete the blank credit note below.

CREDIT NOTE

Hadleigh toy importers, Longlea buisiness park middleton Co. Cork

No. 086239143
VAT No. IE 5592/3
Date 12/7/11

Order No. 666-785

TO Dalys toy Emporium, Main street Drogheda, Co Louth

Quantity	Description	Unit Price	Total (Ex. VAT)
3	Monopoly sets	€19	€57
2	Baby all gone dolls	€30	€60

Total (Ex. VAT)	117
25% **Less Trade Discount**	29.25
	87.75
20% **Add VAT**	€17.55
Total	105.30

E&OE

Invoice/Credit Note Combined

9. K&L Garages, Birr, Co. Offaly, received an invoice from Leeside Motor Factors, Mardyke, Co. Cork, dated 20 July 2011 for the following goods:
   - 2 dozen spark plugs Ref X212 @ €8 per dozen
   - 4 dozen oil filters Ref X714 @ €15 per dozen
   - 14 sets of brake pads Ref X492 @ €8 per set

VAT is to be charged at 10% and there is a trade discount of 20%.

The terms of sale are 5% cash discount for accounts settled within 1 month.

On 27 July, K&L Garages returned part of the consignment of goods invoiced on 20 July because they were faulty, consisting of six spark plugs and four sets of brake pads. They received a credit note dated 31 July.

Complete the blank invoice and credit note below.

INVOICE

Leeside motor
Factors Mardyke
Co Cork

Order No. _KML337_

TO _K&L and_
L garages
Birr Co. Offaly

No. _0853219_
VAT No. _IE457891_
Date _20/7/2011_

Quantity	Description	Unit Price	Total (Ex. VAT)
2	dozen sparkplug Ref X212	€8	€16
4	dozen oil filters X714	€15	€60
14	sets of brake pads X492	€8	€112
	Total (Ex. VAT)		€188
	20% Less Trade Discount		€37.60
			149.4
	10% Add VAT		€14.40
	Total		164.30

E&OE

Check Maths

207

CREDIT NOTE

K and I
garages, Birr Co
offaly

Order No. 11157321

TO Leeside motor
factors Markdyke
co.cork

No. 085992111
VAT No. ie 556712
Date 20/7/11

Quantity	Description	Unit Price	Total (Ex. VAT)
2	dozen spark plug	€8	€16
4	dozen oil filters	€15	€60
14	sets of brake pads	€8	€112

Total (Ex. VAT)	€118	
Less Trade Discount	€37.60	
	119.40	
Add VAT	$14.40	
Total	164.30	

X Only 2 items
2 sparks
4 brake pads.

E&OE

10. Maguire Electrical Wholesalers, Pearse Avenue, Waterford, sent an invoice dated
13 November to Discount Electric, Belgard Road, Tallaght, Dublin 24, for the following goods:

- 6 LX DVD recorders @ €250 each
- 4 20" televisions @ €340 each
- 8 iPod chargers @ €20 each

VAT is to be charged at 20% and there is a trade discount of 25%.

The terms of sale are 5% cash discount for accounts settled within 2 weeks and 3% for
accounts settled within 1 month.

On 18 November, Discount Electric returned two of the DVD recorders and four of the iPod
chargers, which had been damaged in transit. They received a credit note dated
22 November.

Complete the blank invoice and credit note on the next page.

580
× 25
= 100

INVOICE

Maguire Electrical
whole salers, pearse,
avenue, waterford

Order No. 143119

TO Discount Electic,
belgard road
tallaght, Dublin 24,
Dublin 24

No. 678
VAT No. 4869
Date 13/11/12

Quantity	Description	Unit Price	Total (Ex. VAT)
6	LX Dvd recorders	€250	€1500
4	20"	€340	€1360
8	iPod chargers	€20	€160
		Total (Ex. VAT)	3,020
-28%		Less Trade Discount	755
			2265
+20%		Add VAT	453
		Total	2716

E&OE

CREDIT NOTE

? Maguire Electrical

0

?

0

Order No. _____

TO _____
_____
_____
_____

No. 648
VAT No. 4867
Date _____

Quantity	Description	Unit Price	Total (Ex. VAT)
4 2	Dvd recorder	€250	€500
4 4	Ipod chargers	€20	€80
2			
		Total (Ex. VAT)	€580
-25%		Less Trade Discount	€2,32 €1,35
			€174
20		Add VAT	522
		Total	€522

580
- 145
____
435
8.7

E&OE

443.70

Please practice

435
× 20
÷ 100

12/1

Statements

11. The following transactions took place during the month of March 2011 between Electrical Wholesalers Ltd, Ocean View Place, Lifford, Co. Donegal, and McCormack Electrical, 72 Maidstone Way, Manorhamilton, Co. Leitrim.

March	1	Opening account balance	350
March	3	Invoice no. 243	1,200
March	7	Invoice no. 249	1,500
March	8	Credit note no. 261	210
March	12	Cheque no. 224	2,000
March	14	Invoice no. 273	1,500
March	16	Credit note no. 267	170
March	19	Cheque no. 288	1,600

= Credit

Complete the statement of account that Electrical Wholesalers Ltd sent to McCormack Electrical on 31 March. Terms of sale were 5% cash discount for accounts settled within 1 month.

STATEMENT

Eletrical whole salers Ltd, ocean view place Lifford Co. Donegal

Account No. 1245
VAT No. 2134
Date 3/3/11

TO Mc Cormak Eletrical 72 madison way

Date	Details	Debit	Credit	Balance
1/3/11	Opening account balance			350
3/3/11	invoice no. 243	1200		1200
7/3/11	invoice no. 249	1500		1500
8/3/11	credit no. 261		210	2840
12/3/11	cheque no 224	2000		2000
14/3/11	invoice no. 273	4500		9340
16/3/11	credit no. 267		170	4170
19/3/11	cheque no. 288	1600		6970

E&OE

Do Maths again

12. The following transactions took place during the month of October 2011 between LF Publications, Blackglen Park, Cork, and the Bookworm Bookshop, 24 Castle Street, Ennis, Co. Clare.

Date	Details	Amount
October 1	Opening account balance	470
October 6	Invoice no. 73	2,400
October 9	Credit note no. 13	140
October 12	Invoice no. 78	1,600
October 15	Cheque no. 226	2,800
October 17	Invoice no. 82	1,600
October 20	Credit note no. 19	250
October 21	Invoice no. 90	2,850
October 26	Cheque no. 255	1,900

Complete the statement of account that LF Publishers sent to the Bookworm Bookshop on 31 October. Terms of sale were 10% cash discount for accounts settled within 1 month.

STATEMENT

LF publications
Blackglen park
Co. Cork.

Account No. 11557
VAT No. 6468
Date 27/10/11

TO Bookworm Book Shop 24 Castel Street Enis Co. Clare

Date	Details	Debit	Credit	Balance
1	opening account balance			470
6	Invoice no.73	2400		2870
9	Credit note no.13		140	2730
12	invoice no. 78	1,600		4330
15	cheque	2,800		7130
17	Invoice no.82	1,600		8730
20	Credit note no.19		250	8480
21	Invoice no.90	2850		11330
26	cheque no.255	1,900		13230

E&OE

Cheques in wrong place.

Delivery Dockets

13. Complete the delivery docket received by Tom's Newsagent, Balbriggan, Co. Dublin, from A&F Wholesalers, Lincoln Place, Ashbourne, Co. Meath. Delivery took place on 2 May. The following goods were delivered:

- 5 boxes of Mars Bars
- 8 boxes of Snickers
- 6 boxes of Super Mints
- 24 boxes of crisps

DELIVERY DOCKET

A & F whole salers, Lincoln Place, Ashbourne, Co. Meath

Order No. 2774
TO Tom's news agent, balbriggan Co. Dublin

No. 18876
VAT No. 44899
Date 2/5/15

Quantity	Description
5	boxes of mars bars
8	boxes of snickers
6	Boxes of supermints
24	Boxes of crisps

Comments: Thanks for purchasing our goods.
Signature: Nicholas Dancer
Position: Delivery manager

14. Complete the delivery docket received by Write Well Stationers, Ballyhaunis, Co. Mayo, from Office Supplies Ltd, Main Street, Killarney, Co. Kerry. Delivery took place on 14 September. The following goods were delivered:

- 6 dozen boxes of C1 envelopes
- 200 reams of photocopying paper
- 50 reams of coloured paper
- 12 staplers
- 6 boxes of biros

DELIVERY DOCKET

Office supplies ltd
main street,
killarney, Co. Kerry

Order No. 10921
TO write well
stationers
Ballyhaunis
Co. Mayo

No. _____
VAT No. _____
Date 14/8/15

Quantity	Description
6	dozen ~~book~~ boxes of C1 envelopes
200	reams of photocopying paper
50	reams of coloured paper
12	staplers
6	boxes of biro's

Comments: thanks for ~~ordering~~ purchasing these things have been delivered

Signature: _____

Position: _____

Receipts

15. Complete the receipt issued to Mary O'Keefe, Clothes for All, Leixlip, Co. Kildare, on 7 October 2011. The amount was €1,700 and the receipt was issued by L&J Fashion Supplies, Portmarnock, Co. Dublin.

RECEIPT

Mary OKeefe
Leixlip, Co. Kildare, on
~~October~~

No. 277489
Date 7/10/11

Recieved with thanks

The sum of Leixlip, Co. Kildare, on 7 october 2011.
€1700 one thousand and Seven hundred
Euro

From L & J Fashion &
Supplies portmarnock

Signed *Nicholas Dunca*

16. Complete the receipt issued to John O'Farrell, The Food Store, Cobh, Co. Cork, on 15 March 2011. The receipt was for €850 and was issued by ND Wholesalers Ltd, Ballybrack, Co. Dublin.

RECEIPT

John O'farrel
The food store
cobh, Co Cork

No. 45598
Date 15/3/11

Recieved with thanks

The sum of €850 Eight hundred and fifty euro

From ND wholesalers
Ltd ballybrack

Signed _____

Combined Questions

17. The following details refer to the sale of goods on credit by O'Reilly Ltd, Blackwater Industrial Estate, Cork, to B.P. Byrne Ltd, 25 Sycamore Avenue, Dublin 24, during the month of September.

On 1 September 2011 there was a balance of €570 due to O'Reilly Ltd in B.P. Byrne's account.

Sept	5	O'Reilly sent invoice no. 4 to B.P. Byrne	€4,500
Sept	8	O'Reilly sent invoice no. 6 to B.P. Byrne	€16,900
Sept	12	O'Reilly sent credit note no. 46 to B.P. Byrne	€1,200
Sept	15	O'Reilly sent invoice no. 10 to B.P. Byrne	€18,500
Sept	19	O'Reilly received cheque from B.P. Byrne	€5,700
Sept	24	O'Reilly sent credit note no. 56 to B.P. Byrne	€352
Sept	26	O'Reilly gave allowance to B.P. Byrne	€120
Sept	29	O'Reilly sent invoice no. 24 to B.P. Byrne	€15,700

(a) Complete the statement sent by O'Reilly Ltd to B.P. Byrne Ltd on 30 September 2011 on the blank statement on the next page.

(b) The returns on 24 September relate to 10 telephone tables that were damaged in transit. The tables were priced at €40 each. Trade discount was 20% and VAT was charged at 10%. Complete the blank credit note on the next page.

(c) Suggest three methods O'Reilly Ltd could use to check the creditworthiness of B.P. Byrne Ltd before agreeing to sell goods to them on credit.

1. paypath 2. A standing orders

2. standing order

3 A Bank draft

(d) In the case of B.P. Byrne Ltd, suggest two checks that their bookkeeper should carry out before paying the amount due on the statement.

Check delivered, Check the math.

STATEMENT

Oreiley ltd blackwater
industrial state
Co. Cork

Account No. F115916
VAT No. 91185
Date 5/8/11

TO Sp byrne ltd
Sycamore Avenue
Dublin 24

You left out the balance.

Date	Details	Debit	Credit	Balance
sept 5	Invoice no.4	4500		4500
sept 8	Invoice no.6	16,900		21400
sept 12	Credit no.46		1200	20200
sept 15	invoice no.10	18,500		38700
sept 19	Cheque	5700		44600
sept 24	Credit note no.56		352	44068
sept 26	Allowance	120		44168
sept 29	Invoice no 24	15700		59868
Sept 1	Blanc Balance			520

E&OE

CREDIT NOTE

SP Byrne Ltd
Sycamore Avenue
Dublin 24

No. 662002
VAT No. 101154
Date 24/8/16

Order No. _____
TO Oreiley ltd
blackwater
industrial state
Co. Cork

Quantity	Description	Unit Price	Total (Ex. VAT)
10	telephone ~~totts~~ labels	€40	€400
	~~totts~~	€40	
	Total (Ex. VAT)		€400
	− 20% Less Trade Discount		€80
			€320
	+ 10% Add VAT		€32
	Total		€352

E&OE

18. On 6 June 2011, L. Ryan, an office supplies retailer, 125 Duke Street, Athy, Co. Kildare, received an invoice dated 4 June from G. Dennis & Sons, Wholesalers, ABC Industrial Estate, Loughrea, Co. Galway, for the following: &

- 100 pocket calculators, model PC3 @ €20 each

- 40 correspondence trays, model CT19 @ €10 each

- 30 stapling machines, model SM27 @ €15 each

Trade discount on these goods was 30% and they were subject to VAT at 21%.

+2

On 9 June, the wholesalers discovered that the calculators should have been invoiced at €22 instead of €20, so they wrote to the buyer concerning the error and enclosing a debit note to correct the mistake.

(a) Complete the invoice of 4 June 2011 and the debit note of 9 June on the blank documents below.

(b) Outline how L. Ryan should deal with incoming invoices.

He should deal with the like it's a profit for the business and ~~dotto~~ double check his ~~mis~~ calculation

---

INVOICE

G. Denis & sons
wholesalers, Abc industrial
Estate, loughrea Co galway

No. 6620

VAT No. 9/16

Date 6/6/11

Order No. _____

TO L. Ryan 125 Dukes
street, Athy, Co
~~Clare~~ Kildare

Quantity	Description	Unit Price	Total (Ex. VAT)
100	Pocket calculators Model PC3	€20	€2000
40	Correspondence trays, model CT19	€10	€400
30	Stapling machines model SM27	€15	~~€450~~ €450

Total (Ex. VAT) | 2850
−30% Less Trade Discount | 855
| 1995
+21% Add VAT | ~~27~~ 418.95
Total | 2992.5

E&OE

Check Maths

& & &

DEBIT NOTE

R ryan 125 Dukes Street

No. 42091

VAT No. _____

Date 9/6/11

Order No. _____

TO G. Denis R R & & and sons whole Salers

2   200

Quantity	Description	Unit Price	Total (Ex. VAT)
100	Pocket calculators model PC3 €2022	€20 22	2200
40	Cosperant trays model ct19	10	400
30	stapling machines model sm27	15	450

Total (Ex. VAT)	4050
←30% Less Trade Discount	1215
	2835
+21% Add VAT	595.35
Total	3430.35

E&OE

---

19. Louise Malone is the purchasing manager for Pricecuts Electric Ltd, an electrical retailer located at 20 Main Street, Bray, Co. Wicklow. On 13 January 2011 she orders the following goods from the Manager, Wholesale Electric, Bandon Industrial Estate, Co. Cork.

- 20 cookers model XYZ @ €200 each
- 10 televisions model MR7 @ €280 each
- 30 Blu-ray recorders model L91 @ €180 each
- 15 electric kettles model G46 @ €20 each

(a) From the above details, complete order no. 460 using the blank order form on the next page.

All the goods ordered are in stock except the cookers. The televisions, Blu-ray recorders and electric kettles are delivered on 28 January and Louise checks the goods as they arrive and finds they are correct. After she signs the delivery note she is handed invoice no. 819 for the goods by the driver.

(b) From the above details, complete invoice no. 819 using the blank invoice on the next page. VAT on all goods is 20% and trade discount is 30%.

(c) What are the main purposes of a delivery note?

The main purposes is of a delivery note is that you can deliver things.

ORDER

Louise melone Priceculs
Eletric Itd 20
main street Bray
Co. wicklow

TO Manager
wholesales
Eletric bandon
industrial estate
Co. Cork

No. _____

VAT No. _____

Date 13/1/11

Please supply the following as per quotation no. 115421

Quantity	Description	Unit Price
20	Cookers model XYZ	€200
10	television model MY I	€280
30	Blu-ray recorders model C91	€180
15	Electrick Kettles model gl46	€20

Comments: Thanks for delivering it will

Signature: _____

Position: _____

INVOICE

Manager whofesales
Eletric bandon
Industrial estates
Co. Cork

Order No. 8L321

TO Couise melone
Priceculs
Eletrical Itd 20
main street bray
Co. wicklow

No. _____

VAT No. _____

Date _____

Quantity	Description		Unit Price	Total (Ex. VAT)
15	Eletrical Kettles	✓	€20	€600 €300
20	Blu-ray recorders	✓	€180	5400

Total (Ex. VAT)		6000
— 30% **Less Trade Discount**		1800
		4200
+ 20% **Add VAT**		1040
Total		5040

↓

Kettles also

E&OE

Maths? ⊙

20. Word search

Locate the following business documents in the word search below. The answers may read forwards, backwards or diagonally.

- Invoice
- Credit note
- Statement
- Delivery docket
- Debit note
- Order
- Quotation
- Enquiry

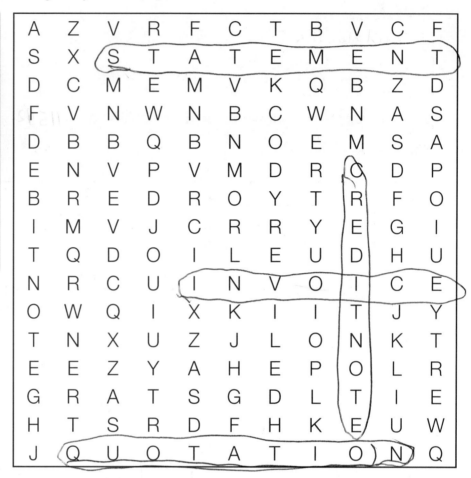

A	Z	V	R	F	C	T	B	V	C	F
S	X	S	T	A	T	E	M	E	N	T
D	C	M	E	M	V	K	Q	B	Z	D
F	V	N	W	N	B	C	W	N	A	S
D	B	B	Q	B	N	O	E	M	S	A
E	N	V	P	V	M	D	R	C	D	P
B	R	E	D	R	O	Y	T	R	F	O
I	M	V	J	C	R	R	Y	E	G	I
T	Q	D	O	I	L	E	U	D	H	U
N	R	C	U	I	N	V	O	I	C	E
O	W	Q	I	X	K	I	I	T	J	Y
T	N	X	U	Z	J	L	O	N	K	T
E	E	Z	Y	A	H	E	P	O	L	R
G	R	A	T	S	G	D	L	T	I	E
H	T	S	R	D	F	H	K	E	U	W
J	Q	U	O	T	A	T	I	O	N	Q

Section A Questions

21. Which of the following documents is sent by the buyer to the seller?

(a) Invoice ✓   (c) Credit note ☐
(b) Order ☐   (d) Quotation ☐

22. Name the source document for each of the following.

(a) Sales book ___Invoice___

(b) Sales returns book ___Credit Note___

(c) Purchases book ___Order___

(d) Purchases returns book ___Debit Note___

23. Tick the correct answer. A receipt is:

(a) Proof that the goods have been paid for ✓

(b) Proof that the goods have been purchased ☐

(c) Proof that the goods have been delivered ☐

Balancing Accounts

1. Balance each of the following accounts. Remember to follow the five steps of balancing in each case.

Dr	VEHICLES ACCOUNT NO. 1							Cr
Date	**Details**	**F**	**Total**	**Date**	**Details**	**F**		**Total**
Oct 1	Balance	b/d	45,000					
Oct 7	Bank	CB1	25,000					

Dr	RENT RECEIVED ACCOUNT NO. 2							Cr
Date	**Details**	**F**	**Total**	**Date**	**Details**	**F**	**Total**
				Sep 1	Balance	b/d	2,390
				Sep 6	Bank	CB1	4,000

Dr	PURCHASES ACCOUNT NO. 3							Cr
Date	**Details**	**F**	**Total**	**Date**	**Details**	**F**	**Total**
Jan 2	Balance	b/d	12,000				
Jan 5	Bank	CB1	23,450				
Jan 7	Creditors	PB1	46,700				

Dr	INSURANCE ACCOUNT NO. 4							Cr
Date	**Details**	**F**	**Total**	**Date**	**Details**	**F**	**Total**
Apr 7	Bank	CB1	12,000	Apr 1	Balance	b/d	2,000
Apr 9	Bank	CB1	13,500				
Apr 12	Cash	CB1	25,780				

Dr				SALES ACCOUNT NO. 5			Cr
Date	**Details**	**F**	**Total**	**Date**	**Details**	**F**	**Total**
Nov 1	Balance	b/d	31,567	Nov 4	Bank	CB1	34,500
				Nov 8	Debtors	SB1	26,700
				Nov 13	Debtors	SB1	68,930

Dr				WAGES ACCOUNT NO. 6			Cr
Date	**Details**	**F**	**Total**	**Date**	**Details**	**F**	**Total**
Aug 1	Balance	b/d	21,300				
Aug 6	Bank	CB1	34,560				
Aug 9	Cash	CB1	46,732				

Dr				BANK ACCOUNT NO. 7			Cr
Date	**Details**	**F**	**Total**	**Date**	**Details**	**F**	**Total**
Jun 1	Balance	b/d	12,450	Jun 5	Wages	GL3	11,000
Jun 4	Grant	GL1	20,000	Jun 8	Insurance	GL4	3,500
Jun 7	Sales	GL2	15,600	Jun 9	Fuel	GL5	2,100
Jun 12	Sales	GL2	21,450	Jun 15	Purchases	GL6	18,900

Dr				BUILDINGS ACCOUNT NO. 8			Cr
Date	**Details**	**F**	**Total**	**Date**	**Details**	**F**	**Total**
Jul 1	Balance	b/d	120,000	Jul 7	Bank	CB1	20,000
Jul 6	Bank	CB1	60,000				

Completing Accounts

In each of the following questions, prepare the relevant accounts in your Business Studies copy using the information provided. Prepare in both traditional and continuous balance format. Balance the accounts where necessary.

2. Machinery and Bank

Jan	1	Opening machinery account balance	25,000
Jan	1	Opening bank account balance	50,000
Jan	3	Purchased machinery by cheque	15,000
Jan	8	Sold old machinery and received cheque	8,000
Jan	11	Purchased machinery by cheque	30,000

3. Equipment and Bank

Feb	1	Opening equipment account balance	12,000
Feb	1	Opening bank account balance	35,000
Feb	6	Purchased equipment by cheque	22,000
Feb	8	Purchased equipment by cheque	30,000
Feb	9	Sold old equipment and received cheque	10,000

4. Purchases and Bank

Mar	1	Opening bank account balance	30,000
Mar	3	Purchased goods for resale and paid by cheque	15,000
Mar	5	Purchased goods for resale and paid by cheque	12,000

5. Sales and Bank

Apr	1	Opening bank account balance	45,000
Apr	8	Sold goods and received cheque	22,000
Apr	15	Sold goods and received cheque	18,000

6. Wages and Bank

May	1	Opening bank account balance	18,000
May	9	Paid wages by cheque	6,000
May	15	Paid wages by cheque	6,000

7. Postage and Stationery and Bank

June	1	Opening bank account balance	22,000
June	4	Purchased stationery and paid by cheque	800
June	8	Paid postage by cheque	900
June	14	Purchased stationery and paid by cheque	250
June	18	Returned stationery and received cheque refund	100
June	20	Paid postage by cheque	1,000

Converting Accounts

In the following questions you are required to transfer the information in the two-sided account into continuous balance format.

8.

Dr								Cr
Date	Details	F	Total	Date	Details	F		Total
Jan 31	Balance	c/d	470	Jan 7	Bank	CB1		220
				Jan 9	Bank	CB1		250
			470					470
				Feb 1	Balance	b/d		470

SALES ACCOUNT NO. 1

9.

Dr								Cr
Date	Details	F	Total	Date	Details	F		Total
Feb 1	Balance	b/d	200	Feb 28	Balance	c/d		940
Feb 5	Bank	CB1	340					
Feb 7	Bank	CB1	400					
			940					940
Mar 1	Balance	b/d	940					

INSURANCE ACCOUNT NO. 1

10.

Dr								Cr
Date	Details	F	Total	Date	Details	F		Total
Jan 1	Balance	b/d	360	Jan 7	Telephone	GL2		120
Jan 5	Sales	GL1	470	Jan 18	Purchases	GL3		400
Jan 10	Sales	GL1	900	Jan 22	Insurance	GL4		110
				Jan 31	Balance	c/d		1,100
			1,730					1,730
Feb 1	Balance	b/d	1,100					

BANK ACCOUNT NO. 1

11.

Dr								Cr
Date	Details	F	Total	Date	Details	F		Total
Apr 1	Balance	b/d	2,400	Apr 30	Balance	c/d		17,828
Apr 6	Bank	CB1	4,700					
Apr 17	Bank	CB1	5,950					
Apr 24	Bank	CB1	4,778					
			17,828					17,828
May 1	Balance	b/d	17,828					

PURCHASES ACCOUNT NO. 1

In the following questions you are required to transfer the information in the continuous balance account into the two-sided account format.

12.

Dr	SALES ACCOUNT NO. 1				Cr
Date	Details	F	Debit	Credit	Balance
Oct 1	Balance				700
Oct 8	Sales	GL1	580		1,280
Oct 11	ESB	GL2		65	1,215
Oct 18	Sales	GL1	1,000		2,215
Oct 24	Purchases	GL3		800	1,415
Oct 29	Telephone	GL4		100	1,315

13.

Dr	SALES ACCOUNT NO. 1				Cr
Date	Details	F	Debit	Credit	Balance
Jun 5	Cash	CB1		1,200	1,200
Jun 7	Cash	CB1		2,300	3,500
Jun 13	Bank	CB1		3,400	6,900

14.

Dr	INSURANCE ACCOUNT NO. 1				Cr
Date	Details	F	Debit	Credit	Balance
Jan 1	Balance	b/d			560
Jan 5	Bank	CB1	440		1,000

15.

Dr	WAGES ACCOUNT NO. 1				Cr
Date	Details	F	Debit	Credit	Balance
Mar 1	Balance	b/d	1,400		1,400
Mar 7	Bank	CB1	2,300		3,700
Mar 14	Bank	CB1	2,150		5,850
Mar 21	Bank	CB1	2,200		8,050
Mar 28	Bank	CB1	3,000		11,050

31 ⭐ The Trial Balance

Preparing the Trial Balance

For each of the questions 1 to 4, you are required to prepare a trial balance from the following accounts.

1. AB Ltd

Dr		PURCHASES ACCOUNT NO. 1					Cr
May 31	Balance b/d	6,500					

Dr		SALES ACCOUNT NO. 2					Cr
			May 31	Balance b/d		10,000	

Dr		VEHICLES ACCOUNT NO. 3					Cr
May 31	Balance b/d	20,000					

Dr		EQUIPMENT ACCOUNT NO. 4					Cr
May 31	Balance b/d	12,000					

Dr		BANK ACCOUNT NO. 5					Cr
May 31	Balance b/d	2,750					

Dr		DEBTORS ACCOUNT NO. 6					Cr
May 31	Balance b/d	4,500					

Dr		CREDITORS ACCOUNT NO. 7					Cr
			May 31	Balance b/d		3,600	

Dr		WAGES ACCOUNT NO. 8					Cr
May 31	Balance b/d	3,000					

Dr		INSURANCE ACCOUNT NO. 9					Cr
May 31	Balance b/d	2,100					

Dr				SALES RETURNS ACCOUNT NO. 10				Cr
May 31	Balance b/d		400					

Dr				PURCHASES RETURNS ACCOUNT NO. 11				Cr
				May 31	Balance b/d			600

Dr				BANK LOAN ACCOUNT NO. 12				Cr
				May 31	Balance b/d			10,000

Dr				CAPITAL ACCOUNT NO. 13				Cr
				May 31	Balance b/d			27,050

2. CD Ltd

Dr				CAPITAL ACCOUNT NO. 1				Cr
				Oct 31	Balance b/d			72,340

Dr				SALES ACCOUNT NO. 2				Cr
				Oct 31	Balance b/d			34,500

Dr				DELIVERY VANS ACCOUNT NO. 3				Cr
Oct 31	Balance b/d		32,000					

Dr				EQUIPMENT ACCOUNT NO. 4				Cr
Oct 31	Balance b/d		23,000					

Dr				BANK ACCOUNT NO. 5				Cr
Oct 31	Balance b/d		12,300					

Dr				DEBTORS ACCOUNT NO. 6				Cr
Oct 31	Balance b/d		34,700					

Dr				CREDITORS ACCOUNT NO. 7				Cr
				Oct 31	Balance b/d			21,400

Dr				LIGHT AND HEAT ACCOUNT NO. 8				Cr
Oct 31	Balance b/d		9,000					

Dr				INSURANCE ACCOUNT NO. 9				Cr
Oct 31	Balance b/d		13,400					

Dr				SALES RETURNS ACCOUNT NO. 10				Cr
Oct 31	Balance b/d		1,000					

Dr				PURCHASES RETURNS ACCOUNT NO. 11				Cr
				Oct 31	Balance b/d		560	

Dr				BANK LOAN ACCOUNT NO. 12				Cr
				Oct 31	Balance b/d		20,000	

Dr				PURCHASES ACCOUNT NO. 13				Cr
Oct 31	Balance b/d		23,400					

3. EF Ltd

Dr				CAPITAL ACCOUNT NO. 1				Cr
				Dec 31	Balance b/d		100,000	

Dr				SALES ACCOUNT NO. 2				Cr
				Dec 31	Balance b/d		65,000	

Dr				PREMISES ACCOUNT NO. 3				Cr
Dec 31	Balance b/d		130,000					

Dr				FURNITURE ACCOUNT NO. 4				Cr
Dec 31	Balance b/d		35,000					

Dr				BANK ACCOUNT NO. 5				Cr
				Dec 31	Balance b/d		12,400	

Dr			DEBTORS ACCOUNT NO. 6				Cr
Dec 31	Balance b/d		34,760				

Dr			CREDITORS ACCOUNT NO. 7				Cr
				Dec 31	Balance b/d		17,800

Dr			OFFICE EXPENSES ACCOUNT NO. 8				Cr
Dec 31	Balance b/d		7,600				

Dr			MARKETING ACCOUNT NO. 9				Cr
Dec 31	Balance b/d		12,940				

Dr			SALES RETURNS ACCOUNT NO. 10				Cr
Dec 31	Balance b/d		3,400				

Dr			PURCHASES RETURNS ACCOUNT NO. 11				Cr
				Dec 31	Balance b/d		2,500

Dr			BANK LOAN ACCOUNT NO. 12				Cr
				Dec 31	Balance b/d		50,000

Dr			PURCHASES ACCOUNT NO. 13				Cr
Dec 31	Balance b/d		24,000				

4. GH Ltd

Dr			PURCHASES ACCOUNT NO. 1				Cr
Jan 31	Balance b/d		36,700				

Dr			SALES ACCOUNT NO. 2				Cr
				Jan 31	Balance b/d		65,500

Dr			VEHICLES ACCOUNT NO. 3				Cr
Jan 31	Balance b/d		42,000				

Dr			FURNITURE AND FITTINGS ACCOUNT NO. 4				Cr
Jan 31	Balance b/d		24,000				

Dr			BANK ACCOUNT NO. 5				Cr
Jan 31	Balance b/d		13,500				

Dr			DEBTORS ACCOUNT NO. 6				Cr
Jan 31	Balance b/d		21,300				

Dr			CREDITORS ACCOUNT NO. 7				Cr
				Jan 31	Balance b/d		3,600

Dr			TRANSPORT COSTS ACCOUNT NO. 8				Cr
Jan 31	Balance b/d		12,700				

Dr			SUNDRY EXPENSES ACCOUNT NO. 9				Cr
Jan 31	Balance b/d		15,600				

Dr			SALES RETURNS ACCOUNT NO. 10				Cr
Jan 31	Balance b/d		2,300				

Dr			PURCHASES RETURNS ACCOUNT NO. 11				Cr
				Jan 31	Balance b/d		1,500

Dr			CAPITAL ACCOUNT NO. 12				Cr
				Jan 31	Balance b/d		97,500

5. Enter the following transactions into the ledger accounts, balance the accounts and extract a trial balance.

Feb 2	P. Sharpe invested capital into her business	€30,000
Feb 5	Purchased new vehicle by cheque	€14,000
Feb 8	Purchased materials and paid by cheque	€4,800
Feb 9	Sold goods and received money by cheque	€8,500
Feb 12	Paid rent by cheque	€2,500
Feb 17	Sold goods and received money by cheque	€7,900
Feb 22	Purchased materials and paid by cheque	€8,400
Feb 23	Paid insurance by cheque	€3,500

6. Enter the following transactions into the ledger accounts, balance the accounts and extract a trial balance.

Apr	4	L. Mortimer invested capital into his business	€25,000
Apr	6	Purchased new computers by cheque	€8,500
Apr	9	Purchased materials and paid by cheque	€6,900
Apr	13	Sold goods and received money by cheque	€12,400
Apr	15	Paid transport costs by cheque	€6,500
Apr	19	Sold goods and received money by cheque	€11,200
Apr	25	Purchased materials and paid by cheque	€10,400
Apr	27	Paid wages by cheque	€5,500

7. Enter the following transactions into the ledger accounts, balance the accounts and extract a trial balance.

Oct	1	D. Rhynhart invested capital into her business	€30,000
Oct	2	Purchased new showcases by cheque	€4,600
Oct	5	Purchased materials and paid by cheque	€8,900
Oct	12	Sold goods and received money by cheque	€14,700
Oct	16	Paid administration costs by cheque	€7,900
Oct	17	Sold goods and received money by cheque	€12,700
Oct	22	Purchased materials and paid by cheque	€11,200
Oct	24	Paid rates by cheque	€3,200

8. Enter the following transactions into the ledger accounts, balance the accounts and extract a trial balance.

June	4	P. Fortune invested capital into his business	€40,000
June	10	Sold goods and received payment by cheque	€9,900
June	15	Paid electricity bills by cheque	€1,700
June	17	Purchased new equipment by cheque	€12,000
June	18	Purchased materials and paid by cheque	€8,750
June	19	Sold goods and received money by cheque	€12,800
June	22	Sold goods and received money by cheque	€15,800
June	22	Received rent from tenant	€2,400
June	25	Purchased materials and paid by cheque	€6,400
June	27	Paid advertising by cheque	€4,500

In each of the following questions, you are required to enter each transaction in the purchases and purchases returns book, post to the creditors and general ledger, balance the accounts and extract a trial balance. All amounts are in euro.

1. Hannah Dunne Ltd

June	1	Purchased goods on credit from L. Fitzgerald .... 35,600 plus VAT @ 10%
June	3	Received an invoice from P. Lyons .... 27,000 plus VAT @ 10%
June	5	Returned goods to L. Fitzgerald.................................. 600 plus VAT @ 10%
June	9	Received an invoice from P. Lyons .... 19,000 plus VAT @ 10%
June	11	Received a credit note from P. Lyons .... 600 plus VAT @ 10%
June	12	Purchased goods on credit from M. O'Sullivan......... 46,700 plus VAT @ 10%
June	17	Received an invoice from L. Fitzgerald .... 26,000 plus VAT @ 10%
June	26	Purchased goods on credit from P. Lyons................. 16,900 plus VAT @ 10%
June	28	Received a credit note from P. Lyons .... 1,000 plus VAT @ 10%

2. Sanders Ltd

Dec	4	Purchased goods on credit from Deasy Ltd.............. 20,000 plus VAT @ 10%
Dec	12	Purchased goods on credit from Deasy Ltd.............. 28,000 plus VAT @ 10%
Dec	15	Purchased goods on credit from Stone & Sons .... 24,200 plus VAT @ 10%
Dec	21	Returned goods to Deasy Ltd .... 4,500 plus VAT @ 10%
Dec	23	Purchased goods on credit from Stone & Sons .... 21,000 plus VAT @ 10%
Dec	24	Purchased goods on credit from Robinson Ltd .... 27,000 plus VAT @ 10%
Dec	26	Returned goods to Robinson Ltd .... 2,300 plus VAT @ 10%
Dec	31	Purchased goods on credit from Deasy Ltd............... 5,000 plus VAT @ 10%
Dec	31	Returned goods to Stone Ltd...................................... 2,300 plus VAT @ 10%

Sales and Sales Returns (HL)

In each of the following questions, you are required to enter each transaction in the sales and sales returns book, post to the debtors and general ledger, balance the accounts and extract a trial balance. All amounts are in euro.

1. McGrath & Daughter

Apr	3	Sold goods on credit to SDS Supplies	22,300 plus VAT @ 10%
Apr	8	Sold goods on credit to SDS Supplies	34,530 plus VAT @ 10%
Apr	12	Sold goods on credit to P. Deeley Ltd	25,660 plus VAT @ 10%
Apr	16	SDS Supplies returned goods	4,450 plus VAT @ 10%
Apr	19	Sold goods on credit to P. Deeley Ltd	43,700 plus VAT @ 10%
Apr	22	Sold goods on credit to Elaine Macken Ltd	32,450 plus VAT @ 10%
Apr	24	Elaine Macken Ltd returned goods	6,700 plus VAT @ 10%
Apr	25	Sold goods on credit to SDS Supplies	35,600 plus VAT @ 10%

2. David McElroy Ltd

May	6	Sold goods on credit to Colclough & Sons	28,500 plus VAT @ 10%
May	7	Sold goods on credit to Jean Lacey Ltd	33,800 plus VAT @ 10%
May	8	Sold goods on credit to Colclough & Sons	40,400 plus VAT @ 10%
May	10	Colclough & Sons returned goods	3,500 plus VAT @ 10%
May	15	Sold goods on credit to Jones Ltd	33,600 plus VAT @ 10%
May	16	Sold goods on credit to Jean Lacey Ltd	35,400 plus VAT @ 10%
May	22	Jones Ltd returned goods	4,300 plus VAT @ 10%
May	24	Sold goods on credit to Colclough & Sons	50,500 plus VAT @ 10%
May	25	Colclough & Sons returned goods	3,400 plus VAT @ 10%
May	30	Sold goods on credit to Jean Lacey Ltd	36,200 plus VAT @ 10%

3. Scott Mason Ltd

June	5	Sold goods on credit to S. Mernagh	185,600 plus VAT @ 10%
June	7	Sent an invoice to N. Deegan	212,000 plus VAT @ 10%
June	8	S. Mernagh returned goods	21,600 plus VAT @ 10%
June	12	Sent an invoice to N. Deegan	219,500 plus VAT @ 10%
June	16	Sent a credit note to N. Deegan	31,800 plus VAT @ 10%
June	18	Sold goods on credit to D. Carey	246,100 plus VAT @ 10%
June	23	Sent an invoice to S. Mernagh	218,000 plus VAT @ 10%
June	24	Sold goods on credit to N. Deegan	211,500 plus VAT @ 10%
June	27	Sent a credit note to N. Deegan	35,000 plus VAT @ 10%

In each of the following questions you are required to prepare the sales, purchases, sales returns and purchases returns day books, post to the ledger and extract a trial balance. All amounts are in euro.

1. D. Ruddle & Co. Ltd

Apr	1	Sold goods on credit to S. Boyle Ltd............................34,500 plus VAT @ 10%
Apr	4	Sold goods on credit to D. Cotter Ltd ....56,000 plus VAT @ 10%
Apr	9	D. Cotter returned goods...2,500 plus VAT @ 10%
Apr	14	Purchased goods on credit from Fields & Co...............57,000 plus VAT @ 10%
Apr	15	Sold goods on credit to S. Boyle Ltd............................49,000 plus VAT @ 10%
Apr	17	S. Boyle Ltd returned goods..5,000 plus VAT @ 10%
Apr	19	Purchased goods on credit from JCV & Sons ....21,000 plus VAT @ 10%
Apr	21	Returned goods to Fields & Co. ....5,600 plus VAT @ 10%
Apr	24	Sold goods on credit to D. Cotter Ltd ....90,000 plus VAT @ 10%
Apr	26	Purchased goods on credit from JCV & Sons ....45,000 plus VAT @ 10%
Apr	29	Purchased goods on credit from Fields & Co...............52,000 plus VAT @ 10%

2. Dalton Pharmaceuticals Ltd

Sept	3	Sold goods on credit to E. Fitzpatrick Ltd ....77,300 plus VAT @ 10%
Sept	6	Sold goods on credit to F. Gilligan...............................88,900 plus VAT @ 10%
Sept	7	F. Gilligan returned goods...2,600 plus VAT @ 10%
Sept	12	Purchased goods on credit from Geraldine Harvey......54,900 plus VAT @ 10%
Sept	14	Sold goods on credit to E. Fitzpatrick Ltd ....74,900 plus VAT @ 10%
Sept	16	E. Fitzpatrick Ltd returned goods ....4,300 plus VAT @ 10%
Sept	18	Purchased goods on credit from Henry Systems Ltd...34,100 plus VAT @ 10%
Sept	20	Returned goods to Geraldine Harvey ....3,700 plus VAT @ 10%
Sept	22	Sold goods on credit to F. Gilligan...............................90,100 plus VAT @ 10%
Sept	25	Purchased goods on credit from Henry Systems Ltd...50,400 plus VAT @ 10%
Sept	27	Purchased goods on credit from Geraldine Harvey......28,700 plus VAT @ 10%

3. EGD Furniture Supplies Ltd

Oct	3	Purchased goods on credit from Jenson Ltd ....35,500 plus VAT @ 10%
Oct	5	Purchased goods on credit from Kirby & Sons............40,700 plus VAT @ 10%
Oct	8	Returned goods to Jenson Ltd..................................4,000 plus VAT @ 10%
Oct	10	Sold goods on credit to Leemore & Co. ....30,200 plus VAT @ 10%
Oct	12	Purchased goods on credit from Kirby & Sons............38,800 plus VAT @ 10%
Oct	15	Leemore & Co. returned goods ....5,400 plus VAT @ 10%
Oct	17	Sold goods on credit to Maureen Delany Supplies ......48,000 plus VAT @ 10%
Oct	20	Purchased goods on credit from Jenson Ltd ....27,000 plus VAT @ 10%
Oct	22	Sold goods on credit to Leemore & Co. ....16,000 plus VAT @ 10%
Oct	25	Returned goods to Jenson Ltd..................................3,800 plus VAT @ 10%
Oct	27	Sold goods on credit to Maureen Delany Supplies ......53,000 plus VAT @ 10%

4. Danmore & Co.

Nov	4	Sold goods on credit to Noleen & Co.......................... 34,700 plus VAT @ 10%
Nov	6	Received an invoice from Orpington Ltd.................... 23,000 plus VAT @ 10%
Nov	8	Sent an invoice to Penrose & Sons .... 42,000 plus VAT @ 10%
Nov	11	Noleen & Co. returned goods....................................... 1,600 plus VAT @ 10%
Nov	14	Purchased goods from Romancheu Ltd .... 30,000 plus VAT @ 10%
Nov	17	Received a credit note from Orpington Ltd.................. 7,500 plus VAT @ 10%
Nov	20	Sent an invoice to Penrose & Sons .... 36,000 plus VAT @ 10%
Nov	23	Sold goods on credit to Noleen & Co.......................... 40,000 plus VAT @ 10%
Nov	25	Received an invoice from Romancheu Ltd................. 36,000 plus VAT @ 10%

5. Novikovas & Sons Ltd

Dec	1	Sold goods on credit to Quality Supplies Ltd............. 44,500 plus VAT @ 10%
Dec	4	Sold goods on credit to Ryan Stephenson .... 66,000 plus VAT @ 10%
Dec	9	Ryan Stephenson returned goods .... 8,400 plus VAT @ 10%
Dec	14	Purchased goods on credit from Sean Tobin Ltd........ 47,000 plus VAT @ 10%
Dec	15	Sold goods on credit to Quality Supplies Ltd............. 59,000 plus VAT @ 10%
Dec	17	Quality Supplies Ltd returned goods........................... 8,000 plus VAT @ 10%
Dec	19	Purchased goods on credit from Ultra Services Ltd ... 31,500 plus VAT @ 10%
Dec	21	Returned goods to Sean Tobin Ltd .... 9,600 plus VAT @ 10%
Dec	24	Sold goods on credit to Ryan Stephenson .... 78,000 plus VAT @ 10%
Dec	26	Purchased goods on credit from Ultra Services Ltd ... 55,000 plus VAT @ 10%
Dec	29	Purchased goods on credit from Sean Tobin Ltd........ 48,000 plus VAT @ 10%

In each of the following you are required to:

    (a) Record the transactions in either the analysed cash book

        or the cash receipts and lodgements book and the cheque payments book.

    (b) Post to the appropriate ledger accounts.

1. Conor McKeon

Use the following analysis columns:

Receipts: Bank; Sales; VAT; Debtors; Capital.

Payments: Bank; Purchases; VAT; Telephone; Creditors.

Opening bank balance €5,000

Nov 2	Cash sales lodged €20,000 plus VAT @ 10%
Nov 4	Paid telephone €300 by cheque no. 27
Nov 6	Purchased materials for resale €12,000 plus VAT @ 10% by cheque no. 28
Nov 9	Cash sales lodged €17,000 plus VAT @ 10%
Nov 12	Paid R. Ryan & Co., a creditor, €1,700 by cheque no. 28
Nov 14	Received €7,000 by cheque from J. Boylen, a debtor
Nov 16	Purchased materials for resale €22,000 including VAT @ 10% by cheque no. 29
Nov 18	Cash sales lodged €27,500 including VAT @ 10%
Nov 27	Shareholders invested a further €10,000 into the business, which was lodged in the bank

2. Peter Flanagan

Use the following analysis columns:

Receipts: Bank; Sales; VAT; Furniture.

Payments: Bank; Purchases; VAT; Electricity; Motor vehicle.

Opening bank balance €10,000

April 3	Cash sales lodged in bank €12,400 plus VAT @ 10%
April 5	Paid electricity bill €345 by cheque no. 175
April 7	Purchased new motor vehicle €33,000 by cheque no. 176
April 9	Purchased materials for resale €17,350 plus VAT @ 10% by cheque no. 177
April 12	Sold second-hand furniture for €5,600 and lodged cheque
April 17	Cash sales lodged in bank €28,900 plus VAT @ 10%
April 21	Purchased materials for resale €15,600 plus VAT @ 10% by cheque no. 178

3. Daniel O'Kelly

Use the following analysis columns:

Receipts: Bank; Sales; VAT; Debtors.

Payments: Bank; Purchases; VAT; Rent; Equipment; Creditors.

Opening bank balance €12,400

Oct	5	Cash sales lodged in bank €44,400, which included VAT @ 10%
Oct	7	Paid rent €1,400 by cheque no. 233
Oct	8	Received €13,560 by cheque from David O'Brien, a debtor
Oct	9	Purchased new equipment €5,700 by cheque no. 234
Oct	12	Purchased materials for resale €16,800 plus VAT @ 10% by cheque no. 235
Oct	15	Paid €12,400 by cheque no. 236 to Alan Devlin, a creditor
Oct	18	Cash sales lodged in bank €32,400 plus VAT @ 10%
Oct	23	Purchased materials for resale €14,600 plus VAT @ 10% by cheque no. 237
Oct	24	Received €10,000 by cheque from Simon Daly, a debtor

4. William Noonan Ltd

Use the following analysis columns:

Receipts: Bank; Sales; VAT; Debtors; Capital.

Payments: Bank; Purchases; VAT; Telephone; Machinery; Creditors; Rent.

Opening bank balance €8,950

Nov	2	Cash sales lodged in bank €23,600 plus VAT @ 10%
Nov	5	Paid telephone €1,750 by cheque no. 111
Nov	7	Purchased materials for resale €22,000, which included VAT @ 10%, by cheque no. 112
Nov	8	Received €15,600 by cheque from Darragh Nolan, a debtor
Nov	9	Purchased new machinery €25,000 by cheque no. 113
Nov	13	Purchased materials for resale €12,400 plus VAT @ 10% by cheque no. 114
Nov	16	Paid €8,650 by cheque no. 115 to Ken Walsh, a creditor
Nov	19	Paid rent €2,400 by cheque no. 116
Nov	19	Cash sales lodged in bank €45,000 plus VAT @ 10%
Nov	25	Paid €15,800 by cheque no. 117 to Tom Byrne, a creditor

Opening Assets and Liabilities

In each of the following questions, you are required to prepare the general journal to record the opening assets and liabilities of each firm and, where necessary, to calculate the opening ordinary share capital. Post each entry to the appropriate ledger account.

1. Della Dowd Ltd

Assets: Premises €224,000; Vehicles €23,000; Machinery €42,000; Debtors: B. Black €13.450 and Smith & Co. €19,870; Stock €18,900; Bank deposit a/c €12,900.

Liabilities: Creditors: L. Mosley €8,700 and Hilliard & Sons €21,350; Bank overdraft €7,400; Ordinary share capital – ?

2. Jendle & Co.

Assets: Buildings €196,000; Machinery €95,000; Furniture €34,000; Debtors: J. Jones €9,700 and Mabel & Co. €15,600; Stock €12,600; Bank deposit a/c €9,690; Bank current a/c €5,540.

Liabilities: Creditors: L. Dodd €17,900 and Manley & Son €15,800; 5-year loan €40,000; Ordinary share capital – ?

Purchase and Sale of Fixed Assets

In each of the following questions you are required to record the transactions in the general journal and post them to the correct ledger accounts.

3. Jane Daly, Fashion Designer

June 7   Purchased new sewing machines on credit from AB Machines Ltd for €2,500

June 10   Sold old hanging racks on credit to DF Merchants for €500

4. Peter O'Malley, Computer Store

Nov 2   Purchased new repair centre premises on credit for €25,000 and paid by cheque

Nov 8   Sold old furniture on credit to S. Smith for €300

5. Goodnight Hotel

Mar 3   Sold old beds on credit to Young's Hostel for €1,200

Mar 9   Purchased new reservations system on credit from DS Peripherals for €12,500 plus VAT @ 10%

6. Brightair, Budget Airline

Dec 6   Purchased new seating for reservations area on credit from Super Seating Ltd for €1,900

Dec 12   Sold old computers to GDS Computer Repairs on credit for €1,200

Bad Debts

In each of the following questions you are required to record the transactions in the general journal and post them to the correct ledger accounts.

7. Nov 11   S. Sloan, a debtor who owes €900, made a first and final payment of 30c in the euro. The remainder is to be written off as a bad debt.

8. July 16   V. Black, a debtor who owed €2,700, made a first and final payment of 38c in the euro. The remainder is to be written off as a bad debt.

9. June 14   L. Sands, a debtor who owed €2,110, made a first and final payment of 22c in the euro. The remainder is to be written off as a bad debt.

10. Nov 11   G. Moran, a debtor who owes €750, made a first and final payment of 50c in the euro. The remainder is to be written off as a bad debt.

11. July 16   R. James, a debtor who owed €1,500, made a first and final payment of 35c in the euro. The remainder is to be written off as a bad debt.

1. The following general journal was extracted from the books of Langton Supplies Ltd on 1 May 2011.

Premises	GL1	80,000	
Motor vans	GL2	40,000	
Bank	CB1	6,000	
Debtor: LD Ryan Ltd	DL1	4,000	
Creditor – Sennet & Co.	CL1		50,000
Issued share capital	GL3		80,000
		130,000	130,000

Credit transactions during May 2011 were as follows:

4/5/11 Purchased goods on credit from Sennet & Co. inv. no. 78...€35,000 + VAT @ 20%

10/5/11 Sold goods on credit to MDD Ltd inv. no. 36 ....€8,000 + VAT @ 20%

17/5/11 Sold goods on credit to LD Ryan Ltd inv. no. 37.................€45,000 + VAT @ 20%

The following bank transactions took place during May 2011:

6/5/11 Cash sales lodged.. €9,000 (this includes €1,500 VAT)

8/5/11 Paid wages by cheque no. 223 .... €2,100

16/5/11 Purchased materials by cheque no. 224 ....€2,400 + VAT @ 20%

23/5/11 LD Ryan Ltd settled their account in full by cheque, which was lodged to the bank

27/5/11 Paid Sennet & Co. by cheque no. 225 .... €40,000

You are required to:

(a) Post the balances on 1 May given in the general journal to the relevant accounts.

(b) Record the transactions for the month of May in the appropriate books of first entry. Post the relevant figures to the ledger.

Note: Analyse the bank transactions using the following money column headings:

Debit side: Bank; Sales; VAT; Debtors.

Credit side: Bank; Purchases; VAT; Creditors; Wages.

(c) Balance the accounts on 31 May 2011 and extract a trial balance on that date.

2. The books of Exco Ltd showed the following balances on 1 Feb 2011.

Buildings €150,000	
Creditor: Best & Co. €12,500	

(a) Enter these balances in the general journal, find the ordinary share capital balance and post this balance to the ledger.

(b) Post the relevant figures from the purchases book and sales book below to the ledgers.

SALES BOOK PAGE 1					
Date	Details	F	Amount (Ex. VAT)	VAT	Total
Feb 6	Worst Ltd inv. no. 47	DL1	25,000	5,250	30,250
		GL1	25,000	5,250	30,250

PURCHASES BOOK PAGE 1					
Date	Details	F	Amount (Ex. VAT)	VAT	Total
Feb 12	Best Ltd inv. no. 56	CL1	14,000	2,940	16,940
		GL1	14,000	2,940	16,940

(c) Record the following bank transactions for the month of February. Post the relevant figures to the ledger.

Note: Analyse the bank transactions using the following money column headings:

Debit side: Bank; Sales; VAT; Debtor.

Credit side: Bank; Purchases; VAT; Creditors; Advertising.

Bank transactions:

5/2/11 Cash sales lodged ....€50,000 + VAT @ 21%	
9/2/11 Paid advertising by cheque no. 34.. €1,700	
15/2/11 Paid Best Ltd by cheque no. 35... €15,500	
15/2/11 Purchased goods for resale by cheque no. 36 ....€9,000 + VAT @ 21%	
20/2/11 Worst Ltd paid part of its account by cheque... €14,000	

(d) Balance the accounts on 28 February and extract a trial balance on that date.

3. The following transactions took place during the month of March 2011.

Credit transactions:

2/3/11	Purchased goods on credit from Downwell Ltd inv. no. 7 ..€12,000 + VAT @ 10%
8/3/11	Purchased goods on credit from Ceder & Co. inv. no. 34...€34,700 + VAT @ 10%
15/3/11	Sold goods on credit to L. Mantle inv. no. 79 ....€44,200 + VAT @ 10%

Bank transactions:

1/3/11	Shareholders invested €50,000 and this was lodged
4/3/11	Purchases for resale by cheque no. 6................................€15,000 + VAT @ 10%
12/3/11	Cash sales lodged ....€21,800 + VAT @ 10%
17/3/11	Paid telephone by cheque no. 7 .... €170
22/3/11	Received cheque from L. Mantle in full settlement of her account
25/3/11	Paid Downwell by cheque no. 8... €8,000
27/3/11	Paid general expenses by cheque no. 9... €2,800

You are required to:

(a) Record the transactions for the month of March 2011 in the appropriate books of first entry. Post the relevant figures to the ledger.

Note: Analyse the bank transactions using the following money column headings:

Debit side: Bank; Sales; VAT; Debtor; Share capital.

Credit side: Bank; Purchases; VAT; Creditors; Telephone; Expenses.

(b) Balance the accounts on 31 March 2011 and extract a trial balance on that date.

Correcting Bank Accounts

1. Gerard Stevens prepared his bank account for July, which indicated a balance on 31 July of €345. When he received his bank statement, however, he discovered the following items had been omitted from his records. You are required to prepare a corrected bank account showing Gerard's amended bank account balance.
   - Bank charges..€35
   - Credit transfer into account...€120
   - Standing order..€224

2. Pauline Mockler prepared her bank account for June, which indicated a balance on 30 June of €144. When she received her bank statement, however, she discovered the following items had been omitted from her records. You are required to prepare a corrected bank account showing Pauline's amended bank account balance.
   - Credit transfer into account...€235
   - Standing order..€125
   - Bank charges..€24
   - Direct debit to mortgage account..€160

3. The Big Box Company prepared their bank account for August, which indicated a balance on 31 August of €1,320. When they received their bank statement, however, they discovered the following items had been omitted from their records. You are required to prepare a corrected bank account showing the firm's amended bank account balance.
   - Wages paid by direct debit...€13,500
   - Bank charges..€55
   - Credit transfer from customers..€27,500

Preparing Bank Reconciliation Statements

4. Maire Cravin received her bank statement on 31 October. It showed she had a balance in the bank of €275. Maureen's own records indicated that certain transactions had been omitted from the bank statement. From the following information, you are required to prepare a bank reconciliation statement showing Maureen's amended bank balance.

   Cheques paid by Maureen but which had not yet been presented to the bank:
   - No. 25 for groceries...€46
   - No. 29 for school books...€28
   - No. 31 for telephone bill..€78

   Cheques lodged by Maureen but which had not yet been credited to her account:
   - Wages €100
   - Child Benefit €30

5. Dan Murphy received his bank statement on 31 March. It showed he had a balance in the bank of €560. Dan's own records indicated that certain transactions had been omitted from the bank statement. From the following information, you are required to prepare a bank reconciliation statement showing Dan's amended bank balance.

Cheques paid by Dan but which had not yet been presented to the bank:

- No. 16 for car service €120

- No. 19 for house insurance..€215

- No. 22 for petrol..€25

Cheques lodged by Dan but which had not yet been credited to his account:

- Dividends from shares €80

- Salary €960

6. Signia Ltd received their bank statement on 31 May. It showed they had a balance in the bank of €13,160. Signia's own records indicated that certain transactions had been omitted from the bank statement. From the following information, you are required to prepare a bank reconciliation statement showing Signia's amended bank balance.

Cheques lodged by Signia but which had not yet been credited to their account:

- J. Costello & Sons €10,000

- P. Mulholland & Sons €35,000

- Desmond Ltd €12,300

Cheques paid by Signia Ltd but which had not yet been presented to the bank:

- No. 2543 for wages €9,800

- No. 2560 for telephone €700

- No. 2561 for supplies...€5,600

- No. 2562 for VAT...€22,600

Combined Bank Account and Reconciliation Statements

In each of the questions below, correct the customers' own records and then prepare a bank reconciliation statement.

7.

Dr								
Date	**Details**	**F**	**Total**	**Date**	**Details**	**F**	**Total**	
May 1	Balance	b/d	100	May 5	Kiely Motors (1)		160	
31	Salary		850	12	Tesco (2)		72	
				18	ATM		50	
				22	Furnish World (3)		190	
				31	Balance		478	
			950				950	
June 1	Balance	b/d	478					

Header: BANK ACCOUNT – LISA SHANAHAN (Cr)

BANK STATEMENT

Bank of Ireland, Merson Street, Carlow

To: Lisa Shanahan, 32 St. Patrick's Road, Carlow   Date 31/05/11

Account No. 22345887

DATE	TRANSACTION DETAILS	Dr	Cr	BALANCE
May 1	Balance			100
7	Cheque no. 1	160		60dr
12	Cheque no. 2	72		132dr
15	Credit transfer		170	38
18	ATM	50		12dr
22	Charges	15		27dr

8.

Dr					BANK ACCOUNT – JAMES KELLY			Cr
Date	Details	F	Total	Date	Details	F	Total
Oct 1	Balance	b/d	270	Oct 7	Esso (1)		20
7	Salary		1,250	12	Groceries (2)		75
20	Lodgement		100	15	Petrol (3)		25
				18	Groceries (4)		82
				31	Balance	c/d	1,418
			1,620				1,620
Nov 1	Balance	b/d	1,418				

BANK STATEMENT

Ulster Bank, Leixlip, Co. Kildare

To: James Kelly, 72 Beech Green, Lucan, Co. Dublin   Date 31/10/11

Account No. 14427893

DATE	TRANSACTION DETAILS	Dr	Cr	BALANCE
Oct 1	Balance			270
9	Cheque no. 1	20		250
10	Lodgement		1,250	1,500
14	Standing order	140		1,360
16	Cheque no. 3	25		1,335
21	Cheque no. 4	82		1,253
25	Bank charges	42		1,211

9.

Dr					BANK ACCOUNT – SIMON O'BRIEN			Cr
Date	**Details**	**F**	**Total**	**Date**	**Details**	**F**	**Total**
Feb 1	Balance	b/d	155	Feb 2	Purchases (1)		80
2	Wages		870	3	Telephone (2)		92
15	Bonus		180	8	ATM		60
				9	Petrol (3)		25
				10	Purchases (4)		72
				12	ATM		55
				14	Gas (5)		75
				18	Holiday dep. (6)		100
				28	Balance	c/d	646
			1,205				1,205
Mar 1	Balance	b/d	646				

BANK STATEMENT

AIB, Leixlip, Co. Kildare

To: Simon O'Brien, 16 The Meadows, Leixlip, Co. Kildare   Date 28/02/11

Account No. 57883400

DATE		TRANSACTION DETAILS	Dr	Cr	BALANCE
Feb	1	Balance			155
	5	Lodgement		870	1,025
	5	Cheque no. 1	80		945
	6	Cheque no. 2	92		853
	7	Standing order	110		743
	8	Withdrawal ATM	60		683
	12	Withdrawal ATM	55		628
	14	Credit transfer		150	778
	17	Cheque no. 5	75		703
	21	Cheque no. 6	100		603
	24	Charges and fees	22		581

10.

Dr				BANK ACCOUNT – LIAM TYRELL			Cr
Date	Details	F	Total	Date	Details	F	Total
Nov 1	Balance	b/d	243.00	Nov 3	Gerry Ryan (14)		81.40
3	Wages		1,000.00	5	ATM		60.00
8	ATM		100.00	8	Laser – Smiths		140.00
29	Insurance		67.00	10	Jones Ltd (15)		88.00
				12	ATM		40.00
				16	N. Murray (16)		141.70
				18	ATM		40.00
				22	Leeson Ltd (17)		24.00
				30	Balance	c/d	794.90
			1,410.00				1,410.00
Dec 1	Balance	b/d	794.90				

BANK STATEMENT

Bank of Ireland, Gorey

To: Liam Tyrell, 16 Lakeside, Gorey, Co. Wexford   Date 30/11/11

Account No. 324290769

DATE		TRANSACTION DETAILS	DR	Cr	BALANCE
Nov	1	Balance			243.00
	3	Allen Plc		1,000.00	1,243.00
	6	Cheque no. 14	81.40		1,161.60
	6	ATM withdrawal	60.00		1,101.60
	8	ATM lodgement		100.00	1,201.60
	8	Laser – POS	140.00		1,061.60
	9	Standing order – IP Plc	340.00		721.60
	10	New chequebook	1.75		719.85
	12	ATM – withdrawal	40.00		679.85
	14	Credit transfer		150.00	829.85
	19	Cheque no. 16	141.70		688.15
	20	Fees – Sept/Oct	15.00		673.15
	20	ATM – withdrawal	40.00		633.15
	25	Cheque no. 17	24.00		609.15

Exam-style Questions

11. Mary Buckley has an account with AIB, Killarney. She received the following statement on 3 May 2011.

Tel: 066-4366287	**AIB, Main Street**
Fax: 066-4366299	**Killarney, Co. Kerry**
Branch Code: 93-71-47	**Statement of Account**

Branch ID Code: AIBKIE5H

Ms Mary Buckley	**Account Name:**
Muckross Road	Mary Buckley No. 1 Account
Killarney	**Account Number:** 25496813
Co. Kerry	**IBAN:** IE39 AIBK 9371 4725 4968 13
Statement Number: 495	**Statement Date:** 30 April 2011

DATE	TRANSACTION DETAILS	Dr	Cr	BALANCE
01 Apr 2011	Balance forward			626.00
06 Apr 2011	Paypath		1,670.00	2,296.00
09 Apr 2011	Cheque no. 50021	2,350.00		54.00dr
15 Apr 2011	DD – Eircom	124.00		178.00dr
18 Apr 2011	ATM – AIB Dingle	160.00		338.00dr
20 Apr 2011	Paypath		1,670.00	1,332.00
22 Apr 2011	SO – Vodafone	33.00		1,299.00
29 Apr 2011	Bank charges	14.00		1,285.00
30 Apr 2011	INET – AIB Visa	308.00		977.00

(A) (i) Is Mary's bank account a deposit or current account? Give one reason for your answer.

_____

(ii) Explain 'Paypath' and state **two** advantages of Paypath to Mary.

_____

_____

_____

(iii) Explain the difference between the transactions that occurred on 15 April 2011 and 22 April 2011.

_____

_____

(iv) What do the initials 'ATM' stand for? Explain **three** services that are available to Mary through the ATM.

_____

_____

_____

_____

(v) Explain why 'dr' appears in the Balance column after three transactions on the statement.

_____

(vi) State **two** possible items that may be included in the entry dated 29 April.

_____

_____

(B) (i) Mary's bank statement does not include the following two items:

- A cheque (no. 50022) of €178.00 written by Mary on 12 April.
- A credit transfer of €95.00 on 30 April.

Calculate her bank balance after taking **both** of the above items into consideration.

_____

_____

(ii) Explain the difference between **each** of the following.

- Stale cheque and dishonoured cheque.
- General crossing and special crossing.

_____

_____

_____

_____

Section A Questions

12. Write down three possible reasons why the balance on a customer's bank statement may not agree with the balance in their own records.

_____

_____

_____

13. The following letters appeared on a bank statement. What do they stand for?

(a) SO _____

(b) OD _____

Control Accounts

In each of the following questions, you are required to prepare a debtors or creditors control account from the figures given in both traditional and continuous balance format.

1. Debtors Control Account

Jan	1	Total debtors balance	34,000
Jan	31	Total credit sales including VAT	56,000
		Total returns including VAT	3,200
		Total receipts from debtors	42,000

Dr	DEBTORS CONTROL ACCOUNT						Cr
Date	Details	F	Total	Date	Details	F	Total

2. Creditors Control Account

June	1	Total creditors balance	27,500
June	30	Total credit purchases including VAT	43,560
		Total returns including VAT	4,500
		Total payments to creditors	31,400

Dr	CREDITORS CONTROL ACCOUNT						Cr
Date	Details	F	Total	Date	Details	F	Total

3. Debtors Control Account

Feb 1	Total debtors balance	47,000
Feb 28	Total credit sales including VAT	93,000
	Total returns including VAT	8,700
	Total receipts from debtors	62,930

Dr	DEBTORS CONTROL ACCOUNT						Cr
Date	Details	F	Total	Date	Details	F	Total

4. Creditors Control Account

July 1	Total creditors balance	45,200
July 31	Total credit purchases including VAT	67,000
	Total returns including VAT	5,100
	Total payments to creditors	35,500

Dr	CREDITORS CONTROL ACCOUNT						Cr
Date	Details	F	Total	Date	Details	F	Total

5. Debtors Control Account

Apr 1   Total debtors balance 48,000

Apr 30   Total credit sales including VAT 134,000

Total returns including VAT 18,400

Total cash receipts from debtors 24,000

Total cheque receipts from debtors 78,000

Dr						DEBTORS CONTROL ACCOUNT		Cr
Date	**Details**	**F**	**Total**	**Date**	**Details**	**F**	**Total**

6. Creditors Control Account

Sept 1   Total creditors balance 178,300

Sept 30   Total credit purchases including VAT 278,500

Total returns including VAT 43,800

Total cash payments to creditors 97,200

Total cheque payments to creditors 167,000

Dr						CREDITORS CONTROL ACCOUNT		Cr
Date	**Details**	**F**	**Total**	**Date**	**Details**	**F**	**Total**

40 The Petty Cash Book

1. Peter Smith is the office manager in CDS Ltd. He uses a petty cash book to keep an account of small office expenses. He begins each month with an imprest of €350. The following were his petty cash expenses during October 2011.

Oct 1   Balance (imprest) on hand €350

2   He bought writing paper (stationery) for €24 – petty cash voucher no. 1

6   He bought envelopes for €20 – petty cash voucher no. 2

7   He paid €16 for postage – petty cash voucher no. 3

10   He paid €32 for cleaning materials for the office – petty cash voucher no. 4

11   He paid €10 bus fares – petty cash voucher no. 5

14   He paid €35 train fare for the sales manager – petty cash voucher no. 6

18   He paid the office cleaner €45 – petty cash voucher no. 7

22   He paid €26 for repairs to the alarm system – petty cash voucher no. 8

23   He paid €16 to a courier to have a parcel delivered – petty cash voucher no. 9

26   He purchased computer paper (stationery) for €35 – petty cash voucher no. 10

27   He paid €20 to a local charity – petty cash voucher no. 11

29   He paid €16 for postage – petty cash voucher no. 12

Write up the petty cash book for the month of May using the analysis columns Postage, Stationery, Travel, Cleaning, Other and post the totals of the analysis columns to the ledger.

2. Stephen Mulligan is the office manager of Seemore Ltd and uses a petty cash book to keep an account of small office expenses. He begins each month with an imprest of €450. The following were the petty cash expenses during September 2011.

Sept 1   Balance (imprest) on hand €450

6   He paid €31 for postage – petty cash voucher no. 1

7   He paid €46 for repairs to a lock – petty cash voucher no. 2

9   He paid €40 to an employee running a marathon for charity – voucher no. 3

12   He bought envelopes (stationery) for €34 – petty cash voucher no. 4

14   He paid €70 for repairs to a computer – petty cash voucher no. 5

17   He paid €45 to DFAST Couriers to deliver a parcel (postage) – petty cash voucher no. 6

20   He paid €55 for a taxi to bring some clients to lunch – petty cash voucher no. 7

21   He paid €124 for extra cleaning – petty cash voucher no. 8

24   He paid €40 for a staff lunch after the firm got an award – petty cash voucher no. 9

25   He purchased new ink cartridges (stationery) for €95 – petty cash voucher no. 10

26   He paid train fare €35 for the sales manager – petty cash voucher no. 11

29   He paid €54 for postage – petty cash voucher no. 12

Write up the petty cash book for the month of September using the analysis columns Travelling, Postage, Repairs, Cleaning, Other and post the totals of the analysis columns to the ledger.

3. Mohammed Mohsen is the office manager in DY Solutions. He uses a petty cash book to keep an account of small office expenses. He begins each month with an imprest of €1,000. The following were his petty cash expenses during June 2011.

June 1   Balance (imprest) on hand €1,000

  2   He bought writing paper (stationery) for €120 – petty cash voucher no. 1

  5   He paid €25 for postage – petty cash voucher no. 2

  8   He paid the office cleaner €60 – petty cash voucher no. 3

  10   He purchased computer paper (stationery) for €60 – petty cash voucher no. 4

  12   He paid €96 for repairs to the sprinkler system – petty cash voucher no. 5

  14   He paid €40 train fare for the HR manager – petty cash voucher no. 6

  15   He paid €37 to a courier to have a parcel delivered – petty cash voucher no. 7

  18   He paid €20 bus fares – petty cash voucher no. 8

  21   He paid €30 to a national charity – petty cash voucher no. 9

  23   He paid €45 for cleaning materials for the office – petty cash voucher no. 10

  27   He bought envelopes (stationery) for €40 – petty cash voucher no. 11

  29   He paid €55 for postage – petty cash voucher no. 12

(a) Write up the petty cash book for the month of June using the analysis columns Postage, Stationery, Travel, Cleaning, Other and post the totals of the analysis columns to the ledger.

(b) How much will Mohammed receive from the chief cashier to enable him to start next month with an imprest of €1,000? _____

Exam-style Question

4. Rita Whyte is the office manager in Quinlan Ltd. She uses a petty cash book to keep an account of small office expenses. She begins each month with an imprest of €250.
On 1 April 2011, the petty cash book had a balance on hand of €250. The following were her petty cash transactions during April 2011.

April 2   She paid €15 for postage – petty cash voucher no. 31

  4   She bought writing paper (stationery) for €11 – petty cash voucher no. 32

  8   She paid €20 to a local charity for raffle tickets – petty cash voucher no. 33

  9   She bought envelopes (stationery) for €18 – petty cash voucher no. 34

  11   She paid €17 to the window cleaner – petty cash voucher no. 35

  16   She paid €16 for cleaning materials for the office – petty cash voucher no. 36

  18   She paid €14 for repairs to a filing cabinet – petty cash voucher no. 37

  21   She paid €25 for cleaning the office – petty cash voucher no. 38

  22   She paid €32 for repairs to an office desk – petty cash voucher no. 39

  25   She paid €8 to post a large packet to a customer – petty cash voucher no. 40

  28   She paid €15 for toll charges – petty cash voucher no. 41

  29   She bought copying paper (stationery) for €23 – petty cash voucher no. 42

(A) Write up the petty cash book for the month of April using the following analysis columns: Postage, Stationery, Cleaning, Repairs, Other. Total each analysis column and balance the petty cash book at the end of April.

(B) How much money will Rita receive from the chief cashier to enable her to start the following month with an imprest of €250? _____

Final Accounts 1: The Trading Account

1. From the following information, prepare a trading account for R. Rock for the year ended 31/12/11.

   Purchases €43,000; Sales €62,700; Carriage inwards €2,340; Opening stock €8,700; Closing stock €10,200; Sales returns €2,700; Purchases returns €3,000.

2. From the following information, prepare a trading account for T. Hunt for the year ended 31/12/11.

   Purchases €73,845; Sales €112,964; Returns inwards €2,643; Returns outwards €3,557; Customs duties €2,446; Opening stock €7,576; Closing stock €13,491.

3. From the following information, prepare a trading account for J. Stack for the year ended 31/12/11.

   Purchases €113,780; Sales €262,556; Sales returns €4,540; Returns outwards €2,200; Carriage inwards €4,268; Opening stock €17,580; Closing stock €21,550.

4. From the following information, prepare a trading account for W. Reilly for the year ended 31/12/11.

   Purchases €245,669; Sales €324,550; Sales returns €19,770; Purchases returns €12,600; Carriage inwards €6,668; Opening stock €19,000; Closing stock €31,550.

Section A Questions

5. Gross profit is which of the following?

   (a) Sales minus purchases ☐

   (b) Sales minus sales returns ☐

   (c) Sales minus cost of sales ☐

Final Accounts 2: The Profit and Loss Account

Combined Trading and Profit and Loss Accounts

1. From the following information, prepare the trading and profit and loss account for Deirdre Power for the year ended 31/12/11.

   Sales €26,500; Carriage outwards €2,300; Sales returns €2,400; Advertising €2,100; Opening stock €4,500; Insurance €1,600; Purchases €15,400; Carriage inwards €1,750; Light and heat €5,400; Purchases returns €1,700; Office expenses €1,120; Closing stock €5,600; Rent received €4,300.

2. From the following information, prepare the trading and profit and loss account for John Lacken for the year ended 31/12/11.

   Sales €56,700; Purchases €24,500; Carriage inwards €1,200; Customs duties €2,450; Salaries €4,560; Carriage outwards €2,650; Sales returns €2,300; Rent received €2,550; Light and heat €4,400; Opening stock €6,800; Closing stock €7,900; Bank interest paid €2,400; Marketing and advertising €2,500; Postage and stationery €1,400.

3. From the following information, prepare the trading and profit and loss account for Lena Dunne for the year ended 31/12/11.

   Sales €165,780; Purchases €88,300; Opening stock €11,780; Closing stock €14,740; Carriage inwards €1,750; Electricity €2,700; Wages and salaries €31,670; Overdraft interest €2,500; Rent and rates €6,780; Advertising €11,200.

4. From the following information, prepare the trading and profit and loss account for Joe Donoghue for the year ended 31/12/11.

   Opening stock €9,700; Purchases €32,800; Purchases returns €3,500; Interest received €1,699; Bad debts €1,230; Travelling expenses €5,600; Sales €78,900; Light and heat €4,500; Salaries €18,700; Closing stock €7,300; Insurance €8,900; Cleaning €1,770; Sales returns €3,200.

5. From the following information, prepare the trading and profit and loss account for Niamh Finn for the year ended 31/12/11.

   Sales €147,800; Carriage outwards €12,300; Sales returns €7,600; Advertising €12,100; Opening stock €9,500; Insurance €21,500; Purchases €95,400; Carriage inwards €13,850; Light and heat €15,400; Purchases returns €3,700; Office expenses €31,120; Closing stock €15,600; Rent received €3,300.

Section A Questions

6. A firm's gross profit was €85,000 for the year in which the total overheads (expenses) were €34,670. Calculate the net profit for the year. _____

7. A firm's gross loss was €21,500 for the year in which the total overheads (expenses) were €37,912. Calculate the net loss for the year. _____

1. In each of the following, prepare a combined trading, profit and loss and appropriation account.

(a) Net sales €150,000; Cost of sales €80,000; Gains €5,000; Expenses €35,000; Dividends €10,000

(b) Net sales €235,000; Cost of sales €146,780; Gains €11,300; Expenses €67,900; Dividends €23,500

(c) Net sales €146,800; Cost of sales €96,150; Gains €2,500; Expenses €21,500; P&L balance 1/1/11 €23,600; Dividends €20,000

(d) Net sales €78,600; Cost of sales €38,900; Gains €358; Expenses €15,700; P&L balance 1/1/11 €12,600; Dividends €15,000

(e) Net sales €96,400; Cost of sales €68,700; Gains €1,200; Expenses €45,250; P&L balance 1/1/11 €30,400; Dividends €4,000

(f) Net profit €128,900; Cost of sales €78,400; Gains €1,400; Expenses €23,000; P&L balance 1/1/11 €32,000; Dividends €6,000

(g) Net sales €235,200; Cost of sales €134,250; Gains €4,500; Expenses €52,500; P&L balance 1/1/11 €13,800; Dividends €25,000

(h) Net sales €169,600; Cost of sales €99,200; Gains €1,438; Expenses €35,700; P&L balance 1/1/11 €22,600; Dividends €25,000

(i) Net sales €296,600; Cost of sales €158,700; Gains €6,200; Expenses €95,150; P&L balance 1/1/11 €20,100; Dividends €24,000

(j) Net profit €327,200; Cost of sales €168,200; Gains €8,400; Expenses €113,000; P&L balance 1/1/11 €42,000; Dividends €36,000

Combined Trading, Profit and Loss, Appropriation Account and Balance Sheet

1. From the following information relating to Dandrillow Ltd, prepare the trading, profit and loss and appropriation account for the year ended 31/12/11 as well as a balance sheet on that date. Dandrillow Ltd has an authorised share capital of 400,000 €1 ordinary shares.

	Dr	Cr	Position
Purchases and sales	76,500	236,580	
Opening stock	23,500		
Import duties	2,700		
Insurance	9,780		
Light and heat	8,400		
Dividends paid	16,000		
Motor vehicles	56,000		
Issued share capital – 200,000 €1 ord. shares		200,000	
Bank overdraft		14,500	
Carriage out	5,500		
Repairs	8,100		
Premises	216,000		
Office expenses	26,300		
Cash on hand	2,300		
	451,080	451,080	
Closing stock	24,000		

2. From the following information relating to Patrick Ltd, prepare the trading, profit and loss and appropriation account for the year ended 31/12/11 as well as a balance sheet on that date. Patrick Ltd has an authorised share capital of 400,000 €1 ordinary shares.

	Dr	Cr	Position
Wages	34,000		
Buildings	195,000		
Purchases and sales	55,400	194,550	
Equipment	82,000		
Long-term loan		65,000	
Administration expenses	39,500		
Rent and rates	26,600		
Bank	32,000		
Cash on hand	4,400		
Marketing and advertising	18,600		
Opening stock	12,500		
Office expenses	6,300		
Carriage inwards	1,250		
Issued share capital – 260,000 €1 ord. shares		260,000	
Dividends paid	12,000		
	519,550	519,550	
Closing stock	25,000		

Higher Level

3. From the following information relating to Reddy Ltd, prepare the trading, profit and loss and appropriation account for the year ended 31/12/11 as well as a balance sheet on that date. Reddy Ltd have an authorised share capital of 400,000 €1 ordinary shares.

	Dr	Cr	Position
Bank overdraft		13,950	
Land and buildings	270,000		
Equipment	45,000		
Purchases and sales	54,000	196,000	
Salaries and wages	18,300		
Selling expenses	7,100		
Sales returns	2,600		
Rent received		6,600	
Furniture and fittings	18,000		
Advertising	2,600		
Dividends paid	10,000		
Import duties	3,700		
Insurance	3,900		
Bank deposit account	9,600		
Debtors and creditors	17,650	13,900	
Opening stock 1/1/11	8,900		
Bad debts	2,400		
Motor van repairs	1,700		
Long-term loan		25,000	
Issued share capital – 220,000 €1 ord. shares		220,000	
	475,450	475,450	
Stock 31/12/11	21,300		

4. From the following information relating to Corinna Ltd, prepare the trading, profit and loss and appropriation account for the year ended 31/12/11 as well as a balance sheet on that date. Corinna Ltd has an authorised share capital of 400,000 €1 ordinary shares.

	Dr	Cr	Position
Long-term loan		74,500	
Premises	190,000		
Purchases and sales	85,000	230,000	
Issued share capital – 140,000 €1 ord. shares		140,000	
Motor vehicles	35,000		
Carriage	5,000		
Telephone and postage	1,700		
Opening stock 1/1/11	12,850		
Equipment	24,000		
Sales returns and purchases returns	4,000	2,500	
Debtors and creditors	22,500	14,800	
Marketing and advertising	5,850		
Salaries	33,000		
Distribution expenses	6,900		
Bank deposit account	8,700		
Bank overdraft		3,400	
Cash on hand	1,000		
Electricity	2,700		
Dividends paid	27,000		
	465,200	465,200	
Stock 31/12/11	31,500		

Carriage is divided between purchases (carriage in) and sales (carriage out) in the ratio 2 : 3.

5. From the following information relating to Dodder Ltd, prepare the trading, profit and loss and appropriation account for the year ended 31/12/11 as well as a balance sheet on that date. Dodder Ltd has an authorised share capital of 500,000 €1 ordinary shares.

	Dr	Cr	Position
Dividends paid	30,000		
Premises	208,000		
Motor vehicles	44,000		
Purchases and sales	224,000	454,000	
Long-term loan		30,000	
Postage and telephone	5,040		
Sales returns and purchases returns	11,500	9,000	
Equipment	27,000		
Electricity	10,600		
Insurance	4,950		
Debtors and creditors	42,500	51,840	
Import duties	2,700		
Bank deposit account	8,900		
Cash on hand	250		
Salaries and wages	38,900		
Stock 1/1/11	37,000		
Interest received		500	
Issued share capital – 150,000 €1 ord. shares		150,000	
	695,340	695,340	
Stock 31/12/11	41,000		

6. From the following information relating to Elder Ltd, prepare the trading, profit and loss and appropriation account for the year ended 31/12/11 as well as a balance sheet on that date. Elder Ltd has an authorised share capital of 500,000 €1 ordinary shares.

	Dr	Cr	Position
Bank overdraft		24,500	
Land and buildings	315,000		
Equipment	56,000		
Purchases and sales	98,000	295,450	
Salaries and wages	35,800		
Selling expenses	9,200		
Sales returns	6,400		
Interest received		12,500	
Furniture and fittings	45,000		
Advertising	14,600		
Dividends paid	20,000		
Import duties	5,900		
Insurance	8,400		
Bank deposit account	23,800		
Debtors and creditors	24,550	18,500	
Opening stock 1/1/11	16,900		
Bad debts	1,500		
Motor van repairs	4,900		
Long-term loan		65,000	
Issued share capital – 270,000 €1 ord. shares		270,000	
	685,950	685,950	
Stock 31/12/11	43,500		

7. From the following information relating to Edfu Ltd, prepare the trading, profit and loss and appropriation account for the year ended 31/12/11 as well as a balance sheet on that date. Edfu Ltd has an authorised share capital of 500,000 €1 ordinary shares.

	Dr	Cr	Position
Long-term loan		90,000	
Premises	250,000		
Purchases and sales	165,000	340,000	
Issued share capital – 280,000 €1 ord. shares		280,000	
Motor vehicles	55,000		
Carriage	8,000		
Telephone and postage	4,500		
Opening stock 1/1/11	18,500		
Equipment	54,000		
Sales returns and purchases returns	6,000	10,240	
Debtors and creditors	41,400	36,800	
Marketing and advertising	15,700		
Salaries	53,000		
Distribution expenses	37,800		
Bank deposit account	15,000		
Bank overdraft		9,400	
Cash on hand	4,000		
Electricity	13,540		
Dividends paid	25,000		
	766,440	766,440	
Stock 31/12/11	22,500		

Carriage is divided between purchases (carriage in) and sales (carriage out) in the ratio 2 : 3.

8. From the following information relating to Murphy Ltd, prepare the trading, profit and loss and appropriation account for the year ended 31/12/11 as well as a balance sheet on that date. Murphy Ltd has an authorised share capital of 500,000 €1 ordinary shares.

	Dr	Cr	Position
Dividends paid	40,000		
Premises	350,000		
Motor vehicles	65,000		
Purchases and sales	288,000	606,770	
Long-term loan		98,000	
Postage and telephone	6,500		
Sales returns and purchases returns	18,900	23,000	
Equipment	65,000		
Electricity	18,900		
Insurance	23,880		
Debtors and creditors	56,780	75,900	
Import duties	5,600		
Bank deposit account	15,900		
Cash on hand	950		
Salaries and wages	78,600		
Stock 1/1/11	33,000		
Interest received		3,340	
Issued share capital – 260,000 €1 ord. shares		260,000	
	1,067,010	1,067,010	
Stock 31/12/11	54,000		

Section A Questions

9. Place a tick in the appropriate box to show where each of the following would appear in the final accounts of a company.

	Trading A/C	Profit and Loss A/C	Balance Sheet
(a) Purchases of goods for resale	☐	☐	☐
(b) Wages due	☐	☐	☐
(c) Issued share capital	☐	☐	☐
(d) Carriage inwards	☐	☐	☐
(e) Closing stock of goods for resale	☐	☐	☐
(f) Light and heat	☐	☐	☐

10. Which of the following form part of the fixed assets of a limited company?

(a) Bank loan ☐

(b) Plant and machinery ☐

(c) Issued share capital ☐

11. A firm's final accounts showed that it had made a net profit of €51,800. It later realised it had left out sales returns of €2,400 from the final accounts. Calculate the correct net profit after the error has been corrected. _____

12. Give two examples of fixed assets you are likely to find in the balance sheet of a vegetable shop.

(a) _____

(b) _____

Preparation of Accounts

1. From the following information relating to Samir & Co. Ltd, prepare the trading, profit and loss and appropriation account for the year ended 31/12/11 as well as a balance sheet on that date. Samir & Co. Ltd has an authorised share capital of 440,000 €1 ordinary shares.

	Dr	Cr	Position
Opening stock	9,700		
Rent received		18,500	
Sundry expenses	32,400		
Premises	175,000		
Purchases and sales	189,000	351,510	
Machinery	54,000		
Debtors and creditors	32,200	27,700	
Salaries	39,400		
Import duties	1,760		
Sales returns	5,500		
Postage and stationery	5,700		
Motor vans	35,000		
Insurance	8,400		
Carriage outwards	7,200		
Bank	22,450		
Issued share capital – 220,000 €1 shares		220,000	
	617,710	617,710	

You are asked to take the following information into account:

- Stock 31/12/11   15,500
- Rent received prepaid   800
- Insurance due   700
- Sundry expenses prepaid   5,300
- Depreciation on machinery 15%
- Depreciation on motor vans 20%

2. From the following information relating to Simone & Co. Ltd, prepare the trading, profit and loss and appropriation account for the year ended 31/12/11 as well as a balance sheet on that date. Simone & Co. Ltd has an authorised share capital of 400,000 €1 ordinary shares.

	Dr	Cr	Position
Issued share capital – 250,000 €1 ord. shares		250,000	
Buildings	230,000		
Machinery	55,000		
Purchases and sales	145,600	319,810	
Rent received		5,800	
Wages and salaries	46,900		
Light and heat	23,820		
Fixtures and fittings	44,000		
Sales returns and purchases returns	9,550	7,660	
Repairs	1,200		
Carriage in	1,500		
Selling expenses	13,400		
Debtors and creditors	45,200	37,300	
Customs duties	4,600		
Cash on hand	2,600		
Stock 1/1/11	35,400		
Transport and fuel	15,800		
15-year loan		90,000	
Bank	36,000		
	710,570	710,570	

You are asked to take the following information into account:

- Stock 31/12/11   46,850
- Rent received due   1,500
- Light and heat due   4,600
- Dividends declared 12%
- Depreciation on machinery 25%
- Depreciation on fixtures and fittings 20%

Section A Questions

3. Dividend due but not yet paid is an example of a:

   (a) Current liability ☐

   (b) Current asset ☐

   (c) Fixed asset ☐

   (d) Debtor ☐

4. Insurance paid in advance is an example of a:

   (a) Current liability ☐

   (b) Current asset ☐

   (c) Fixed asset ☐

   (d) Debtor ☐

Prepayments

1. Ibrahim & Sons had an opening balance (prepayment) of €750 in their rent account on 1 January 2011. Rent is paid in three instalments each year on 1 April, 1 August and 1 December and each instalment is €1,000. You are required to show the following for the year ended 31 December:

(a) The rent account

(b) The amount to be transferred to the P&L account

(c) The amount to be entered in the balance sheet

2. James Ltd has an opening balance (prepayment) of €500 in their security account on 1 January 2011. Security charges are paid every 3 months on 1 February, 1 May, 1 August and 1 November and each payment is €1,500. You are required to show the following for the year ended 31 December:

(a) The security account

(b) The amount to be transferred to the P&L account

(c) The amount to be entered in the balance sheet

Amounts Due

3. Desmond Ltd pay rent every 3 months and each payment is €2,700. On 1 January, Desmond Ltd owed 2 months' rent. Rent was paid on 1 February, 1 May, 1 August and 1 November. You are required to show the following for the year ended 31 December:

(a) The rent account

(b) The amount to be transferred to the P&L account

(c) The amount to be entered in the balance sheet

4. Cantwell Ltd pay telephone bills every 2 months and each payment is €240. On 1 January, Cantwell Ltd owed for 1 month's telephone. Telephone bills were paid on 1 February, 1 April, 1 June, 1 August, 1 October and 1 December. You are required to show the following for the year ended 31 December:

(a) The telephone account

(b) The amount to be transferred to the P&L account

(c) The amount to be entered in the balance sheet

Depreciation

5. MN Ltd purchased a new motor vehicle on 1/1/2012 for €30,000. Depreciation is charged at the rate of 20% per year. You are required to show the following for 5 years:

(a) The motor vehicles account

(b) The provision for depreciation account

(c) Relevant extracts from the profit and loss account and balance sheet

6. OP Engineering Ltd purchased new machinery on 1/1/2012 for €80,000. Depreciation is charged at the rate of 25% per year. You are required to show the following for 4 years:

(a) The machinery account

(b) The provision for depreciation account

(c) Relevant extracts from the profit and loss account and balance sheet

Assessing the Business (HL)

Exam-style Question

1. (A) Martin Kelly of 10 Laois Street, Carlow, was reading the financial pages of a daily newspaper when he noticed the following business terms:

Issued share capital	Collateral	Overtrading	Solvency

Assume that you are Brenda Nolan, finance consultant, 14 Quay Street, Waterford. Martin asks for your help in explaining any **three** of these terms. Write a report, on today's date, to Martin Kelly explaining any **three** of the above terms.

(B) JONES Ltd supply the following results for the year ending 31 May 2012:

Rate of stock turnover .... 5 times

Net profit percentage 12%

Acid test ratio .... 3.5 : 1

Return on capital employed 4%

JONES Ltd supply the following information for the year ending 31 May 2013:

Net sales €300,000

Opening stock €40,000

Closing stock €20,000

Cost of sales €150,000

Net profit €45,000

Current assets (including closing stock) €360,000

Current liabilities €110,000

Capital employed €750,000

(i) Using the above 2013 information, calculate the following ratios:

- Rate of stock turnover
- Net profit percentage (margin)
- Acid test ratio
- Return on capital employed

(ii) Compare the performance of JONES Ltd in 2013 with 2012.

Section A Questions

2. Study the following trading account and answer the questions that follow.

Trading Account of PJH Ltd for Y/E 31/12/11

Sales		45,000
Less cost of sales		
Opening stock	2,700	
Purchases	30,600	
	33,300	
Closing stock	3,300	
Cost of sales		30,000
Gross profit		15,000

(a) Calculate the average stock. _____

(b) Calculate the stock turnover. _____

3. A retailer's final accounts showed the following figures:

Cost of sales €180,000; Sales €277,500; Sales returns €7,500.

(a) Calculate the turnover for the period. _____

(b) Calculate the percentage gross profit. _____

4. A firm's final accounts showed the following figures.

Sales €450,000; Total expenses €90,000; Net profit €60,000.

(a) Calculate the gross profit for the year. _____

(b) Calculate the net profit percentage. _____

5. The following figures were taken from the balance sheet of Stockwell Ltd.

Fixed assets €330,000; Current assets €120,000; Current liabilities €112,500; Issued share capital €225,000; Revenue reserves €75,000; Long-term loan €37,500.

(a) What is the figure for retained profits? _____

(b) If the net profit for the year was €67,500, calculate the return on capital employed.

_____

48 Club Accounts

Analysed Cash Book/Analysed Receipts and Payments Account

1. St Patrick's GAA Club had the following receipts and payments for the month of November. You are required to prepare an analysed cash book (analysed receipts and payments account) for the month of November. The balance in their bank account on 1 November was €1,200. Use the following analysis columns:

Receipts: Total, Subscriptions, Bar, Other.
Payments: Total, Bar, Match expenses, Club expenses, Other.

Nov 3	Received subscriptions...................2,300	
5	Bar purchases.................1,890	
6	Transport to matches..........400	
9	Bar receipts.....................4,300	
10	Electricity 250	
13	Paid competition entry fees 300	
15	Administration expenses...........................569	
16	Received subscriptions...................1,700	
19	Bar wages 1,250	
21	Referee's expenses.............160	
22	Receipts from fundraising dance...............800	
24	Insurance 450	
25	Transport to matches..........200	
27	Receipts from Mini-World Cup competition 1,200	
28	Bar receipts.....................2,540	
29	Purchase of new outdoor goals..................1,600	
30	Printing and stationery 200	

2. From the following information, prepare an analysed receipts and payments account (analysed cash book) for the Mountain Hockey Club for the month of April. They had €2,000 in their bank account on 1 April. Use the following analysis columns:

Receipts: Total, Subscriptions, Fundraising, Hire, Other.
Payments: Total, Transport, Club expenses, Catering, Equipment, Other.

Apr 3	Received subscriptions...................1,200	
4	Receipts from hire of pitches 200	
6	Competition entry fees.........120	
8	Receipts from fundraising disco...............1,500	
9	Purchase of new line-marker..........................500	
12	Transport costs 315	
14	Grant from Irish Hockey Federation..........................600	
17	Hire of caterers....................560	
19	Lighting and heating 230	
21	Received subscriptions........800	
22	Postage and stationery 220	
23	Receipts from fundraising .... bingo night..........................650	
24	Receipts from hire of pitches 200	
25	Sale of old equipment..........300	
25	Purchase of new equipment 400	
25	Postage and stationery 110	
26	Printing costs 200	
27	Hire of caterers....................300	
28	Transport costs 240	

Income and Expenditure Account

3. Study the receipts and payments account below for the Castlecourt Golf Club and prepare an income and expenditure account for the year ended 31/12/12.

Receipts and Payments Account for Y/E 31/12/12

Balance b/d	9,780	Purchase of grass cutter	3,200
Subscriptions	5,700	Wages	4,300
Dance receipts	1,230	Committee expenses	1,970
Sale of old machine	300	Competition prizes	800
Competition receipts	2,000	Electricity	554
Sale of refreshments	1,200	Insurance	1,600
GUI affiliation fee	800		
Postage and stationery	1,280		
Balance c/d	5,706		
	20,210		20,210
Balance b/d	5,706		

Combined Questions

4. The following receipts and payments relate to the Riverglen Golf and Bowling Club for the year ended 31/12/12.

Receipts		Payments	
Bar receipts	76,680	Bar purchases	47,120
Table quiz receipts	500	Table quiz expenses	300
Subscriptions	147,800	Wages	32,500
Green fees	2,500	Light and heat	3,300
Lotto draw	1,400	Printing, postage and telephone	700
Dance proceeds	3,400	Dance expenses	1,300
New lawnmower	15,000		
Secretarial expenses	4,500		
Lotto prizes	900		

At 1 January 2012 the club owned a clubhouse and course costing €300,000, bar stock €3,700 and cash at bank €14,400. At 31 December 2012 the bar stock was €5,100.

The following information is also to be taken into account:

- Subscriptions prepaid 31/12/12 €150
- Subscriptions due 31/12/12 €4,780
- Telephone prepaid €60
- Secretarial expenses due €140

(a) Calculate the bank balance on 31/12/12. _____

(b) Prepare the accumulated fund at 1/1/12.

(c) Prepare the bar trading account and an income and expenditure account for the year ended 31/12/12 and a balance sheet on that date.

5. The following trial balance is for the Bus Workers' Social Club. From the trial balance and additional information given below, prepare an income and expenditure account for the year ended 31/12/13 and a balance sheet on that date.

	Dr	**Cr**
Raffle expenses	2,310	
Cost of keep fit classes	2,030	
Rent of club premises	10,500	
Subscriptions received		15,540
Bank	2,807	
Electricity	2,660	
Telephone	700	
Sports equipment	6,300	
Accumulated fund 1/1/13		5,131
Raffle receipts		8,400
Cash on hand	462	
Repairs to club premises	1,302	
	29,071	29,071

The following information is available on 31/12/13:

- Subscriptions paid in advance €280
- Raffle ticket monies owing from collectors €840
- Electricity due €250
- Depreciate sports equipment by 20%

6. The following trial balance is for the Midland Cricket Club. From the trial balance and additional information given below, prepare a bar trading account and income and expenditure account for the year ended 31/12/14 and a balance sheet on that date.

	Dr	**Cr**
Advertising	500	
Rent	360	
Bar purchases	31,960	
Subscriptions		8,000
Tournament expenses	386	
Tournament receipts		546
Printing and stationery	146	
Raffle ticket sales		1,200
Insurance	550	
Secretary's salary	5,250	
Catering profit		3,600
Bank	3,450	
Bar sales		52,600
Clubhouse	120,000	
Bar stock 1/1/14	2,500	
Equipment	16,000	
Minibus	15,000	
Accumulated fund		130,156
	196,102	196,102

The following information is available on 31/12/14:
- Rent due €140; Advertising prepaid €250
- Subscriptions due €50; Subscriptions paid in advance €75
- Equipment owned on 31/12/14 is to be depreciated at the rate of 10% p.a.
- Bar stock 31/12/14 €4,500

7. The Redwood Concert Band holds two concerts during the year in June and December. On 1/1/11 they had an overdraft of €455 in the bank. The following extracts show the totals of the cash received and lodgement book and the cheque payments book for the year ending 31/12/11.

Analysed Cash Receipts and Lodgement Book						
Date	Details	Total	Disco	Concert	Subs	Refreshments
31/12/11	Total	5,690	850	3,830	650	360

Analysed Cheque Payments Book						
Date	Details	Total	Disco	Instruments	Advert	Theatre Hire	Refreshments
31/12/11	Total	3,180	410	1,100	230	1,200	240

The following information is available on 31/12/11:

- Subscriptions due €40; Subscriptions paid in advance €25
- Advertising due €100
- Instruments owned on 31/12/11 are to be depreciated at the rate of 4% per year

You are required to prepare:

(a) The receipts and payments account for the year ended 31/12/11.
(b) The income and expenditure account for the year ended 31/12/11.

Exam-style Questions
Ordinary Level

8. The Tiger Pitch and Putt Club use an analysed receipts and payments account (analysed cash book). The club runs regular competitions for its members and organises a club lotto to raise funds. The annual membership fee is €75. All money received is lodged in a current account and all bills are paid by cheque. On 1 March 2011, the club had a balance of €455 in the bank. The club had the following transactions during March 2011.

March	2	Paid for trophies for competition (cheque no. 421)	€360
	4	Received competition entry fees	€545
	6	Received annual membership fee from 20 members	
	7	Paid for posters to advertise the club lotto (cheque no. 422)	€180
	9	Paid wages to ground staff (cheque no. 423)	€850
	12	Received money from sale of club lotto tickets	€2,350
	13	Received annual membership fee from 25 members	
	15	Received money from sale of club lotto tickets	€1,650
	16	Bought prizes for competition (cheque no. 424)	€400
	17	Received competition entry fees	€450
	22	Paid for repairs to greens mower (cheque no. 425)	€540
	23	Paid wages to ground staff (cheque no. 426)	€900
	29	Paid the winner of club lotto draw (cheque no. 427)	€3,000

(A) Write up the analysed receipts and payments account (analysed cash book) of the Tiger Pitch and Putt Club for the month of March 2011. Use the following money column headings:
Debit (receipts) side: Bank, Competitions, Lotto, Membership fees.
Credit (payments) side: Bank, Competitions, Lotto, Wages, Other.

Total **each** analysis column and balance the Bank columns at the end of March.

(B) Calculate the surplus or deficit that the club made on the lotto during March. Show your answer and workings.

Higher Level

9. Bulben Sailing Club, Bundoran, Co. Donegal, had the following assets and liabilities on 1 January 2012: Yachts €110,000, Clubhouse €320,000, Cash €14,000, Long-term loan €128,500. Below is a summary of the club's financial transactions for the year ending 31 December 2012.

Receipts:	€	Payments:	€
Subscriptions	8,700	Light and heat	1,680
Regatta entry fees	19,360	Purchase of equipment	15,600
Annual sponsorship	850	General expenses	3,460
Club lotto	2,750	Regatta expenses	8,220
		Insurance	1,870

Additional information on 31 December 2012:

- Light and heat due   €210
- Subscriptions prepaid   €600
- Equipment to be depreciated by 15%
- Yachts to be depreciated by 10%
- Insurance prepaid   €160

(A) Prepare a statement calculating the club's accumulated fund on 1 January 2012.

(B) Prepare:

   (i) A receipts and payments account for the year ending 31/12/2012.
   (ii) An income and expenditure account for the year ending 31/12/2012.

(C) Name **two** of Bulben Sailing Club's assets and **one** of the club's liabilities.

Section A Questions

10. The Middleton Social Club had the following receipts and expenses relating to a disco held last Christmas. Calculate the profit (surplus) made by the club on the disco.
Hire of hall €220; Hire of DJ €245; Printing of tickets €20; Ticket sales €1,760.
Profit: _____

11. Which of the following should the purchase of a new machine for marking the lines on the soccer pitches by the Greenwood Soccer Club be included in?

  (a) Receipts and payments account only   ☐

  (b) Receipts and payments account and income and expenditure account   ☐

  (c) Receipts and payments account and balance sheet   ☐

12. List two duties of a club treasurer.

  (a) _____

  (b) _____

13. The capital of a club is called the:

  (a) Excess of income   ☐   (c) Accumulated fund   ☐

  (b) Net assets   ☐   (d) Liquid capital   ☐

Farm Accounts

1. Study the trial balance below.

Details	Dr	Cr
Land and buildings	140,000	
Equipment	48,000	
Machinery	39,000	
Purchase of livestock	32,000	
Sale of livestock		84,000
Sale of milk		30,000
Bank overdraft		7,000
Rent	3,400	
Telephone	3,800	
Purchase of feed	9,200	
Long-term loan		70,000
Creditors		5,000
Capital		174,000
Insurance	5,600	
Opening stock of livestock	52,000	
Wages	32,200	
Cash	900	
Vet's fees	3,900	
	370,000	370,000

The following additional information is available:

- Closing stock: Livestock €32,000; Feed €400
- Machinery to be depreciated by 20%
- Telephone due €40

You are required to prepare:

(a) An income and expenditure account for the year ended 31/12/14.

(b) A balance sheet on 31/12/14.

Exam-style Questions
Ordinary Level

2. Nora Lydon is a farmer who keeps an analysed receipts and payments book (analysed cash book). All money received is lodged in her bank current account on the same day and all payments are made by cheque. On 1 April 2011, Nora had a balance in the bank of €5,600. She had the following transactions during April 2011:

April 2 Sold cattle at the mart for €11,450 (receipt no. 855)

6 Purchased cattle feed for €1,850 (cheque no. 321)

7 Purchased cattle (calves) for €6,000 (cheque no. 322)

8	Paid for repairs to tractor €1,900 (cheque no. 323)
9	Received an EU grant of €7,500 (receipt no. 856)
15	Paid for repairs to machinery €2,450 (cheque no. 324)
16	Sold cattle at the mart for €14,500 (receipt no. 857)
20	Paid for fertilizers €900 (cheque no. 325)
21	Purchased cattle feed for €3,650 (cheque no. 326)
24	Received a state grant of €6,000 (receipt no. 858)
27	Purchased cattle (calves) for €6,500 (cheque no. 327)
28	Received a tax refund €750 (receipt no. 859)
29	Paid farm insurance €3,500 (cheque no. 328)

Write up the analysed receipts and payments book (analysed cash book) of Nora Lydon for the month of April 2011, using the following analysis columns:

Receipts side: Bank; Cattle; Grants; Other.
Payments side: Bank; Cattle; Feed; Repairs; Other.

Total each analysis column and balance the bank columns at the end of April.

Service Firm Accounts

3. Study the information below relating to The Medical Centre, Ennis, and prepare an income and expenditure account for the year ended 31/12/14 and a balance sheet on that date.

Trial Balance

Details	Dr	Cr
Income from fees		265,000
Buildings	200,000	
Petrol	1,200	
Motor vehicles	30,000	
Wages	80,000	
Light and heat	2,700	
Bank	12,500	
Purchase of supplies	24,000	
Telephone	890	
Equipment	2,000	
Postage and stationery	1,300	
Cash	200	
Insurance	12,000	
Creditors for supplies		2,790
Rates	1,000	
Capital		25,000
Loan from building society		75,000
	367,790	367,790

You are required to take the following information into account:

- Wages due €1,000
- Insurance prepaid €100
- Depreciation on equipment 20%

Exam-style Question
Higher Level

4. Fiddle Sticks, an Irish music group, will launch their latest CD on the French and German markets on 1 July 2012. The CDs will sell at €18 each. The group will receive 15% of the sales income. The five members of the group will divide this income equally between them.

(A) State **three** of the most suitable methods of promotion that Fiddle Sticks may use to launch their CD. Give **one** reason for each of the methods stated.

_____

_____

_____

(B) (i) Calculate how much each member of the group will receive if 250,000 CDs are sold.

_____

    (ii) Apart from An Post, recommend **three** other types of financial institutions in which group members might save some of their earnings. Give **one** different reason for choosing each of the institutions you recommended.

_____

_____

_____

(C) Prepare the **income and expenditure account** of Fiddle Sticks for the year ended 31 May 2012 from the following information:

	€
Income from playing concerts	800,000
Endorsement income	300,000
Promotional expenses	200,000
Transport and accommodation expenses	260,000
Royalty income	250,000
Voice coach expenses	80,000
Wages	600,000
Clothes	30,000
Repairs to equipment	9,000

Management fees will be 12½% of total income.

50 Information Technology

Exam-style Question

1. Joe Byrne contacted The Computer Store Ltd, Main Street, Castlebar, and spoke to the manager, Fiona Twomey. 'I know nothing about computers or information technology,' said Joe, 'but my friends tell me I should buy a computer. Please send me some information. My address is The Cottage, Ballina, Co. Mayo.'

Fiona wrote a letter to Joe thanking him for his telephone enquiry. In the letter, dated 7 June 2011, she listed **three** examples of information technology which could be found in the home and which Joe could be using every day without realising it. She also stated **three** advantages for Joe of using a computer. She concluded by inviting Joe to visit the shop someday so that she could show him the latest computer models.

(A) Write the letter that Fiona Twomey sent to Joe Byrne on 7 June 2011.

(B) State **three** examples of information technology in banking.

_____

_____

_____

(C) **Hardware** and **software** are well-known computer terms. Clearly explain **each** of these terms (one sentence in each case).

Hardware _____

Software _____

2. Word search

Locate the following terms in the word search below. The terms may read forwards, backwards or diagonally.

Computer	ICT	Keyboard	Mouse
Printer	Broadband	Scanner	Speakers
VDU	USB	Spreadsheet	Joystick
Memory stick	Proofread	Modem	Podcast
CPU	ROM	RAM	CAD
Wireless	Database	Hard drive	Qwerty

```
D  Q  W  C  E  R  T  Y  U  I  O  P  A  S  D
A  F  S  P  R  E  A  D  S  H  E  E  T  G  H
E  C  Z  U  A  S  P  D  D  F  D  G  S  H  J
R  O  M  N  B  V  R  C  C  X  Z  A  A  S  D
F  M  Q  W  M  A  I  E  R  O  M  R  C  T  E
O  P  S  D  O  F  N  G  E  A  H  J  D  K  V
O  U  Z  B  U  X  T  C  N  V  M  B  O  N  I
R  T  Y  Q  S  W  E  E  N  R  T  Y  P  V  R
P  E  C  Z  E  B  R  O  A  D  B  A  N  D  D
K  R  A  I  S  D  F  G  C  H  M  J  K  U  D
Q  S  R  E  K  A  E  P  S  W  E  E  R  T  R
O  P  A  B  S  D  F  G  H  J  D  K  L  Z  A
Z  X  S  K  C  I  T  S  Y  R  O  M  E  M  H
Q  U  E  R  T  Y  Q  W  E  R  M  T  Y  U  I
A  S  K  C  I  T  S  Y  O  J  D  F  G  H  J
Z  X  C  V  B  E  S  A  B  A  T  A  D  N  M
Q  W  I  R  E  L  E  S  S  A  S  D  F  G  H
```

Notes

Notes

Notes

Notes

Notes

Notes

Notes

Notes